Foreign Direct Investment and the Multinational Enterprise

CESifo Seminar Series
Edited by Hans-Werner Sinn

Measuring the Tax Burden on Capital and Labor
Peter Birch Sørensen, editor

A Constitution for the European Union
Charles B. Blankart and Dennis C. Mueller, editors

Labor Market Institutions and Public Regulation
Jonas Agell, Michael Keen, and Alfons J. Weichenrieder, editors

Venture Capital, Entrepreneurship, and Public Policy
Vesa Kanniainen and Christian Keuschnigg, editors

Exchange Rate Economics: Where Do We Stand?
Paul De Grauwe, editor

Prospects for Monetary Unions after the Euro
Paul De Grauwe and Jacques Mélitz, editors

Structural Unemployment in Western Europe: Reasons and Remedies
Martin Werding, editor

Institutions, Development, and Economic Growth
Theo S. Eicher and Cecilia García-Peñalosa, editors

Competitive Failures in Insurance Markets: Theory and Policy Implications
Pierre-André Chiappori and Christian Gollier, editors

Japan's Great Stagnation: Financial and Monetary Policy Lessons for Advanced Economies
Michael M. Hutchison and Frank Westermann, editors

Tax Policy and Labor Market Performance
Jonas Agell and Peter Birch Sørensen, editors

Privatization Experiences in the European Union
Marko Köthenbürger, Hans-Werner Sinn, and John Whalley, editors

Recent Developments in Antitrust: Theory and Evidence
Jay Pil Choi, editor

Schools and the Equal Opportunity Problem
Ludger Woessmann and Paul E. Peterson, editors

Economics and Psychology: A Promising New Field
Bruno S. Frey and Alois Stutzer, editors

Institutions and Norms in Economic Development
Mark Gradstein and Kai A. Konrad, editors

Pension Strategies in Europe and the United States
Robert Fenge, Georges de Ménil, and Pierre Pestieau, editors

Foreign Direct Investment and the Multinational Enterprise
Steven Brakman and Harry Garretsen, editors

See http://mitpress.mit.edu for a complete list of titles in this series.

Foreign Direct Investment and the Multinational Enterprise

edited by Steven Brakman and Harry Garretsen

CESifo Seminar Series

The MIT Press
Cambridge, Massachusetts
London, England

For information about special quantity discounts, please email special_sales@mitpress.mit.edu

This book was set in Palatino on 3B2 by Asco Typesetters, Hong Kong.
Printed and bound in the United States of America.

Library of Congress Cataloging-in-Publication Data

Foreign direct investment and the multinational enterprise / edited by Steven Brakman and Harry Garretsen.
    p.   cm. — (CESifo seminar series)
Includes bibliographical references and index.
ISBN 978-0-262-02645-1 (hardcover : alk. paper)
1. Investments, Foreign. 2. International business enterprises. I. Brakman, Steven. II. Garretsen, Harry.
HG4538.F619198   2008
332.67′214—dc22   2007032377

10 9 8 7 6 5 4 3 2 1

Contents

Contributors   vii
Series Foreword   ix

1   **Foreign Direct Investment and the Multinational Enterprise: An Introduction**   1
Steven Brakman and Harry Garretsen

I   **Theory**   11

2   **Trade Costs and Foreign Direct Investment**   13
J. Peter Neary

3   **Investment Liberalization and the Geography of Firm Location**   39
Anders N. Hoffmann and James R. Markusen

4   **Outsourcing, Contracts, and Innovation Networks**   67
Alireza Naghavi and Gianmarco Ottaviano

5   **Agglomeration and Government Spending**   89
Steven Brakman, Harry Garretsen, and Charles van Marrewijk

6   **Transfer Pricing and Enforcement Policy in Oligopolistic Markets**   117
Oscar Amerighi

7   **Gains from Trade and Fragmentation**   155
Alan V. Deardorff

II Empirics   171

8 Spacey Parents: Spatial Autoregressive Patterns in Inbound FDI   173

Bruce A. Blonigen, Ronald B. Davies, Helen T. Naughton, and Glen R. Waddell

9 Do Italian Firms Improve Their Performance at Home by Investing Abroad?   199

Giorgio Barba Navaretti and Davide Castellani

10 Is Human Capital Losing from Outsourcing? Evidence for Austria and Poland   225

Andzelika Lorentowicz, Dalia Marin, and Alexander Raubold

11 Is It Strategic to Attract the Service Activities of Multinational Firms? Some Empirical Evidence   259

Fabrice Defever

Index   277

Contributors

Oscar Amerighi, CORE, Université catholique de Louvain

Bruce A. Blonigen, Department of Economics, University of Oregon and NBER

Steven Brakman, Department of Economics, University of Groningen, and CESifo

Davide Castellani, Faculty of Economics, University of Urbino "Carlo Bo"

Ronald B. Davies, Department of Economics, University of Oregon

Alan V. Deardorff, University of Michigan

Fabrice Defever, Centre for Economic Performance, London School of Economics

Harry Garretsen, Utrecht School of Economics, Utrecht University, and CESifo

Andzelika Lorentowicz, University of Munich

Charles van Marrewijk, Department of Economics, Erasmus University

Anders N. Hoffmann, Division of Research and Analysis, FORA, Danish Ministry of Economic and Business Affairs

Dalia Marin, University of Munich and CESifo

James R. Markusen, University of Colorado, University College Dublin, NBER, CEPR, and CEBR (Copenhagen)

Alireza Naghavi, Università di Modena e Reggio Emilia

Helen T. Naughton, Department of Economics, University of Oregon

Giorgio Barba Navaretti, Centro Studi Luca d'Agliano, Department of Economics, University of Milan

J. Peter Neary, University of Oxford and CEPR

Gianmarco Ottaviano, Università
di Bologna, FEEM and CEPR

Alexander Raubold, OECD, Paris

Glen R. Waddell, Department of
Economics, University of Oregon

Series Foreword

This book is part of the CESifo Seminar Series. The series aims to cover topical policy issues in economics from a largely European perspective. The books in this series are the products of the papers and intensive debates that took place during the seminars hosted by CESifo, an international research network of renowned economists organized jointly by the Center for Economic Studies at Ludwig-Maximilians-Universität, Munich and the Ifo Institute for Economic Research. All publications in this series have been carefully selected and refereed by members of the CESifo research network.

1   Foreign Direct Investment and the Multinational Enterprise: An Introduction

Steven Brakman and Harry Garretsen

1.1 Introduction

One of the stylized facts about today's world economy is the importance of foreign direct investment (FDI). Figure 1.1 compares the growth of world gross domestic product (GDP), world trade, and FDI.

What is particularly striking about this figure is that from 1990 onward, FDI grows far more rapidly than world GDP and world trade. The sharp decline of FDI growth around 2000 corresponds to the worldwide fall of share prices that not only ended all speculation about the wonders of the new economy but also signaled a (temporary) halt to cross-border mergers and acquisitions, one of the main vehicles for FDI. Figure 1.1 is just one example of the importance of FDI. Similar bursts of rapid FDI growth occured in earlier periods (Eichengreen 2003, Obstfeld and Taylor 2003), and it might be expected that such a salient characteristic of the world economy would have been closely scrutinized by theoreticians and empirical researchers alike. It also seems reasonable to suppose that by now, a vast amount of literature that focuses on FDI—its causes and consequences—would exist. Until quite recently, however, this was not the case. The reason is that it is far from trivial to formalize and analyze FDI and its determinants.

The standard theories of international trade—in the absence of trade costs—have no need for international factor mobility and so do not encompass FDI. In the neoclassical view of the world, factor price equalization (FPE) removes all incentives for international factor mobility. Indeed, in Heckscher-Ohlin-Samuelson (HOS) types of trade models, trade and factor mobility are perfect substitutes. In the transition period toward a new equilibrium, both trade and factor mobility are equally capable of restoring FPE. The literature traditionally focuses

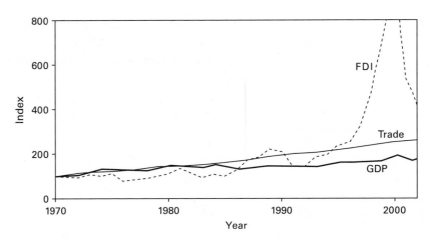

Figure 1.1
Growth of world GDP, FDI, and trade
Note: 1970 = 100.
Source: World Bank (2004).

on the trade channel as the means of restoring equilibrium, because (final) goods are assumed to be more mobile than factors of production. Similarly, in situations where a market distortion is present—for example, a tariff resulting in a failure of FPE—trade and capital flows are substitutes in the sense that capital inflow eliminates trade (Mundell 1957). Figure 1.1 suggests, however, that this may not be the case: FDI growth mirrors the growth of international trade, even though FDI grows much faster than trade.[1] This implies that the HOS trade model will not do and that alternative theoretical explanations are required to explain FDI and the presence of multinational enterprises (MNEs).

Becoming an MNE has obvious disadvantages: the need to set up a foreign plant or a sales network, to try to overcome cultural and legal differences, to bear the risk of expropriation, and, of course, exchange rate risks. Models that explain the existence of MNEs must highlight the potential benefits of production in foreign markets and show that these are larger than, for instance, the costs of setting up a plant in a foreign market. An early attempt to do so is the so-called OLI approach of Dunning (1977). The *O* refers to ownership advantage. A firm must have a product or asset that is uniquely associated with this firm because of a patent, a brand name, a special production process, or some other characteristic unique to it. This provides the firm with market power since it supplies a product that is different from others in the market. The L refers to location advantages. Instead of exporting, a MNE chooses instead to produce in a foreign country because it is more profitable. The additional profits come from the fact that by setting up a foreign plant, the firm is able to avoid barriers to trade, like tariffs or transportation costs, which reduce competitiveness should the firm choose to export. A different location-related motive for FDI is to benefit from lower factor costs in foreign markets. The I refers to the internalization advantage. It recognizes that even if the O and the L conditions are satisfied, a firm does not necessarily need to set up a foreign plant. It may simply choose to license a foreign firm to produce, that is, it might outsource part of its production. However, this could reduce long-run profits if the foreign partner decides to defect on the original arrangement and start for itself (after gaining knowledge of the production process). In-house production reduces these risks. Assuming that the location issue has been solved and the firm opts for foreign production, the internalization issue is basically about whether this foreign production should be in the form of FDI or outsourcing.

Although interesting, Dunning's approach is more an organizing framework than a model. It is useful because it identifies elements that should be the ingredients for any full-fledged model of the MNE and FDI, such as imperfect competition (the O of OLI), barriers to trade like transportation costs (the L of OLI), and internalization aspects (the I of OLI). The seminal contribution of Dixit and Stiglitz (1977), which provides an elegant and tractable way of incorporating these elements in a formal model, paved the way for the recent burst of MNE and FDI research activity in the field of international economics. The development of the modern theory of MNEs resembles the development of other trade (related) theories, like the new trade theory and the new economic geography, where the workhorse model of Dixit and Stiglitz (1977) proved to be important as well because of the need to model imperfect competition. The elegant formalization provided by the Dixit-Stiglitz model allows the analysis of increasing returns, imperfect competition, and product differentiation, elements that are crucial to understanding intraindustry trade. The addition of transportation costs in this model leads to the famous home market effect, which is fundamental to the explanation of agglomeration (see the contributions in Brakman and Heijdra 2004).

Helpman (1984) is one of the first attempts to apply the Dixit-Stiglitz framework to MNEs. It is a two factor of production model with monopolistic competition in the sector that can potentially locate headquarters activities in a different country from where production is carried out. In this model, it is assumed that headquarter services and production are characterized by different factor intensities. This gives rise to multinational behavior if headquarters and production can be separated. As usual in a three-commodity, two-factor model, the trade pattern is ambiguous, because many trade patterns are consistent with full employment. Allowing multinational behavior also implies that the employment of resources by a country might differ from its endowments, indicating that the so-called factor-price-equalization set is larger in the case of multinational production than in a world without MNEs. Helpman's model applies to vertical FDI—production is located in only one country. Horizontal FDI is not possible by assumption, which is a serious drawback of the model, as most FDI is in the form of horizontal FDI. Furthermore, the bulk of FDI is between developed countries, implying that FDI is mostly market seeking rather than factor-cost seeking (Markusen 2002).

The integration of imperfect competition and horizontal FDI was the central element of the research program Markusen started in the 1980s and is summarized in Markusen (2002). If a firm decides to set up two plants in different countries and each plant sells to only the local market, a critical element is transportation costs. A firm has an incentive to become multinational if the additional costs of setting up a foreign subsidiary—the plant-specific fixed costs—are offset by avoiding costs associated with barriers to trade. This implies that transportation or trade costs become an essential element of these models. The most general model in Markusen (2002), called the *knowledge-capital model*, combines both vertical and horizontal multinational behavior at the same time. Not surprisingly, given the prevalence of horizontal FDI in the data, tests of the knowledge-capital model reveal that the horizontal FDI model is empirically more relevant than the vertical FDI model (Carr, Markusen, and Maskus 2001).

These two examples of FDI and MNE modeling by Helpman and Markusen have been important for the development of modern MNE theory, but neither of these two approaches considers the question why the foreign plant has to be internalized (the *I* of the OLI approach) and why outsourcing will not do. Alternatives to full ownership are, for example, a joint venture or licensing to a foreign firm. The basic question is thus whether to insource or outsource. The existence of market failures implies that this is a nontrivial decision for the firm to make. The topic goes back to Coase (1937) and was elaborated by Williamson (1975, 1985). A few issues stand out: the hold-up problem, the asset specificity problem, the principal-agent problem (whether it can be expected that a foreign agent reveals the true nature of the foreign market), and various matching problems (see Rauch 2001 for the latter). The recent literature now also addresses these problems (Helpman 2006).

Although this introduction is far from complete, it sketches the background against which the chapters in this book were written. The book consists of two parts. In the chapters in part I, "Theory," the modern theory on FDI and MNE as outlined above is taken as a starting point, and the common denominator is to show how the basic framework of this theory could or should be extended. In the second part of this book, "Empirics," several of the empirical hypotheses concerning the determinants and effects of FDI associated with the modern theory of FDI and MNEs are tested.

1.2   Part I: Theory

In the chapter 2, Neary identifies an empirical puzzle that he solves theoretically. As noted, horizontal FDI is more prevalent than vertical FDI. And remarkably, the increased integration of the European Union (EU)—or ongoing globalization for that matter—continues hand-in-hand with ever increasing FDI. This is puzzling because according to theory, a decrease of FDI is expected: a fall in trade costs should be accompanied by a decrease in horizontal FDI. Neary suggests two solutions for this puzzle. The first is the existence of hubs or export platforms for FDI. Foreign firms still jump over trade barriers to gain access to an integrated market that has low internal trade costs, markets like the EU, and will select a host country from where they will export goods to the rest of that market. The second solution to the puzzle comes from the application of his so-called GOLE (General OLigopolistic Equilibrium) model. In a series of papers, Neary has developed a model that, unlike the Dixit and Stiglitz (1977) framework, allows strategic interaction between firms within a general equilibrium framework (see Neary 2003, 2007, 2004). Interestingly, this model implies that increased integration leads to cross-border mergers and acquisitions. And since most horizontal FDI takes place through cross-border mergers and acquisitions, this does offer a solution to the puzzle. In this approach, Neary addresses the O of the OLI framework. In chapter

3, Hoffman and Markusen extend the modern MNE literature by explicitly combining Markusen's (2002) knowledge-capital model with elements of the new economic geography approach, and thereby deal explicitly with the L of the OLI framework. The authors focus on the effects of investment liberalization and find, using simulation experiments, that over a wide range of parameters, headquarters tend to agglomerate but plants tend to spread. Headquarters become more concentrated in countries that are relatively well endowed with skilled labor or countries that are large. The increased spread of plants alters the general conclusion of new economic geography models—that the symmetric or spreading equilibrium is unstable for a wide range of parameter settings, since spreading now becomes the stable equilibrium. The I of the OLI approach is addressed in chapter 4 by Naghavi and Ottaviano. Innovation does not take place in isolation; it is a global phenomenon. The central idea is that while outsourcing increases transaction costs, it also lowers the costs of governance. In this chapter, the static framework of Grossman and Helpman (2002) is reformulated as a dynamic framework. Naghavi and Ottaviano show that product innovation and matching probability are strongly interrelated.

The final three chapters in part I take a closer look at issues that surround FDI: tax competition, how to avoid taxes, and, last but not least, the general welfare consequences of factor mobility. Brakman, Garretsen, and van Marrewijk use a new economic geography model in chapter 5 to show that when the focus is not on government taxation but on government spending, a different conclusion may emerge compared to the traditional tax competition literature. In a new economic geography setting, it is not only the existence of an agglomeration rent that may prevent firms from relocating when the corporate tax rate is lower in other countries. A higher level of government spending can also help countries to attract mobile (footloose?) firms, despite relative high taxes. In their model, the provision of public goods fosters agglomeration. In chapter 6, Amerighi sets up a two-country oligopoly model where two MNEs compete on quantities and try to avoid taxation by using transfer prices. The two national governments have to simultaneously decide on both the corporate tax rate and enforcement policies. Amerighi shows that increased international ownership of the MNEs implies a race to the bottom in tax rates as well as enforcement policies, but that the lowering of trade costs ultimately, when trade costs have become very low, leads to an increase of the corporate tax rates and enforcement policies. Finally, Deardorff discusses in chapter 7 the welfare effects of fragmentation, when production can be split into separate parts. Fragmentation can apply to both FDI and outsourcing. A main question for policymakers is what the gains from trade are from fragmentation. Deardorff shows that, similar to international trade in final goods, it is not hard to come up with examples where fragmentation hurts particular groups or even the whole world. Having said this, he then makes the case that it is most likely that fragmentation will increase world income. Therefore, when all is said and done, the policy conclusion is that any interference with the fragmentation process should be avoided.

1.3   Part II: Empirics

In the first contribution to the part II, Blonigen, Davies, Naughton, and Waddell extend in chapter 8 the existing empirical literature on the determinants of FDI by explicitly considering the effect of many parents. They use U.S. inbound FDI to show that FDI from different home countries in a given host actually compete for resources. Especially for the EU countries, this crowding-out effect is significant, and it is a forceful reminder that FDI cannot be studied in isolation as a bilateral transaction concerning only a single home and host country. Next, in chapter 9, Barba Navaretti and Castellani look at productivity effects of FDI for Italian MNEs. They address the difficult question of what would have happened to an MNE had it not invested abroad. Their findings for their sample of Italian firms suggest that becoming a MNE and facing additional competition raises total factor productivity. The implication of their findings suggests that wages increase. Surprisingly, however, this need not always be the case, as is shown in chapter 10 by Lorentowitz, Marin, and Raubold. They show that the common belief regarding outsourcing—that skilled workers gain from outsourcing in skill-abundant countries—is not necessarily true. For Austria, a skill-abundant country, they find that relative skill-intensive stages of the production process are outsourced. This reduces the skill premium on wages in Austria. For Poland the results are the opposite to those of Austria: Poland is outsourcing unskilled-intensive stages of the production process. Although the research focuses on only these two countries, the findings suggest that care should be taken before jumping to conclusions about the effects of outsourcing. Using a unique data set for individual firms covering almost 11,000 location choices during the period 1997–2002, chapter 11 by Defever closely examines the location decisions of MNEs. The emphasis is on the location of MNE services' production in the enlarged EU. A main finding is that agglomeration or clustering effects of MNE activity arise at the sectoral level for production activities and at the functional level for service activities.

Notes

The chapters in this book were presented at the workshop "Recent Developments in International Trade" at the CESifo Venice Summer Institute, July 18–19, 2005, in Venice. We thank CESifo for its hospitality and its assistance in the organization and funding of the workshop. The selection of speakers and papers to be presented was our responsibility (see http://www.cesifo.de for the full program). For this book, each chapter was refereed by two anonymous referees (selected by us) and the complete manuscript was refereed as well (by MIT Press). We thank all the referees for their efforts. Last, but not least we would like to thank Thijs Knaap for his indispensable help translating the manuscript into LaTex, and Beverly H. Miller (MIT Press copy editor) for preventing us and some others from making embarrassing mistakes regarding our English.

1. The evidence with regard to this issue is mixed. Bloningen (2001) finds evidence that FDI is both a substitute and a complement to imports.

References

Bloningen, B. A. (2001). In Search of Substitution between Foreign Production and Exports. *Journal of International Economics* 53, 81–104.

Brakman, S., and B. J. Heijdra, eds. (2004). *The Monopolistic Competition Revolution in Retrospect*, Cambridge: Cambridge University Press.

Carr, D. L., J. R. Markusen, and K. Maskus. (2001). Estimating the Knowledge-Capital Model of the Multinational Enterprise. *American Economic Review* 91, 693–708.

Coase, R. (1937). The Nature of the Firm. *Economica* 4(3), 386–405.

Dixit, A., and J. Stiglitz. (1977). Monopolistic Competition and Optimum Product Diversity. *American Economic Review* 67, 297–308.

Dunning, J. H. (1977). The Determinants of International Production, *Oxford Economic Papers* 25, 289–330.

Eichengreen, B. (2003). *Capital Flows and Crises*. Cambridge, Mass.: MIT Press.

Grossman, G., and E. Helpman (2002). Integration vs Out sourcing in Industry Equilibrium, *Journal of European Association* 1, 317–327.

Helpman, E. (1984). A Simple Theory of International Trade with Multinational Corporations. *Journal of Political Economy* 92, 451–471.

Helpman, E. (2006). Trade, FDI, and the Organization of Firms. *Journal of Economic Literature* 44, 589–630.

Markusen, J. R. (2002). *Multinational Firms and the Theory of International Trade.* Cambridge, Mass.: MIT Press.

Mundell, R. A. (1957). International Trade and Factor Mobility. *American Economic Review* 47, 321–335.

Neary, J. P. (2003). Globalization and Market Structure. *Journal of the European Economic Association* 1, 245–271.

Neary, J. P. (2004). Monopolistic Competition and International Trade Theory. In S. Brakman and B. J. Heijdra (eds.), *The Monopolistic Competition Revolution in Retrospect.* Cambridge: Cambridge University Press.

Neary, J. P. (2007). Cross-Border Mergers as Instruments of Comparative Advantage. *Review of Economic Studies*, 74, 1229–1274.

Obstfeld, M., and A. M. Taylor. (2003). Globalization and Capital Markets. In M. D. Bordo, A. M. Taylor, and J. G. Williamson, *Globalization in Historical Perspective.* Chicago: University of Chicago Press.

Rauch, J. (2001). Business and Social Networks in International Trade. *Journal of Economic Literature* 39, 1177–1203.

Williamson, O. E. (1975). *Markets and Hierarchies: Analysis and Antitrust Implications.* New York: Free Press.

Williamson, O. E. (1985). *The Economic Institutions of Capitalism.* New York: Free Press.

World Bank. (2004). *World Bank Indicators.* CD-ROM.

I   Theory

2   Trade Costs and Foreign Direct Investment

J. Peter Neary

2.1   Introduction

Foreign direct investment (FDI) is one of the key features of the modern globalized world. Some traders maintained international links in the late medieval and early modern periods, and multinational firms became important in many industries in the late nineteenth century, but the period since World War II, and in particular since about 1985, has seen an explosion in FDI in both absolute terms and relative to the levels of trade and gross domestic product (GDP).[1]

Matching these real-world developments, an extensive economic literature has developed that attempts to explain the nature, causes, and consequences of FDI.[2] The central plank of the now standard theoretical framework used in this literature is the so-called proximity-concentration trade-off. This suggests that FDI occurs when the benefits of producing in a foreign market outweigh the loss of economies of scale from producing exclusively in the firm's home plant. As we will see, there is much to be said for this model and a lot of empirical evidence in support of it. However, it makes a key prediction that seems to run counter to the experience of the 1990s. If FDI is driven primarily by the proximity-concentration trade-off, then falls in trade costs should discourage it as the benefits of concentrated production increasingly outweigh the gains from improved market access. Yet the worldwide boom in FDI during the 1990s coincided with dramatic falls in both technological and policy-induced barriers to trade. This is especially true within Europe, where artificial trade barriers were significantly reduced under the European Union's (EU) single market program, even as FDI boomed.[3]

This apparent paradox is the organizing principle of this chapter, which presents a selective overview of the theory and empirics of FDI.

It first outlines the simplest case of horizontal FDI and then considers in turn vertical FDI, export platform FDI, and cross-border mergers and acquisitions. Throughout I try to present results as simply as possible, paring the models down to their essentials to focus attention on the key assumptions, and making use of diagrams where possible. As we will see, there are many ways of explaining the paradox, but their relative empirical importance remains to be determined.

2.2   The Proximity-Concentration Trade-Off

I begin with the simplest framework in which the proximity-concentration trade-off can be illustrated.[4] Consider a single potential multinational, which is the monopoly supplier of a product and seeks to determine the optimal mode of serving a foreign market. The assumption that the firm is a monopoly can be related to the O in the OLI (ownership-location-internalization framework) of Dunning (1973): the firm possesses unique advantages in terms of product quality, marketing, organization, or R&D, which give it an ownership advantage over other potential firms. It is also consistent with models of monopolistic competition: many firms compete against each other, each producing a symmetrically differentiated product, but from the perspective of an individual firm, the demand function it faces is given. Of course, the assumption is not consistent with perceived interdependence between oligopolistic firms, which seems a priori likely to characterize the markets in which many multinational corporations operate. However, the main points I want to make do not require an oligopolistic setting, and I postpone consideration of oligopoly until section 2.5. I also concentrate throughout the chapter on a single industry in partial equilibrium. Embedding such an industry in general equilibrium is essential for a complete analysis, and much recent research in the theory of FDI (including my own) has done just this. However, the points I wish to highlight can be adequately addressed in partial equilibrium.

The operating profits that the firm earns in the foreign market depend on many factors, some under its control (such as output and advertising) and others not. Assume in this section that these factors are independent of how the firm serves the market. In particular, there is no comparative advantage reason that makes it cheaper or more expensive to produce in the firm's home country or in the host country. In that case we can focus on a single key determinant of operating profits—the unit cost of serving the market, denoted by t. Part of this cost too is independent of how the market is served: marketing, distribution, and after-sales service costs, for example. However, for our purposes, it makes sense to focus on the incremental cost of serving the market from abroad, so t should be understood as a measure of the external trade barrier, which is zero if the firm locates in the market and otherwise includes both tariffs and transport costs. Hence we can write the firm's operating profits as a reduced-form function of t, $\pi(t)$, where all the other determinants of operating profits, which are independent of how the market is served, are subsumed into the π function. It is easy to check that a rise in t reduces both sales and profits in the market, so π' is negative. (See the chapter appendix for more details.)

We can now state the firm's profits from alternative ways of serving the market. If it does so by exports, then its total profits Π^X are simply $\pi(t)$. Of course, the firm also incurs fixed costs in its home country: these are an important determinant of its willingness to serve the foreign market at all, but they are independent of how it does so, so little is lost by ignoring them. By contrast, investing in a local plant to serve the market will incur additional fixed costs, which we denote f. (It is convenient to interpret fixed costs as measured with respect to the size of the domestic market; see Rowthorn 1992 for a justification.) The benefit from this proximity is the saving on trade costs, which boosts operating profits to $\pi(0)$. Hence the total profits from engaging in FDI, which we denote Π^F, equal $\pi(0) - f$. The choice between FDI and exports therefore depends on the trade-cost-jumping gain, which we denote $\gamma(t, f)$

$$\Pi^F - \Pi^X = \gamma(t, f)$$

where

$$\gamma(\underset{+}{t}, \underset{-}{f}) \equiv \pi(0) - f - \pi(t). \tag{2.1}$$

As the signs under the arguments indicate, this gain is increasing in trade costs t but decreasing in fixed costs f.

All this can be illustrated in (f, t) space as in figure 2.1. Profits from exporting, Π^X, are independent of f, decreasing in t, and strictly positive for $t < \tilde{t}$, where $\tilde{t}$ is the threshold tariff at which exports are just profitable, and is defined by $\pi(\tilde{t}) = 0$. By contrast, profits from FDI, Π^F, are independent of t, decreasing in f, and strictly positive for f less than the threshold level of fixed costs $\pi(0)$ at which FDI is just

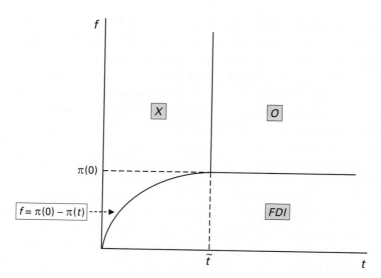

Figure 2.1
Proximity-concentration trade-off I: Trade-cost-jumping motive

profitable. It is now easy to read off the figure the different modes of serving the market that a profit-maximizing firm will choose. If both trade costs and fixed costs are above their threshold values, then the firm cannot make positive profits and so will not serve the market at all: this corresponds to the region denoted O. If only one cost variable exceeds its threshold value, then only one mode of serving the market yields positive profits, and the firm will opt for it. Finally, if both variables are below their threshold values, then both modes are profitable, and the choice between them depends on the sign of $\Pi^F - \Pi^X$ given by equation 2.1. Setting this equal to zero defines the boundary between the regions in figure 2.1 in which the firm will engage in exports and FDI, labeled X and *FDI*, respectively.

This analysis is the foundation of the proximity-concentration trade-off, and its implications are clear. Higher fixed costs favor exporting over FDI, whereas higher trade costs favor FDI over exporting. Furthermore, the same firm never engages in both FDI and trade.[5] The model is a disarmingly simple one, and it is worth teasing out the riches of its implications. It can be interpreted in either a time-series or cross-section context, and though it is stated explicitly in terms of a single firm, it can also be applied at the level of sectors or whole countries. Thus, for comparisons across time, the model implies that falls in trade costs should encourage FDI relative to exports, and vice versa. For comparisons across sectors, it implies that lower trade costs should be associated with more exports relative to FDI and vice versa. And for comparisons across space, it implies that closer markets should be served by exports and farther ones by FDI.

Since I will spend much of the rest of the chapter criticizing these implications, it is only fair to begin by noting that there is considerable, though not overwhelming, evidence in their favor. Consider first the econometric evidence. Brainard (1993) showed that as trade and transport costs rise, the level of outward FDI from the United States (measured by local sales of U.S. affiliates) falls, but the share of FDI in affiliate sales plus U.S. exports rises. Thus, although the predictions of the theory are not borne out in an absolute sense, they are confirmed in relative terms: lower trade costs lead to a substitution away from FDI toward exports. Similar results are found by Carr, Markusen, and Maskus (2001) and by Yeaple (2003b). However, results for the effects of distance (which is positively but not strongly correlated with transport costs) are less favorable to the theory.[6] Both FDI and exports fall with distance, and the effects on the share of FDI are sensitive to the specification used. Of course, distance may be proxying for factors other than trade costs, such as the costs of communicating with foreign subsidiaries, but this is clearly inconsistent with the simple proximity-concentration trade-off.

Over and above this econometric evidence, there is also considerable case study evidence that is consistent with the proximity-concentration trade-off. Indeed, case studies are an important supplement to econometric estimates and often highlight special features that large-sample econometric studies are likely to miss. I mention two. The first is the experience of Ireland in the 1930s, which transformed rapidly from an extremely open economy to a highly protected one following a change of government in 1932.[7] (See Neary and Ó Gráda 1991 for details and further references.) Despite the small size of the Irish market, the theory predicts that the imposition of protection should have induced a large inflow of FDI, yet this did not occur until some years later. The reason is simple: protection had been imposed by the new nationalist government as part of a campaign to reduce British influence in Ireland. When British firms responded by trying to set up affiliates in Ireland, the Irish government passed new legislation prohibiting their doing so. Only when this legislation was relaxed in 1938 did FDI increase significantly. A second case study is that of Japanese electronics firms in the European Community (EC) in the late 1980s by Belderbos and Sleuwaegen (1998). They concluded that the rapid increase in Japanese manufacturing investments in the late 1980s was mainly induced by EC antidumping and other trade-restricting measures aimed at Japanese firms and that such tariff-jumping investment substituted for exports from Japan. But since antidumping duties are a form of contingent protection, the effect of FDI was not merely to evade tariffs but to ensure that they were not imposed in the first place. The busy econometrician (busy because she has hundreds of other data points to worry about) would in the case of Ireland in the mid-1930s observe protection but no FDI, and in the case of EC affiliates of Japanese electronics firms in the late 1980s observe FDI but no protection. Yet both episodes are fully consistent with the logic of the proximity-concentration trade-off once it is supplemented by obvious features of the institutional and political context.

Nevertheless, there remains the puzzle noted in the chapter introduction. How can the theory be reconciled with the enormous increase in FDI in the 1990s, especially into the EU? Clearly tariffs and transport costs fell dramatically, but FDI rose much faster than exports. With Ireland as a prime example of a host country that benefited enormously from this inflow, how is it that the simple theory explains the Irish experience in the 1930s but not in the 1990s? Of course, many other changes were taking place at the same time. Markets grew in size, for example, and it is easy to show that this increases the ratio of FDI to exports in the model of this section. However, it is not evident that this factor was sufficient to offset the effect of the major falls in trade costs.

A clue to resolving the trade costs and FDI paradox comes from an old literature that explored the issue of whether exports and FDI are substitutes or complements in competitive factor-endowment models. This literature was initiated by Mundell (1957), who showed that they are perfect substitutes in the textbook two-sector two-country Heckscher-Ohlin model: barriers to trade encourage international capital flows, which, if unimpeded, raise the output of each country's import-competing sector, eventually leading to an equilibrium identical to that which would obtain under free trade. However, extensions by Markusen (1983), Jones and Neary (1984), and Neary (1995), among others, showed that exports and FDI can be complements if countries differ in either technology or endowments of sector-specific factors. In such cases, trade liberalization can encourage FDI if the induced capital flows lead export sectors to produce more. This literature has fallen out of fashion, as its view of FDI as physical flows of a productive factor has given way to an industrial organization–inspired view of FDI as an intrafirm transfer of intangible assets by multinational corporations.[8] But its insights can help explain the anomalies we have found in the predictions of the proximity-concentration trade-off hypothesis. In the next two sections, we turn to two such approaches.

2.3   Vertical versus Horizontal FDI

The first framework in which FDI may encourage rather than substitute for exports is when it is vertical rather than horizontal. The theory of vertical FDI originated with Helpman (1984), who showed in a Heckscher-Ohlin model that when stages of production differ in their factor intensities, international differences in factor endowments generate incentives for vertical disintegration by firms. More generally, it can arise from any comparative-advantage reason that makes it more profitable to locate one or more stages of production outside the market where the final good is sold.

The simplest example of vertical FDI, and one that is easily linked to the model of the previous section, is where the firm has two stages of production. The first stage produces headquarter services (in Helpman's phrase), which provide internal public goods to the firm, are located in the parent country, and incur fixed costs only. The second, or production, stage incurs both fixed and variable costs and can be located wherever it is most profitable to do so. Assuming for simplicity that each unit of output requires a single unit of labor, we can write the operating profits of serving the parent country market as $\pi^*(c)$, where c includes both factor costs and market access costs. Ignoring demand in the host country for the present, the firm now has two options. If it remains a domestic firm and supplies its home market from its parent plant, where w^* is the local wage rate, its profits will equal $\pi^*(w^*)$, which we can denote Π^D. Alternatively, it can engage in FDI and locate a new plant in the host country, exporting all its output back to the source country and incurring a trade cost of t^*. In that case, it incurs a plant-specific fixed cost f as in the previous section and earns operating profits of $\pi^*(w + t^*)$, where w is the host country wage. The relative profitability of FDI now becomes

$$\Pi^F - \Pi^D = \mu(w + t^*, w^*) - f$$

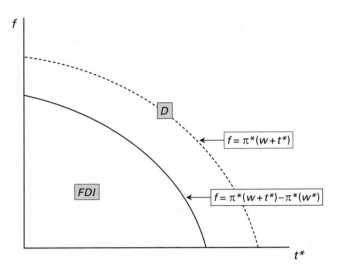

Figure 2.2
Vertical FDI

where

$$\mu(\underset{-}{w+t^*},\underset{+}{w^*}) \equiv \pi^*(w+t^*) - \pi^*(w^*). \tag{2.2}$$

The new element is $\mu(w + t^*, w^*)$, which we can call the *offshoring gain*. Not surprisingly, it depends negatively on the source country wage w^* and positively on the host country wage w, reflecting the importance of comparative advantage. In addition, and crucially for our purposes, it is decreasing in the source country tariff t^*, implying that trade liberalization will encourage FDI. In figure 2.2, FDI makes positive profits below the dashed line and more profits than producing at home below the solid line (assuming that wages in the host country are sufficiently lower than in the source country). Now the FDI region corresponds to low values of both fixed costs and trade costs.

So far we have ignored host country demand. If instead the host country market is nonnegligible, then we get a combination of vertical and horizontal motives. Now the choice between FDI and staying at home (labeled *DX* since it involves producing for both domestic sales and exports) depends on the sum of the tariff-jumping and offshoring gains:

$$\Pi^F - \Pi^{DX} = \gamma(w, w^* + t, f) + \mu(w + t^*, w^*)$$

where

$$\gamma(w, w^* + t, f) \equiv \pi(w) - f - \pi(w^* + t). \tag{2.3}$$

The tariff-jumping gain function γ is identical to that in the previous section, except that now it too depends on wages, in a way that reflects comparative advantage. As for the two tariffs, they have opposite effects on FDI: falls in the host country tariff t tend to discourage it, while falls in the source country tariff t^* tend to encourage it. If both tariffs are reduced in equal proportions, the effect is ambiguous and depends on the relative sizes of the two markets and the differences in wages and trade costs.

Faced with these theoretical ambiguities, it is natural to look at the empirical evidence for guidance on the relative importance of the two motives. At a purely descriptive level, Brainard (1997) and Markusen (2002) note that foreign affiliates of U.S. firms export relatively small amounts of their output back to the United States—between 13 and 15 percent depending on the year—with affiliates in Canada as a noteworthy but not unexpected exception. Turning to econometric evidence, Brainard (1997) finds that FDI is high in industry-country pairs with high transport costs and low plant-scale economies, while international differences in relative factor abundance have little effect on FDI. All of this is consistent with the view that FDI is primarily horizontal rather than vertical. In the same vein, Markusen (2002) finds evidence that bilateral flows of FDI at the industry level are encouraged by similarities in market size and in relative endowments of skilled and unskilled labor between countries, and interprets this as evidence against the importance of vertical FDI.

The results of studies with firm-level data are more ambiguous, however. Braconier and Ekholm (2000) look at the relationship between employment levels in different plants of Swedish multinationals. They find that employment in Sweden is negatively related to employment in foreign affiliates, supporting the horizontal view, but that employment levels in different foreign affiliates are positively related to each other, supporting the vertical view. Yeaple (2003b), while confirming the importance of the proximity-concentration motive, finds that, other things equal, U.S. multinationals in the least skilled-labor-intensive industries invest more in skill-scarce countries than in skill-abundant countries. He notes that this is consistent with a comparative advantage or vertical view of FDI. Finally, a recent study by Defever

(2006) uses data not just at the level of individual firms but at individual stages of production. He finds that the location of logistics and marketing stages by firms engaged in FDI is highly sensitive to market size, but that the location of production is highly sensitive to wages: the latter finding suggests that vertical FDI is important for production.

We can conclude that the case against the vertical FDI model is not proven, although the case in favor is not strong enough to explain the paradox of trade liberalization coexisting with FDI growth.

2.4 Export-Platform FDI

In this section I consider a different way to resolve the paradox noted in section 2.2, drawing on my work on export platform FDI (Neary 2002).[9] Suppose that the model is the same as that in section 2.2, except that the host country is one of two identical countries in a potential economic union. The previous analysis still holds when intraunion barriers are equal to the external barrier t, with the added implication that the FDI option implies establishing two plants—one in each union country.

Now suppose that intraunion barriers are reduced to a level τ, which is less than the common external trade cost t. Clearly this does not affect the profits from exporting to both countries from the firm's country of origin: these continue to equal $\pi(t)$ for each destination country, as in section 2.2, so the total profits from exporting, Π^X, equal twice this, $2\pi(t)$. However, the profits from locating a plant in one of the union countries are now greater then before: in addition to the net profits of serving the host country market $\pi(0) - f$, there is an additional gain from serving the partner country market, $\pi(\tau)$. Hence the total profits from FDI, Π^F, equal $\pi(0) + \pi(\tau) - f$, and the relative attractiveness of FDI is now

$$\Pi^F - \Pi^X = \gamma(t, f) + \chi(t, \tau)$$

where

$$\chi(\underset{+}{t}, \underset{-}{\tau}) \equiv \pi(\tau) - \pi(t). \tag{2.4}$$

Now there are two sources of gain from FDI. As before, $\gamma(t, f) \equiv \pi(0) - f - \pi(t)$ is the trade-cost-jumping gain as the host country market is served from a local plant rather than from exports. In addition, $\chi(t, \tau)$ denotes the gain from serving the partner country market facing the intraunion trade cost τ rather than the higher common external trade cost t. We can call this the *export-platform gain*. Two implications are immediate. First, FDI is now more attractive relative to exporting. Unlike the trade-cost-jumping gain, which can be positive or negative, the export platform gain is always nonnegative. This reflects the fact that the decision to locate a new plant depends not on the size of the host-country market but on the size of the trade-cost-adjusted market that can be served from that plant. Second, and central to the theme of this chapter, the export platform gain is decreasing in the intraunion trade cost τ. Hence, in striking contrast to the simple two-country horizontal FDI model of section 2.2, intrabloc trade liberalization tends to encourage FDI once we recognize the importance of the export-platform motive. Note that a framework with at least three countries is essential for this result. Note also that the external trade cost t continues to exert a positive effect on FDI; indeed, it enhances both the trade-cost-jumping and the export platform motives.

Some further implications of this model can be deduced from figure 2.3. In the region labeled *FDI* in figure 2.1, high trade costs and low fixed costs justify building a plant in both of the union countries. Such a region still exists when τ is less than t, provided τ is strictly positive: in figure 2.3, it is denoted *FDI* (2). However, it is reduced in size by the

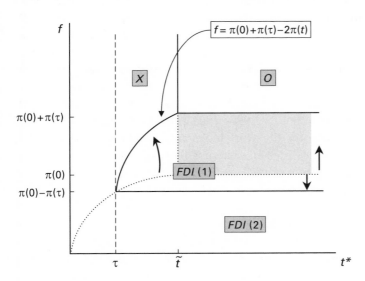

Figure 2.3
Proximity-concentration trade-off II: External trade-cost-jumping + export platform motives

emergence of a new region labeled *FDI* (1): this gives the combinations of f and t where (for given τ) it is profitable to establish a plant in only one market serving both. Thus, as τ falls, the export platform motive favors plant consolidation by firms already engaged in FDI with multiple plants. The new region also expands at the expense of the X region, as implied by equation 2.4. Finally, and more surprising, it expands at the expense of the O region, since export platform FDI is profitable for any fixed cost less than $\pi(0) + \pi(\tau)$ (rather than merely $\pi(0)$ as in section 2.2), provided the common external trade cost is above the threshold level $\tilde{t}$. Thus, as τ falls, the export platform motive not only favors FDI over exporting but it also (for parameter values in the shaded region) favors FDI over not serving the market at all. A final implication of the model is that the same firm engages in both exports and FDI, albeit not across the same frontier: the firm engages in FDI into the host country and also in exports from there to the partner country. Hence exports and FDI become complements rather than substitutes in the aggregate data.

This approach avoids many of the criticisms of the simple horizontal FDI model of section 2.2. How does it relate to the empirical evidence? It is clearly consistent with the experience of the EU in the 1990s, when the dismantling of nontariff barriers to internal trade under the single market program coincided with a huge inflow of extra-EU FDI, especially from the United States. The Irish economy in particular exemplified this pattern, with many firms locating giant plants far larger than needed to service the Irish market, causing both FDI and exports to rise in tandem. The model therefore reinforces the view that FDI, attracted by the deepening of the EU single market, was a major cause of the "Celtic tiger" boom, which saw close to double-digit growth rates in GDP for much of the 1990s. (See Barry 1999.) As for econometric evidence, most of the literature looks only at bilateral flows of FDI, but two recent studies present evidence that supports the importance of the export-platform motive. Head and Mayer (2004) study Japanese FDI in European regions and find that it is encouraged by market potential, which they measure using both host-region GDP and the GDPs of adjacent regions. This is consistent with the export-platform view but could also be due to agglomeration effects (and indeed the authors interpret it as such). Blonigen et al. (2004) throw further light on this by using spatial econometric techniques to measure distance effects beyond adjacent countries. They find evidence against agglomeration effects—higher U.S. FDI in neighboring countries reduces the amount of U.S. FDI into individual European countries—but in favor of the export platform hypothesis—higher GDP in neighboring countries increases U.S. FDI.

As for the prediction that falling intrabloc trade barriers should encourage plant consolidation, Pavelin and Barry (2005) address this in a study of the geographical diversification of 290 leading European firms between 1987 and 1993. Contrary to the hypothesis, they find that diversification increased substantially over this period, which roughly coincides with the deepening of the single market. However, as they note, their sample does not include many U.S. firms; it covers only very large firms, which are likely to be multiproduct and even multi-industry; and they measure the geographical diversification of a firm by the number of countries in which it operates rather than by the variance of its production or sales across countries. By contrast, evidence in favor of the plant consolidation hypothesis can be found in Belderbos (1997), who notes that Japanese electronics firms followed a strategy of locating VCR plants in many EC countries in the early 1980s but divested many of these multiple plants and concentrated on best locations in the late 1980s and early 1990s. Clearly more work is needed on this topic.

2.5   Cross-Border Mergers and Acquisitions

So far I have assumed that all FDI involves constructing a new plant in a foreign country—the so-called greenfield case. However, the most important form of FDI in reality is not the greenfield type but rather cross-border mergers and acquisitions (M&As), where a foreign firm purchases an existing firm in the host country. UNCTAD (2000) documents the importance of M&As in the world economy, noting that they grew rapidly in the 1990s, both absolutely and relative to greenfield FDI: the share of M&As in the total value of world FDI exceeded 80 percent in 1999, and cross-border M&As were particularly important in FDI flows between developed countries.[10] By contrast, the enormous scholarly literature on FDI has concentrated on the greenfield case. In this section I review some of my recent work that attempts to redress this balance, and discuss its implications for the effects of trade costs on FDI.

In discussing M&As, it seems very desirable, for the first time, to adopt an explicitly oligopolistic approach. One reason is empirical: according to UNCTAD (2000), the principal difference between greenfield and M&A FDI is a persistent concentration effect: markets with more mergers and acquisitions are more concentrated. A second reason is conceptual: the theory of industrial organization emphasizes two broad motives for M&As: a strategic motive, as acquiring firms gain from a reduction in competition, and an efficiency motive, as acquisitions lead to synergies through internal technology transfer, economies of scale, and coordination of production and marketing decisions. Of these, the former can be considered only in a model that explicitly allows perceived interdependence between firms, and both suggest that firms are large relative to the markets in which they operate. Hence in this section, I present a model of cross-border mergers in oligopolistic markets introduced in Neary (2003, 2007).[11] This concentrates on the strategic motive for M&As. As we shall see, it also throws light on the theme of the chapter: how trade liberalization can encourage rather than discourage FDI.

The setting is an industry with n home firms, all with unit cost c, and n^* foreign firms, all with unit cost c^*. Assume that the two countries constitute a completely integrated market. Write the total profits of a home firm as a function of all these variables: $\pi(c, c^*; n, n^*)$. (I abstract from firm-level fixed costs, since they would provide a trivial justification for mergers.) It is plausible to assume that profits are decreasing in own costs c, increasing in foreign costs c^*, and that the own effect dominates the cross-effect. Hence I will confine attention to this case.[12] In the absence of foreign rivals, the threshold level of home costs consistent with breaking even is $\tilde{c}$, defined as the price that drives demand to zero.[13] With active foreign rivals, the threshold level of home costs consistent with breaking even is defined as an implicit function of the rivals' costs by $\pi(c, c^*; n, n^*) = 0$. Given my assumptions on the derivatives of π, this yields a locus in $\{c, c^*\}$ space for given numbers of home and foreign firms, which is upward sloping though less steeply sloped than the 45 degree line, as illustrated by the locus labeled $\pi = 0$ in figure 2.4. Similar arguments applied to foreign firms imply the locus labeled $\pi^* = 0$ for their break-even cost level. Hence, with symmetric assumptions concerning foreign firms, the diagram is divided into four regions. In region O it is not profitable for any firms to serve the market; in regions F and H, only firms from foreign or home, respectively, are profitable; and in region HF, both types of firm are profitable. The latter region, or cone of diversification, is the most interesting case, since low- and high-cost firms coexist there. The pattern of trade is

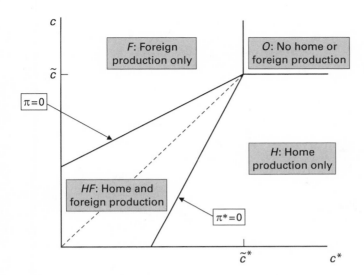

Figure 2.4
Equilibrium production patterns in free trade without FDI

clear: at all points above the 45 degree line, home firms are at a cost disadvantage and so are smaller in size than foreign firms in the same sector. Hence there is a presumption that the home country is the importer for points above the 45 degree line, and this holds exactly if the two countries are symmetric (with equal market size and with the same number of home firms as foreign firms in each industry). In the perfectly competitive case, where entry of new firms into the industry was free, the *HF* region would collapse to the 45 degree line, as only low-cost firms would survive, and so specialization patterns would perfectly reflect the two countries' comparative advantage.

The cone *HF* is also the only region in which mergers may take place. In the *F* and *H* regions, all firms are the same, and a classic result in industrial organization, due to Salant, Switzer, and Reynolds (1983), states that bilateral mergers are not profitable in an industry with more than two identical firms. Salant et al. confined attention to cases where firms have identical costs, whereas Neary (2007) shows that provided costs are sufficiently different, then bilateral mergers are indeed profitable. To see why, define the gain from a takeover of a home firm by a foreign firm as G_{FH}:[14]

$$G_{FH}(c, c^*; n, n^*) = \Delta \pi^*(c, c^*; n, n^*) - \pi(c, c^*; n, n^*). \tag{2.5}$$

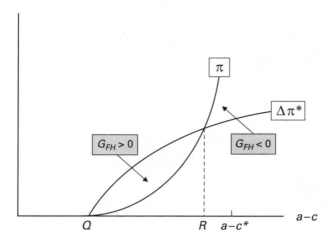

Figure 2.5
Components of gain from a cross-border acquisition by a foreign firm
Source: Adapted from Leahy and Neary (2005).

This consists of two parts. The first is the change in the acquiring firm's profits as the market becomes more concentrated following a takeover which reduces the number of home firms from n to $n-1$: $\Delta\pi^*(c, c^*; n, n^*) \equiv \pi^*(c, c^*; n-1, n^*) - \pi^*(c, c^*; n, n^*)$. Since oligopoly profits are decreasing in the number of firms, this is always positive. The second is the initial profits of the target home firm, $\pi(c, c^*; n, n^*)$, which is the amount that it must be paid to persuade it to sell. Along the boundary between the F and HF regions in figure 2.4, both of these terms are zero, since the home firm's output is zero, so both its own profits, and its impact on other firms' profits if it ceases production, are zero. As c falls, the changes in the two terms can be deduced with the help of figure 2.5. This shows how the two terms change as the cost competitiveness of the home firm rises, holding c^*, n, and n^* constant.[15] Both increase, but the $\Delta\pi^*$ term increases more rapidly at first. Why? Because the home firm is initially very small, and its profits increase with the square of its output. By contrast, eliminating a small firm raises industry price, and so increases the foreign firm's price-cost margin, giving it additional profits on every unit it sells. As the home firm's cost competitiveness continues to rise (moving to the right of point Q in figure 2.5), its initial profits increase more rapidly, whereas the change in the foreign firm's profits from eliminating it rises at a diminishing rate. (See the chapter appendix for details.) At some point,

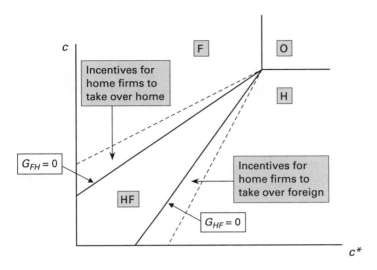

Figure 2.6
Cross-border merger incentives

denoted R in figure 2.5, the two curves intersect, so the gain from taking over the home firm becomes zero: the foreign firm would benefit
greatly from the reduction in competition, but cannot afford to acquire
the by-now relatively large home firm. Finally, from Salant et al., we
know that the gain is strictly negative when the home firm's cost competitiveness rises to the level of the foreign firm, $a - c^*$. All this implies
that there is a range, denoted QR in figure 2.5, within which home
firms make positive profits but are vulnerable to acquisition by foreign
firms. This corresponds to the region indicated in figure 2.6 where, relative to figure 2.4, the F region expands at the expense of the HF region. Symmetric reasoning with the roles of the two countries reversed
implies that there is a second region in figure 2.6 where the H region
expands at the expense of the HF region, as low-cost home firms acquire high-cost foreign ones.

Now consider the implications of this analysis for the effects of trade
liberalization. Starting in autarky, home firms face no competition, so
they produce positive levels of output in that subregion of F where
their cost is less than the threshold level $\tilde{c}$. Trade liberalization alone
eliminates home firms in region F and (in the case of symmetric countries and integrated markets) leads all foreign firms above the 45 degree line to export into the home market. If restrictions on cross-border

M&As are also lifted, then as we have seen, the region within which home firms can survive contracts even further. This gives the first prediction of the model: cross-border mergers take place in the same direction as trade flows (even at the level of individual firms, unlike in section 2.4), and they serve to move the pattern of international specialization closer to what would prevail under perfect competition. In both senses, cross-border mergers can be viewed as instruments of comparative advantage.

The second prediction of the model follows from the fact that G_{FH} is decreasing in the number of home firms n. A takeover of one home firm causes both curves in figure 2.5 to pivot upward around the point Q, but the gain to a takeover $\Delta\pi^*$ rises by more than the cost π. Intuitively, the potential acquiring firm is larger with $n-1$ rivals than with n, so its gain in profits (which equal the increase in its price-cost margin times its total output) rises faster than the profits of the home firm (which are proportional to the square of its output). Hence the acquisition of one home firm increases the incentive for another to be acquired, so that mergers are likely to come in waves, with one bilateral acquisition prompting another until all the small and relatively inefficient firms in the sector have been acquired.

Finally, while the analysis so far has considered the incentives for cross-border M&As when trade is fully liberalized and the markets are integrated, it can be extended to allow intermediate tariff levels, assuming that the markets are segmented.[16] The effects of a small reduction in an existing tariff on the gain from a merger must now take account of the change in the acquiring firm's profits and the initial profits of the target firm in both markets. Trade liberalization increases the home firm's profits on its initial exports, and this in itself makes it a more expensive takeover target, with cross-border M&As therefore less likely. But trade liberalization also increases the foreign firm's profits from exporting as well as reducing both firms' profits in their home markets, both of which make cross-border M&As more likely. In the neighborhood of autarky, the first effect does not arise, and so at high trade costs, a small amount of trade liberalization unambiguously raises the likelihood of cross-border M&As.

Turning finally to empirical evidence, Brakman, Garretsen, and van Marrewijk (2005) is the only paper to date that explicitly tests the instruments of comparative advantage theory of cross-border M&As. They consider data on cross-border M&As between five member countries of the Organization for Economic Cooperation and Development in twenty sectors over the period 1980–2004 and find strong evidence of a role for comparative advantage. Specifically, acquiring firms in cross-border mergers and acquisitions come disproportionately from sectors that have a revealed comparative advantage, as measured by the standard Balassa index. They also find evidence that mergers are positively autocorrelated within sectors, consistent with the hypothesis that mergers occur in waves. Of course, these results may be consistent with other theories too, so further work is needed to test their robustness.

2.6 Conclusion

This chapter has presented a selective review of the theory and empirics of foreign direct investment, using as an organizing principle an apparent conflict between received theory and recent trends in the globalized world. Conventional wisdom holds that the bulk of FDI is horizontal rather than vertical, aimed at replicating production facilities abroad to improve access to foreign markets rather than breaking up the production process to benefit from lower production costs. Furthermore, the standard model of horizontal FDI emphasizes a proximity-concentration trade-off and is consistent with much, though not all, of the empirical evidence. Given this, we should expect trade and FDI to be substitutes, in the sense that falls in trade costs should discourage FDI. However, this prediction conflicts with the experience of the 1990s, when trade and FDI appear to have been complements: trade costs fell dramatically, due to trade liberalization, market integration, and technological change, yet FDI grew much faster than trade. Two possible resolutions to this paradox have been explored. First, horizontal FDI in trading blocs is encouraged by intrabloc trade liberalization, because foreign firms establish plants in one country as export platforms to serve the bloc as a whole. Second, cross-border mergers, which are quantitatively more important than greenfield FDI, are encouraged rather than discouraged by falling trade costs.

One broad conclusion that follows from the literature reviewed here is that the distinction between horizontal and vertical FDI is useful for pedagogic purposes but otherwise not very helpful. In practice, most multinational corporations pursue what Yeaple (2003a), following UNCTAD (1998), calls complex integration strategies, which do not fit neatly into either the horizontal or vertical categories. Export platform FDI as discussed in section 2.4 is one example of such a strategy:

though modeled here as purely horizontal in the sense that no physical intermediate inputs are traded within the firm, it implies that the simple proximity-concentration trade-off does not apply easily to a world with more than two countries. Cross-border mergers and acquisitions are another example, implying that trade and FDI can move in the same direction, even at the level of a single firm. Clearly more analytical and empirical work is required to disentangle the relative importance of these different aspects of FDI.

Appendix 2A

Operating Profits and Trade Costs

Write the operating profits of the foreign firm serving the home market as a function of its output y and the trade cost t:

$$\tilde{\pi}(y,t) = [p(y) - (w+t)]y, \tag{2.6}$$

where $p(y)$ is the inverse demand function and the unit production cost w is ignored in the text until section 2.3. The function used in the text, $\pi(t)$, is the value of $\tilde{\pi}(y,t)$ when y is chosen at the profit-maximizing level:

$$\pi(t) \equiv \underset{y}{\text{Max}}[\tilde{\pi}(y,t)]. \tag{2.7}$$

This exhibits a variant of Hotelling's lemma applied to a firm with monopoly power,

$$\pi' \equiv \frac{d\pi}{dt} = \tilde{\pi}_y \frac{dy}{dt} + \tilde{\pi}_t = \tilde{\pi}_t = -y < 0, \tag{2.8}$$

where the envelope property follows from the first-order condition: $\tilde{\pi}_y = p + yp' - (w+t) = 0$. Totally differentiating the first-order condition gives $\tilde{\pi}_{yy} dy + \tilde{\pi}_{yt} dt = 0$, which implies that output is a decreasing function of the trade cost,

$$\frac{dy}{dt} = -\frac{\tilde{\pi}_{yt}}{\tilde{\pi}_{yy}} = \frac{1}{\tilde{\pi}_{yy}} < 0, \tag{2.9}$$

where the negative sign follows from the second-order condition: $\tilde{\pi}_{yy} = 2p' + yp'' < 0$. This also implies that the boundaries between the X and FDI regions in figures 2.1 and 2.3 and between the D and FDI regions in figure 2.2 are concave.

Merger Gains

To evaluate the merger gain G_{FH}, we make use of the always useful result that a firm's operating profits in any market are proportional to the square of its sales in that market, $\pi = by^2$, which follows from the first-order condition $p - c = by$, where b is the inverse demand slope. (Note that this holds under all market structures and demand systems, though when demand is nonlinear, b depends on the sales of all firms.)

From equation 2.5, the two components of the gain from a merger are $\Delta\pi^*$ and $-\pi$. These depend on the initial outputs of a typical home and foreign firm, which can be written as follows (using $A \equiv a - c$ and $A^* \equiv a - c^*$ to denote each firm's cost competitiveness, and $\bar{n} \equiv n + n^*$ to denote the total number of firms):

$$y(c, c^*; n, n^*) = \frac{(n^* + 1)A - n^*A^*}{b(\bar{n} + 1)}$$

$$y^*(c, c^*; n, n^*) = \frac{(n + 1)A^* - nA}{b(\bar{n} + 1)}. \tag{2.10}$$

Since home output y is linear in A, home profits $\pi = by^2$ must be quadratic in A with first and second derivatives:

$$\frac{\partial\pi}{\partial A} = 2y\frac{\partial y}{\partial A} = 2b\frac{n^* + 1}{\bar{n} + 1}y \quad \text{and} \quad \frac{\partial^2\pi}{\partial A^2} = 2\left(b\frac{n^* + 1}{\bar{n} + 1}\right)^2 > 0. \tag{2.11}$$

Hence the profits of a target home firm are increasing and convex in A, provided its output is strictly positive $(y > 0)$. This is illustrated by the curve labeled π in figure 2.5: note that it is horizontal at Q since $\partial\pi/\partial A = 0$ at $y = 0$.

As for the change in the acquiring foreign firm's profits, $\Delta\pi^*$, this can be factorized as follows:

$$\Delta\pi^*(c, c^*; n, n^*) = b[y^*(c, c^*; n - 1, n^*) + y^*(c, c^*; n, n^*)]$$

$$[y^*(c, c^*; n - 1, n^*) - y^*(c, c^*; n, n^*)]. \tag{2.12}$$

Direct calculations (following Neary 2004) show that

$$y^*(c, c^*; n - 1, n^*) - y^*(c, c^*; n, n^*) = \frac{1}{\bar{n}}y(c, c^*; n, n^*) \tag{2.13}$$

and

$$y^*(c, c^*; n-1, n^*) + y^*(c, c^*; n, n^*)$$

$$= 2y^*(c, c^*; n, n^*) + \frac{1}{\bar{n}} y(c, c^*; n, n^*). \tag{2.14}$$

Hence we can write

$$\frac{\bar{n}}{b} \Delta \pi^* = \left(2y^* + \frac{1}{\bar{n}} y \right) y. \tag{2.15}$$

Differentiating this with respect to A,

$$\frac{\bar{n}}{b} \frac{\partial(\Delta \pi^*)}{\partial A} = 2y \frac{\partial y^*}{\partial A} + 2 \left(y^* + \frac{1}{\bar{n}} y \right) \frac{\partial y}{\partial A}$$

$$= \frac{2}{\bar{n}+1} \left[(n^*+1) y^* - \frac{n\bar{n} - (n^*+1)}{\bar{n}} y \right]. \tag{2.16}$$

This is strictly positive at $y = 0$ (point Q in figure 2.5). Since y is increasing in A and y^* is decreasing in A, it follows that $\partial(\Delta \pi^*)/\partial A$ is decreasing in A. Hence the curve $\Delta \pi^*$ is concave everywhere, as shown in figure 2.5. We know from Salant et al. (1983) that it must lie below the π curve when the two firms are equally competitive (when $A \equiv a - c$ equals $A^* \equiv a - c^*$). It follows that the two curves must have a unique intersection at a point such as R as shown.

Notes

Earlier versions of this chapter were presented to the CESifo Workshop, "Recent Developments in International Trade: Globalization and the Multinational Enterprise," Venice International University, July 2005, to the 2005 European Trade Study Group Conference in University College Dublin, and at the University of Tübingen. I am very grateful to participants on these occasions and to an anonymous referee for comments, and also to Frank Barry, René Belderbos, Ben Ferrett, Keith Head, Dermot Leahy, Philippe Martin, Armando Pires, Charles van Marrewijk, and Stephen Yeaple for helpful discussions. This research is part of the International Trade and Investment Programme of the Geary Institute at UCD.

1. See UNCTAD (2000), Markusen (2002, chapter 1) and Barba Navaretti and Venables (2004, chapter 1) for summaries of the stylized facts about FDI.

2. Markusen (2002) and Barba Navaretti and Venables (2004) give overviews of the theory of FDI and multinational corporations.

3. It is true that measuring either tariffs or transport costs in even the simplest contexts poses major conceptual and practical problems. (See Anderson and van Wincoop 2004

and Anderson and Neary 2005.) Nevertheless, it seems incontrovertible that both fell considerably in the 1990s.

4. The model in this section is standard. See, for example, Smith (1987, section 2) or Markusen (2002, chapter 2). The analytical properties of figure 2.1 are taken from Neary (2002).

5. The model has been extended by Helpman, Melitz, and Yeaple (2004) to allow firms within the same monopolistically competitive industry to have different efficiency levels. This permits two-way flows of FDI, but still predicts that a given firm will engage in either FDI or trade and not both.

6. I am indebted to Stephen Yeaple for these findings.

7. "Ireland" is used here to refer to the political unit that was an independent state from 1922 until 1949, though with a constitutionally ambiguous status in international law, reflected in its official designation as the "Irish Free State." It became a republic in 1949.

8. An exception is an interesting recent paper by Blanchard (2005), which explores the implications of international flows of sector-specific capital for the source country's incentive to levy an optimal tariff.

9. For other discussions of this topic, see Motta and Norman (1996), Yeaple (2003a), Ekholm, Forslid, and Markusen (2003) and Grossman, Helpman, and Szeidl (2004).

10. UNCTAD cautions that the data on greenfield and M&A FDI are not fully comparable. The data on total FDI come from balance-of-payments statistics and those on cross-border M&As from Thompson, a consultancy group, so the latter is not a proper subset of the former. See Head and Ries (2005) for further discussion. However, the importance of cross-border M&As is uncontroversial.

11. Cross-border mergers have been studied in models of large-group monopolistic competition by Barba Navaretti and Venables (2004, chapter 3) and Nocke and Yeaple (2004), and in a model emphasizing the market for corporate control but abstracting from trade flows (and hence from trade costs) by Head and Ries (2005). My approach is closer to the small but rapidly growing literature on cross-border mergers in oligopolistic markets exemplified by Long and Vousden (1995), Falvey (1998), Horn and Persson (2001), Bertrand and Zitouna (2003), and Ferrett (2004).

12. Exact conditions are given in Neary (2002, appendix A.2). As often in oligopoly theory, the properties hold provided that demand is not too convex.

13. The threshold $\tilde{c}$ is independent of c^* and n^*. This follows from the typical home firm's first-order condition in the absence of any foreign firms, which is $p(ny) + yp'(ny) = c$. If the inverse demand function has constant elasticity, $\tilde{c}$ is infinite, while if it is linear $\tilde{c}$ equals its intercept.

14. Strictly speaking, this is a myopic gain, since it does not take account of the effect of one takeover on the profitability of further takeovers between the remaining $n + n^* - 1$ firms. Neary (2007) shows that similar results hold when the model is extended to allow firms to have forward-looking expectations of future takeovers.

15. Figure 2.5 is drawn on the assumption that the demand function is linear with intercept a. The home firm's cost competitiveness is measured by $a - c$.

16. I am very grateful to Philippe Martin for detailed suggestions on this case. See also Long and Vousden (1995).

References

Anderson, James E., and Eric van Wincoop. (2004). Trade Costs. *Journal of Economic Literature* 42, 691–751.

Anderson, James E., and J. Peter Neary. (2005). *Measuring the Restrictiveness of International Trade Policy.* Cambridge, Mass.: MIT Press.

Barba Navaretti, Giorgio, and Anthony J. Venables (2004). *Multinational Firms in the World Economy.* Princeton: Princeton University Press.

Barry, Frank (ed.). (1999). *Understanding Ireland's Economic Growth.* London: Macmillan.

Belderbos, René. (1997). *Japanese Electronics Multinationals and Strategic Trade Policies.* Oxford: Oxford University Press.

Belderbos, René, and Leo Sleuwaegen. (1998). Tariff Jumping DFI and Export Substitution: Japanese Electronics Firms in Europe. *International Journal of Industrial Organization* 16, 601–638.

Bertrand, Olivier, and Hamid Zitouna. (2003). Trade Liberalization and Industrial Restructuring: The Role of Cross-Border Mergers and Acquisitions. Mimeo., Université de Paris I.

Blanchard, Emily J. (2005). Foreign Direct Investment, Endogenous Tariffs, and Preferential Trade Agreements. Mimeo., University of Virginia.

Blonigen, Bruce A., Ronald B. Davies, Glen R. Waddell, and Helen Naughton. (2004). FDI in Space: Spatial Autoregressive Relationships in Foreign Direct Investment. Mimeo., University of Oregon.

Brainard, S. Lael. (1993). An Empirical Assessment of the Factor Proportions Explanation of Multi-National Sales. Working paper no. W4583, National Bureau of Economic Research, Cambridge, Mass.

Brainard, S. Lael. (1997). An Empirical Assessment of the Proximity-Concentration Tradeoff Between Multinational Sales and Trade. *American Economic Review* 87, 520–544.

Brakman, Steven, Harry Garretsen, and Charles van Marrewijk. (2005). Cross-Border Mergers and Acquisitions: On Revealed Comparative Advantage and Merger Waves. Mimeo., University of Gröningen.

Braconier, Henrik, and Karolina Ekholm. (2000). Swedish Multinationals and Competition from High- and Low-Wage Locations. *Review of International Economics* 8, 448–461.

Carr, David, James R. Markusen, and Keith E. Maskus. (2001). Estimating the Knowledge-Capital Model of the Multinational Enterprise. *American Economic Review* 91, 691–708.

Defever, Fabrice. (2006). Functional Fragmentation and the Location of Multinational Firms in the Enlarged Europe. *Regional Science and Urban Economics* 36: 658–677.

Dunning, John H. (1973). The Determinants of International Production. *Oxford Economic Papers*, NS, 25(3), 289–336.

Ekholm, Karolina, Rikard Forslid, and James R. Markusen. (2003). Export-Platform Foreign Direct Investment. Discussion paper no. 3823, Centre for Economic Policy Research, London.

Falvey, Rod. (1998). Mergers in Open Economies. *World Economy* 21, 1061–1076.

Ferrett, Ben. (2004). Greenfield Investment versus Acquisition: Alternative Modes of Foreign Expansion. Mimeo, University of Nottingham.

Grossman, Gene, Elhanan Helpman, and Adam Szeidl. (2004). Optimal Integration Strategies for the Multinational Firm. Working paper no. 10189, National Bureau of Economic Research, Cambridge, Mass.

Head, Keith, and Thierry Mayer. (2004). Market Potential and the Location of Japanese Investment in the European Union. *Review of Economics and Statistics* 86, 959–972.

Head, Keith, and John Ries. (2005). FDI as an Outcome of the Market for Corporate Control: Theory and Evidence. Mimeo., Sauder School of Business, University of British Columbia, May.

Helpman, Elhanan. (1984). A Simple Theory of International Trade with Multinational Corporations. *Journal of Political Economy* 92, 451–471.

Helpman, Elhanan, Marc Melitz, and Stephen Yeaple. (2004). Exports versus FDI with Heterogeneous Firms. *American Economic Review* 94, 300–316.

Horn, Henrik, and Lars Persson. (2001). The Equilibrium Ownership of an International Oligopoly. *Journal of International Economics* 53, 307–333.

Jones, Ronald W., and J. Peter Neary. (1984). The Positive Theory of International Trade. In R. W. Jones and P. B. Kenen (eds.), *Handbook of International Economics*, vol. 1. Amsterdam: North-Holland, 1–62.

Leahy, Dermot, and J. Peter Neary. (2005). Strategic and Efficiency Motives for Cross-Border Mergers. Mimeo., University College Dublin.

Long, Ngo Van, and Neil Vousden. (1995). The Effects of Trade Liberalization on Cost-Reducing Horizontal Mergers. *Review of International Economics* 3, 141–155.

Markusen, James R. (1983). Factor Movements and Commodity Trade as Complements. *Journal of International Economics* 14, 341–356.

Markusen, James R. (2002). *Multinational Firms and the Theory of International Trade*. Cambridge, Mass.: MIT Press.

Motta, Massimo, and George Norman. (1996). Does Economic Integration Cause Foreign Direct Investment? *International Economic Review* 37, 757–783.

Mundell, Robert. (1957). International Trade and Factor Mobility. *American Economic Review* 47, 321–335.

Neary, J. Peter. (1995). Factor Mobility and International Trade. *Canadian Journal of Economics* 28, S4–S23.

Neary, J. Peter. (2002). Foreign Direct Investment and the Single Market. *Manchester School* 70, 291–314.

Neary, J. Peter. (2003). Globalization and Market Structure. *Journal of the European Economic Association* 1, 245–271.

Neary, J. Peter. (2007). Cross-Border Mergers as Instruments of Comparative Advantage. *Review of Economic Studies* 74, 1229–1274.

Neary, J. Peter, and Cormac Ó Gráda. (1991). Protection, Economic War and Structural Change: The 1930s in Ireland. *Irish Historical Studies* 27, 250–266.

Nocke, Volker, and Stephen Yeaple. (2004). Mergers and the Composition of International Commerce. Mimeo., University of Pennsylvania.

Pavelin, Stephen, and Frank Barry. (2005). The Single Market and the Geographical Diversification of Leading Firms in the EU. *Economic and Social Review* 36, 1–17.

Rowthorn, R. E. (1992). Intra-Industry Trade and Investment Under Oligopoly: The Role of Market Size. *Economic Journal* 102, 402–414.

Salant, Stephen, S. Switzer, and R. Reynolds. (1983). Losses due to Merger: The Effects of an Exogenous Change in Industry Structure on Cournot-Nash Equilibrium. *Quarterly Journal of Economics* 98, 185–199.

Smith, Alasdair. (1987). Strategic Investment, Multinational Corporations and Trade Policy. *European Economic Review* 31, 89–96.

UNCTAD. (1998). *World Investment Report: Trends and Determinants*. New York and Geneva: United Nations.

UNCTAD. (2000). *World Investment Report: Cross-Border Mergers and Acquisitions and Development*. New York and Geneva: United Nations.

Yeaple, Stephen. (2003a). The Complex Integration Strategies of Multinational Firms and Cross-Country Dependencies in the Structure of Foreign Direct Investment. *Journal of International Economics* 60, 293–314.

Yeaple, Stephen. (2003b). The Role of Skill Endowments in the Structure of U.S. Outward Foreign Direct Investment. *Review of Economics and Statistics* 85, 726–734.

3 Investment Liberalization and the Geography of Firm Location

Anders N. Hoffmann and
James R. Markusen

3.1 Introduction

The theory of international trade with increasing returns to scale and imperfect competition in production includes analyses of firm location and industry agglomeration that are sometimes referred to as *economic geography*. With increasing returns and interdependencies among firms, parameter changes in trade costs can have interesting and indeed non-monotonic effects on industry location patterns. Recent work by Fujita, Krugman, and Venables (1999), Brakman, Garretsen, and van Marre-wijk (2001), and Baldwin et al. (2003) presents a great deal of research in this interesting and important new subfield.

One limitation of this location literature is that it almost exclusively deals with geographically integrated firms that conduct all activities from R&D to final production in a single location. But when we examine the industries that motivate this literature, we generally find them dominated by multinational firms. A parallel literature to the economic geography approach considers the endogenous formation of multi-national firms. Much of it is reflected in Markusen's (1997, 2002) knowledge-capital model. Firms' location strategies include not just where to locate an integrated operation, but horizontal expansion, pro-ducing roughly the same goods and services in multiple locations, and vertical strategies in which the production process is geographically fragmented into stages such as R&D, component production, and final assembly.

There are now a few relatively new studies that integrate some the new geography models with the multinational models. Important con-tributions include Barry (1996), Gao (1999), Raybaudi-Massilia (2000), Ekholm and Forslid (2001), and Egger et al. (2005). Much of this work concentrates on the question of how changes in trade costs affect location decision when multinational firms form endogenously versus when they are not allowed (the geography models), and the consequences of factor mobility with and without multinationals. They tend to have a particular focus on multiple and unstable equilibria in the geography tradition.[1]

This chapter continues in the tradition of this research, seeking to integrate results from the geography and multinationals models. We use the world Edgeworth box to consider a series of two-country cases in which the countries differ in size or in relative endowments. We use Markusen's knowledge-capital model in which firms may adopt national, horizontal, or vertical strategies. Instead of focusing on trade costs or factor mobility, we focus on investment barriers and the effect of the removal of these barriers on the location of activities holding trade costs constant and factors immobile. The location of firm headquarters (R&D, management, marketing, finance, and so forth) may change in ways quite different from the location and number of production plants.

The model is a two-good, two-factor, two-country general equilibrium model where the X sector has increasing returns and imperfect competition. An X firm is associated with a country where its headquarters is located. If it has a single plant in that same country, it is referred to as a national firm (type n). If it has plants in both countries, it is referred to as a horizontal multinational (type m). If its single plant is in the nonheadquarters country, then it is referred to as a vertical multinational (type v). These three firm types can be headquartered in either country, giving six firm types in all.

The experiment considered here is to remove a prohibitive investment barrier holding the costs of trading X across borders constant. Initially only type n firms can exist.[2] This experiment is repeated over a parameter space represented by points in the world Edgeworth box where each point is a division of the total world endowment of skilled and unskilled labor between the two countries. Thus, the countries are allowed to differ in two dimensions: size and relative factor endowments. We assume that headquarters are more skilled labor intensive than plants, which are in turn more skilled labor intensive than the other sector (Y) of the economy.[3]

We begin with the no-liberalization case and show how firm location depends on both relative country sizes due to scale economies and relative endowments. Investment liberalization tends to lead to headquarter location depending almost exclusively on relative endowments. Plant location depends on a combination of endowment and size differences, with the latter playing a major role. Averaged over all the two-country pairs in the world Edgeworth box, the average Herfindahl index of concentration for plants falls and that for headquarters rises relative to the no-liberalization case. Thus, production may become more dispersed, but corporate headquarters and R&D labs may become more concentrated in a few locations. This result was identified by Ekholm and Forslid (2001).

We consider the effects of investment liberalization on factor prices and the incentives for workers to migrate. We find that investment liberalization creates a substantial factor-price-equalization set in the world Edgeworth box, so migration cannot destabilize countries that are relatively similar.[4] More generally, investment liberalization moves countries toward factor-price equalization, but not completely so. Investment liberalization, while leading to convergence, can still leave a small country with lower real wages for both skilled and unskilled labor. Thus, investment liberalization cannot substitute completely for free trade for a small country trying to build and maintain its skilled-labor workforce. Welfare changes are also considered. Both countries benefit if they are not too different, but the larger or skill-abundant country can lose when the difference is substantial. This result also tends to occur with trade liberalization and is due to a loss of monopoly power in trade or, alternatively, an adverse terms-of-trade change for the large country.

We have not found suitable data for trying to estimate this model but present some suggestive statistics in our final section. We show that the concentration across source countries of outward foreign direct investment (FDI) in the world economy is substantially higher than the concentration of inward FDI across countries and that this difference has been fairly stable and persistent over time. We also find that the concentration across countries of parent firms is more concentrated than foreign affiliates if China is excluded from the data but not if China is included. The count of foreign affiliates in the world economy is more than ten times the number of parents. These results do not directly address or estimate our model, but they are at the very least consistent with the knowledge-capital model itself.

3.2   Model Structure

The model has two countries (h and f) producing two homogeneous goods, Y and X. There are two factors of production, L (unskilled labor) and S (skilled labor). L and S are mobile between industries but internationally immobile. Y will be used as numeraire throughout the chapter.[5]

Subscripts (i, j) will be used to denote the countries (f, h). The output of Y in country i is a constant elasticity of substitution (CES) function, identical in both countries. The production function for Y is

$$Y_i = (aL_{iy}^{\varepsilon} + (1 - a)S_{iy}^{\varepsilon})^{1/\varepsilon} \quad i = h, f, \tag{3.1}$$

where L_{iy} and S_{iy} are the unskilled and skilled labor used in the Y sector in country i. The elasticity of substitution $(1/(1 - \varepsilon))$ is set at 3.0 in the simulation runs reported later in the chapter.

Good X is produced with increasing returns to scale by imperfectly competitive Cournot firms. There are both firm-level (arising from joint inputs such as R&D) and plant-level scale economies. There is free entry and exit of firms, and entering firms choose their "type." The term *regime* denotes the set of firm types active in equilibrium. There are six firm types, defined as follows:

Type m_h—horizontal multinationals that maintain plants in both countries, with headquarters located in country h.

Type m_f—horizontal multinationals that maintain plants in both countries, with headquarters located in country f.

Type n_h—national firms that maintain a single plant and headquarters in country h. Type h firms may or may not export to country f.

Type n_f—national firms that maintain a single plant and headquarters in country f. Type f firms may or may not export to country h.

Type v_h—vertical multinationals that maintain a single plant in country f and headquarters in country h. Type v_h firms may or may not export to country h.

Type v_f—vertical multinationals that maintain a single plant in country h and headquarters in country f. Type v_f firms may or may not export to country f.

Factor-intensity assumptions are crucial to the results that will be derived below. These are guided by evidence presented in Markusen (1997, 2002). First, headquarters activities are more skilled labor intensive than production plants (including both plant-specific fixed costs and marginal costs). This obviously implies that an integrated type n firm with a headquarters and plant in the same location is more skilled labor intensive than a plant alone. Second, we assume that a plant alone (no headquarters) is more skilled labor intensive than the composite Y sector. This is much less obvious, but some evidence suggests that this is probably true for developing countries: branch plants of foreign multinationals are more skilled labor intensive than the economy as a whole.[6] Assumptions on the skilled labor intensity of activities are therefore:

Activities

[headquarters only] > [integrated X] > [plant only] > [Y].

Superscripts (n, v, m) will be used to designate a variable as referring to national firms, vertical multinationals, and horizontal multinational firms, respectively. (m_i, v_i, n_i) will also be used to indicate the number of active m, v, and n firms based in country i. It should always be clear from the context what is being represented (e.g., n_i as a variable in an equation always refers to the number of national firms in country i). Important notation in the model is as follows.

p_i Price of X (in terms of Y) in country i ($i = h, f$)

w_i Wage of unskilled labor in country i

z_i Wage of skilled labor in country i

c Marginal cost of X production in units of L (both countries, all firm types)

τ Transport cost for X in units of L (same in both directions)

M_i Income of country i

X_{ij}^k Sales of a type k firm ($k = n, v, m$), based in country i, sales in market j ($i, j = h, f$)

e_{ij}^k Markup of q type k firm ($k = n, v, m$), based in country i, sales in market j ($i, j = h, f$)

G^k Fixed costs of a type k firm in units of unskilled labor (where relevant: subscript 1 = headquarters' country, subscript 2 = host country)

F^k Fixed costs of a type k firm in units of skilled labor (where relevant: subscript 1 = headquarters' country, subscript 2 = host country)

A national firm undertakes all its production in its base country, so the cost function of one national firm in country i is given by

$$w_i L_i^n + z_i S_i^n = w_i[cX_{ii}^n + (c+\tau)X_{ij}^n + G^n] + z_i F^n, \quad i,j = h,f, \quad i \neq j. \tag{3.2}$$

c, τ, F^n, and G^n are identical across countries.

A horizontal multinational based in country i has sales in country j, X_{ij}^m. It operates one plant in each country incurring fixed costs, (G_1^m, F_1^m) in its base country and fixed costs (G_2^m, F_2^m) in country j. Sales are met entirely from local production, not trade. $L_{ij}^m(S_{ij}^m)$ denotes a country i horizontal multinational firm's demand for unskilled (skilled) labor in country j. A firm type m_i thus has a cost function

$$w_i L_{ii}^m + w_j L_{ij}^m + z_i S_{ii}^m + z_j S_{ij}^m$$

$$= w_i[cX_{ii}^m + G_1^m] + w_j[cX_{ij}^m + G_2^m] + z_i F_1^m + z_j F_2^m. \tag{3.3}$$

Similarly, a vertical multinational based in country i (plant in country j) has sales in country j, X_{ij}^v. $L_{ij}^v(S_{ij}^v)$ denotes a country i vertical multinational firm's demand for unskilled (skilled) labor in country j. A firm type v_i has a cost function

$$w_j L_{ij}^v + z_i S_{ii}^v + z_j S_{ij}^v = w_j[cX_{jj}^m + (c+\tau)X_{ji}^v + G^v] + z_i F_1^v + z_j F_2^v. \tag{3.4}$$

Let $\bar{L}_i$ and $\bar{S}_i$ denote the total labor endowments of country i. Adding labor demand from n_i national firms, v_i and v_j vertical multinationals, and m_i and m_j horizontal multinationals gives country i factor market clearing:

$$\bar{L}_i = L_{iy} + n_i L_i^n + m_i L_{ii}^m + m_j L_{ji}^m + v_j L_{ji}^v$$

$$\bar{S}_i = S_{iy} + n_i S_i^n + m_i S_{ii}^m + m_j S_{ji}^m + v_i S_{ii}^v + v_j S_{ji}^v. \tag{3.5}$$

In equilibrium, the X sector makes no profits, so country i income, denoted M_i, is

$$M_i = w_i \bar{L}_i + v_i \bar{S}_i \quad i = h,f. \tag{3.6}$$

p_i denotes the price of X in country i, and X_{ic} and Y_{ic} denote the consumption of X and Y. Utility of the representative consumer in each country is Cobb-Douglas,

$$U_i = X_{ic}^\alpha Y_{ic}^{1-\alpha}, \quad X_{ic} \equiv n_i X_{ii}^n + n_j X_{ji}^n + m_i X_{ii}^m + m_j X_{ji}^m + v_i X_{ii}^v + v_j X_{ji}^v, \tag{3.7}$$

giving demands

$$X_{ic} = \alpha M_i / p_i, \quad Y_{ic} = (1 - \alpha) M_i. \tag{3.8}$$

Equilibrium in the X sector is the solution to a complementarity problem. First, there are marginal revenue–marginal cost inequalities, associated with outputs per firm. These are:

$$p_i(1 - e_{ii}^n) \leq w_i c \qquad (X_{ii}^n) \tag{3.9}$$

$$p_j(1 - e_{ij}^n) \leq w_i(c + \tau) \qquad (X_{ij}^n) \tag{3.10}$$

$$p_i(1 - e_{ii}^m) \leq w_i c \qquad (X_{ii}^m) \tag{3.11}$$

$$p_j(1 - e_{ij}^m) \leq w_j c \qquad (X_{ij}^m) \tag{3.12}$$

$$p_i(1 - e_{ji}^v) \leq w_i c \qquad (X_{ji}^v) \tag{3.13}$$

$$p_i(1 - e_{ii}^v) \leq w_j(c + \tau) \qquad (X_{ii}^v) \tag{3.14}$$

In a Cournot model with homogeneous products, the optimal markup formula is given by the firm's market share divided by the Marshallian price elasticity of demand in that market. In our model, the price elasticity is one (see equation 3.8), reducing the firm's markup to its market share. This gives (also using demand equations 3.8)

$$e_{ij}^k = \frac{X_{ij}^k}{X_{jc}} = \frac{p_j X_{ij}^k}{\alpha M_j} \quad k = n, m, v \quad i, j = h, f. \tag{3.15}$$

There are six zero-profit conditions corresponding to the numbers of the four firm types. Given equations 3.9 to 3.14, zero profits can be written as the requirement that markup revenues equal fixed costs, with the number of firms as the associated complementary variable:

$$p_h e_{hh}^n X_{hh}^n + p_f e_{hf}^n X_{hf}^n \leq w_h G^n + z_h F^n \qquad (n_h) \tag{3.16}$$

$$p_f e_{ff}^n X_{ff}^n + p_h e_{fh}^n X_{fh}^n \leq w_f G^n + z_f F^n \qquad (n_f) \tag{3.17}$$

$$p_h e_{hh}^m X_{hh}^m + p_f e_{hf}^m X_{hf}^m \leq w_h G_1^m + z_h F_1^m + w_f G_2^m + z_f F_2^m \qquad (m_h) \tag{3.18}$$

$$p_f e_{ff}^m X_{ff}^m + p_h e_{fh}^m X_{fh}^m \leq w_f G_1^m + z_f F_1^m + w_h G_2^m + z_h F_2^m \qquad (m_f) \tag{3.19}$$

$$p_h e_{hh}^v X_{hh}^v + p_f e_{hf}^v X_{hf}^v \leq w_f G^v + z_h F_1^v + z_f F_2^v \qquad (v_h) \qquad (3.20)$$

$$p_f e_{ff}^v X_{ff}^v + p_h e_{fh}^v X_{fh}^v \leq w_h G^v + z_f F_1^v + z_h F_2^v \qquad (v_f) \qquad (3.21)$$

Substitute markups into MR = MC inequalities:

$$X \geq \beta M_i \frac{p_i - w_i c}{p_i^2}, \qquad \text{for} \qquad X_{ii}^n, X_{ii}^m, X_{ji}^v \qquad (3.22)$$

$$X \geq \beta M_j \frac{p_j - w_i(c + \tau)}{p_j^2}, \qquad \text{for} \qquad X_{ij}^n, X_{jj}^v. \qquad (3.23)$$

Substitute these inequalities into the zero-profit conditions in order to derive some awful looking quadratic equations:

$$\beta \left[M_h \left(\frac{p_h - w_h c}{p_h} \right)^2 + M_f \left(\frac{p_f - w_h(c + \tau)}{p_f} \right)^2 \right]$$

$$\leq w_h G^n + z_h F^n \qquad (n_h) \qquad (3.24)$$

$$\beta \left[M_h \left(\frac{p_h - w_f(c + \tau)}{p_h} \right)^2 + M_f \left(\frac{p_f - w_f c}{p_f} \right)^2 \right]$$

$$\leq w_f G^n + z_f F^n \qquad (n_f) \qquad (3.25)$$

$$\beta \left[M_h \left(\frac{p_h - w_h c}{p_h} \right)^2 + M_f \left(\frac{p_f - w_f c}{p_f} \right)^2 \right]$$

$$\leq w_h G_1^m + z_h F_1^m + w_f G_2^m + z_f F_2^m \qquad (m_h) \qquad (3.26)$$

$$\beta \left[M_h \left(\frac{p_h - w_h c}{p_h} \right)^2 + M_f \left(\frac{p_f - w_f c}{p_f} \right)^2 \right]$$

$$\leq w_f G_1^m + z_f F_1^m + w_h G_2^m + z_h F_2^m \qquad (m_f) \qquad (3.27)$$

$$\beta \left[M_h \left(\frac{p_h - w_f(c + \tau)}{p_h} \right)^2 + M_f \left(\frac{p_f - w_f c}{p_f} \right)^2 \right]$$

$$\leq w_f G^v + z_h F_1^v + z_f F_2^v \qquad (v_h) \qquad (3.28)$$

$$\beta \left[M_h \left(\frac{p_h - w_h c}{p_h} \right)^2 + M_f \left(\frac{p_f - w_h(c + \tau)}{p_f} \right)^2 \right]$$

$$\leq w_h G^v + z_f F_1^v + z_h F_2^v. \qquad (v_f) \qquad (3.29)$$

Assume that foreign ownership is initially banned, meaning that initially there are only type n firms active in equilibrium. Consider first the effects of investment liberalization on the incentive for type m firms to enter. Comparing equations 3.26–3.27 to 3.24–3.25, we see that type m firms will have higher markup revenues but also higher fixed costs relative to type n firms. The degree to which markup revenues will be higher will be greater the more similar are the sizes of the two countries. Thus type m firms will enter following liberalization when the two countries are of relatively similar size.

Second, consider the incentives for type v firms to enter. Comparing equations 3.28–3.29 to 3.24–3.25, we see no differences in markup revenues, but type v firms can "arbitrage" factor price differences, locating their headquarters and incurring fixed costs where skilled labor is cheap.

3.3 Effects of Investment Liberalization

The regime shifts induced by investment liberalization are analyzed in Markusen (1997, 2002), and we will not repeat a detailed analysis here. Rather, the effects of liberalization on the location of plants and headquarters will be interpreted in terms of regime shifts as we go along.

Figures 3.1 to 3.7 show world Edgeworth boxes, with skilled labor on the vertical axis and unskilled labor on the horizontal axis. Country h's endowment is measured from the southwest (SW) corner and country f's endowment from the northwest (NE) corner. Along the SW-NE diagonal, the countries differ in size but have identical relative endowments. The locus of points where the countries have roughly equal GDPs runs through the center of the box but is steeper than the NW-SE diagonal.[7] The approximate equal-income locus is show in several of the figures. We limit the dimensions of the box to each country having at least 20 percent of the world endowment of each factor. Not much different happens for a wider range, and this allows more graphical clarity for the interesting part.[8]

The model itself is known as a nonlinear complementarity problem, and we repeatedly solve a numerical version of the model over a grid

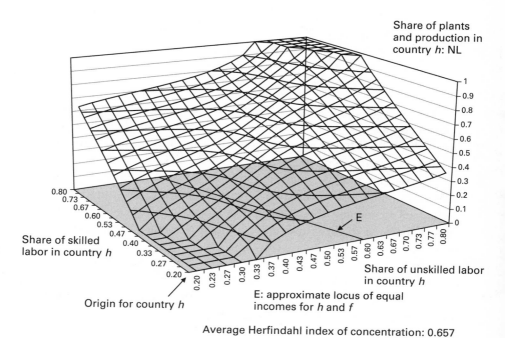

Average Herfindahl index of concentration: 0.657

Figure 3.1
Share of plants and headquarters in country h: No liberalization (NL)

of values of the world endowment of each factor using Rutherford's subsystem MPS/GE of GAMS. Each cell in figures 3.1 to 3.7 is a solution to a particular two-country model with the countries differing in size or relative endowments. The shares are increases in steps of 0.0333 with nineteen steps on each axis. Thus there $19 \times 19 = 361$ cells or solutions to the model in each world Edgeworth box.

Figures 3.1 and 3.2 show the solutions under the assumptions that multinational firms are not permitted. The figures show the share of firms (equals plants equals headquarters) that are located in country h. There are two sources of comparative advantage in the model: country size, due to scale economies, and relative endowments. Figure 3.2 presents two two-dimension curves to help clarify this from the general three-dimension presentation in figure 3.1. The curve labeled "income locus" is the SW-NE diagonal of figure 3.1, where the countries differ in size but not in relative endowments. The curve labeled "relative endowment locus" is the set of endowments where the countries have the same income but differ in relative endowments, line E on the

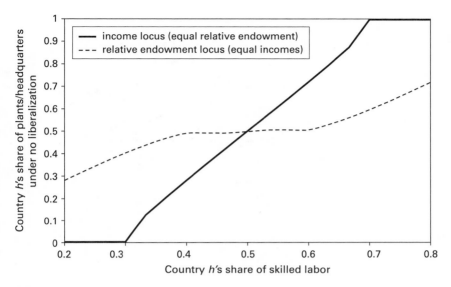

Figure 3.2
Share of plants and headquarters in country h: No liberalization

floor of figure 3.1. Figure 3.2 has country h's share of skilled labor on the horizontal axis, identical to its share of unskilled labor for the income locus, but not for the relative endowment locus (unskilled labor share moves in the opposite direction from the skilled labor share).

Both figures 3.1 and 3.2 make clear the role of country size. Given relatively high trade costs of 20 percent ad valorem, a small country with an income share less than or equal to 30 percent of the world total is shut out of the X sector in equilibrium. In figure 3.2, a country with a 40 percent income share has about 28 percent of the firms, and this, of course, reaches 50 percent when country h has a 50 percent income share. Figures 3.1 and 3.2 also show the role of relative endowment differences, the latter when the countries are of equal size. The relative endowment locus in figure 3.2 seems relatively flat, but remember that this is measuring the share of firms in each country, not the share of production. The skilled-labor-abundant country has more competition, more efficient firms, lower markups, and a share of production that exceeds its share of firms.

Finally, we present a Herfindahl index of concentration at the bottom of figure 3.1. This index squares each country's share of the total number of firms and then sums over the two countries in question. This ranges from 1.0, when all firms are in one country, to 0.50

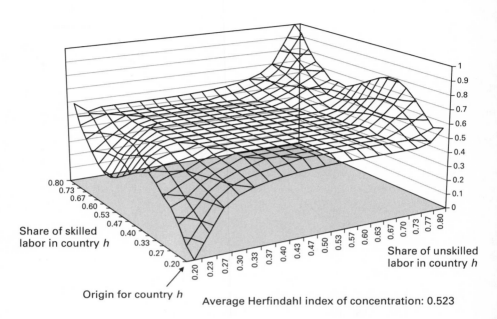

Figure 3.3
Share of plants in country h: With liberalization (IL)

$(0.50^2 + 0.50^2 = 0.50)$, when the firms are equally distributed. The statistic 0.657 presented in figure 3.1 averages this over all 361 country pairs in the simulation.

We then remove all barriers to multinational firms, allowing type m and type v firms to enter when profitable.[9] The shares of plants and headquarters located in country h are shown in figures 3.3 and 3.4, respectively. The difference between the plant and headquarters location patterns is dramatic. Plants are much more divided between any two countries in a cell. The flat area of figure 3.3 is a region dominated by horizontal multinationals, each with plants in both countries. When there are only horizontal firms in equilibrium, the Herfindahl index of plant concentration must be 0.50. When countries become quite different in size, national firms enter in the large country, and so the large country has a larger share of total plants. When a country is quite small but very skilled labor abundant, it becomes the headquarters of vertical firms with plants in the other country, and so its share of plants falls below 0.50. Averaged over all 361 country pairs, the Herfindahl index of concentration falls to 0.523. Similar results are found in Ekholm and Forslid (2001) and Raybaudi-Massilia (2000).

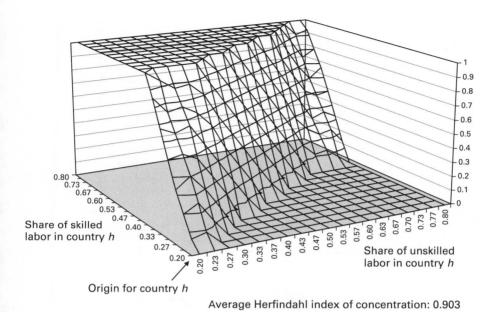

Origin for country *h*

Average Herfindahl index of concentration: 0.903

Figure 3.4
Share of headquarters in country *h*: With liberalization (IL)

Figure 3.4 shows headquarters concentration across country pairs following investment liberalization. The pattern is clearly that investment liberalization increases the share of firms headquartered in the skilled-labor-abundant country. The reason for this is fairly clear from inequalities 3.24 to 3.29. When investment is free, the choice for the location of firm headquarters depends only on factor prices, and not directly on either country size or trade costs. The latter directly influence whether a firm chooses to have one or two plants and where to locate a single plant, but the choice of headquarters is influenced only indirectly by these variables insofar as they have general equilibrium ramifications on factor prices. The Herfindahl index for headquarters averaged over all 361 country pairs is 0.903, much higher than the concentration index for plants.

Figure 3.5 explicitly turns to the changes induced by investment liberalization. Panel A maps the change in the share of plants located in country *h*, and panel B maps the changes in country *h*'s share of headquarters. The equal income locus is drawn in panel A to help make it clear that the change in plant location is driven a lot by country sizes as well as relative endowments. Small countries tend to gain plants

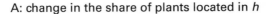

A: change in the share of plants located in *h*

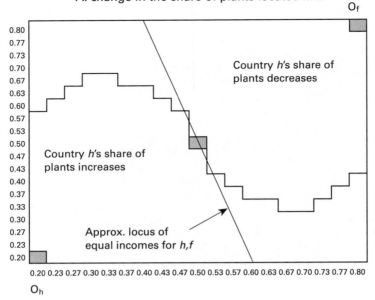

B: change in the share of headquarters located in *h*

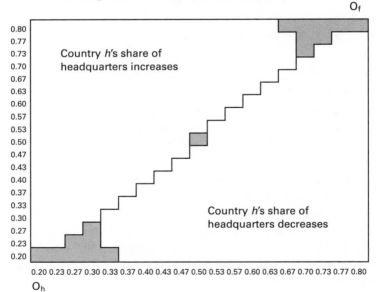

Vertical axes: Country *h*'s share of skilled labor
Horizontal axes: Country *h*'s share of unskilled labor

☐ No change

Figure 3.5
Change in the location of plants following investment liberalization

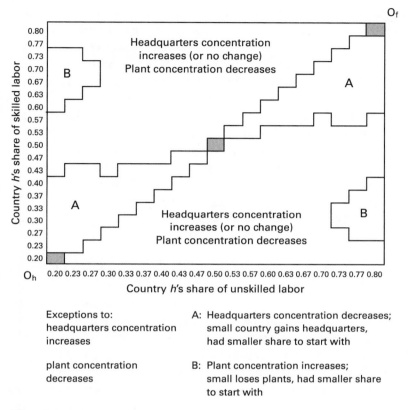

Figure 3.6
Change in the concentration of plant and headquarters following investment liberalization

through horizontal firms replacing national firms headquartered in the large country. But a small, very skilled-labor-abundant country can lose plants. This is because of the entry of vertical firms headquartered in such a country, with plants in the large, unskilled-labor-abundant country.

Panel B of figure 3.5 shows that the change in the share of firms headquartered in country h follows relative factor proportions almost exactly. This is because we are now essentially assuming that headquartersU services are freely traded, and thus they depend only on factor prices, which are only indirectly affected (and apparently not much) by country size.

Figure 3.6 computes changes in the Herfindahl concentration index for firms and plants for each country going from no liberalization to investment liberalization. The dominant outcome, occurring in almost 75 percent of the cells, is that headquarters concentration increases between the two countries and plant concentration decreases. There are no cells where both of those outcomes are reversed. There are, however, several regions where one of the dominant outcomes is reversed. In the regions marked A in figure 3.6, headquarters concentration decreases along with plant concentration. This is because the small country is gaining headquarters, but it had a smaller share to start with, so headquarters concentration is moving toward 0.50 rather than away from it. In the regions marked B in figure 3.6, plant concentration increases while headquarters concentration also increases. This is because the smaller, skilled-labor-abundant country loses plants, concentrating on headquarters of vertical firms. But since that country had a smaller share of plants to begin with, concentration of plants increases.

Figure 3.7 turns to equilibrium factor real prices, nominal returns in terms of Y divided by the price index (cost of buying a unit of utility) in each country. Panel A gives the result for no liberalization. The model is calibrated so that the scale effect on the price index does not overwhelm factor proportions effects, and so countries that differ substantially in relative endowments show the usual Heckscher-Ohlin pattern that factors are expensive where they are scarce. Because of trade costs, the factor-price-equalization (FPE) set is a singular point where the countries are identical. This symmetric equilibrium with identical countries is stable to the movement of one factor alone, in contrast to many of the new geography models that have a single factor used only in the X sector.

There are, however, regions where countries differ in size but not greatly in relative endowments, where both real factor prices are higher in the larger country. This is the scale-economies/imperfect-competition effect that leaves the price of X lower and real factor productivity higher in the larger country. These points can be thought of as unstable with respect to factor mobility, in that the mobility of either factor will necessarily increase the size differences of the countries, and if both factors can move as a bundle, the smaller country can disappear.

Panel B of Figure 3.7 shows real factor price differences under investment liberalization. The big change is in the appearance of a large FPE set. This is a region dominated by two-plant horizontal firms. Each country has the same number of plants, all with the same marginal

A: Factor-price difference under NL

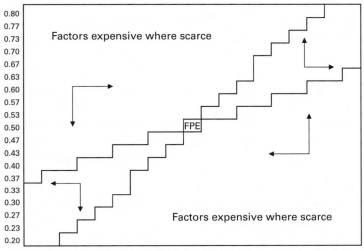

0.20 0.23 0.27 0.30 0.33 0.37 0.40 0.43 0.47 0.50 0.53 0.57 0.60 0.63 0.67 0.70 0.73 0.77 0.80

B: Factor-price differences under IL

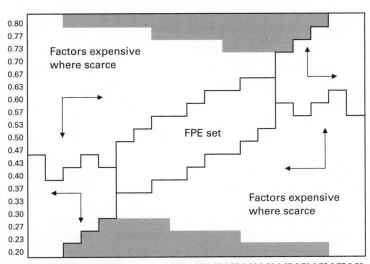

0.20 0.23 0.27 0.30 0.33 0.37 0.40 0.43 0.47 0.50 0.53 0.57 0.60 0.63 0.67 0.70 0.73 0.77 0.80

Vertical axes: Country h's share of skilled labor
Horizontal axes: Country h's share of unskilled labor

Pairs where the price of skilled labor diverges
between countries; all other points, convergence

Figure 3.7
Factor-price differences before and after liberalization

cost, and so the prices and markups in each country are the same. This set contains countries that differ in relative endowments. This is sustained as an FPE equilibrium by allocating the headquarters between the two countries—more to the skilled-labor-abundant country—so as to achieve FPE.

It is also true that almost all cells in panel B show a smaller difference in the real price of each factor between the two countries (including, obviously, the expanded FPE set) relative to panel A. In other words, investment liberalization leads to partial convergence for virtually all pairs of countries, but full convergence for only those in the FPE set of panel B. The exception to this is the shaded cells in panel B of Figure 3.7, where the price of skilled labor diverges between the two members of the country pair. The intuition follows three articles by Feenstra and Hanson (1996a, 1996b, 1997). For these country pairs, investment liberalization shifts plants to the smaller country and headquarters to the larger country. The result is a relative increase in the demand for skilled labor in both countries as each country shifts to a relatively more skill-intensive activity. The real return to skilled labor rises for both countries in these cells but tends to rise more in the unskilled-labor-abundant country. But it was higher there to start with, and so the return to skilled labor diverges.

Figure 3.8, which shows the welfare consequences of liberalization, concludes this section. It is not easy to describe in a single sentence the region where both countries gain. Basically and roughly, both countries gain when the size difference is moderate and the smaller country is moderately skilled labor abundant. Very similar countries, including two identical countries, both gain as horizontal firms replace costly exporting by national firms.

It seems that a country can lose under two circumstances: (1), if it is large and has a relative endowment not much different from its trading partner or (2) if it is more middle sized and very skilled labor abundant. In both cases, the country has an initially strong comparative advantage in X, resulting in a concentration of X production at home and consequently a low price index (recall that trade costs are 20 percent). Investment liberalization shifts plants to the other country, and although there are overall gains in scale and in lower markups, the price index increases in the large or very skilled-labor-abundant country, which leads to an aggregate welfare loss for that country. The price index effect always works against the country losing plants, and note that the region where country h loses in figure 3.8 is a subregion of the

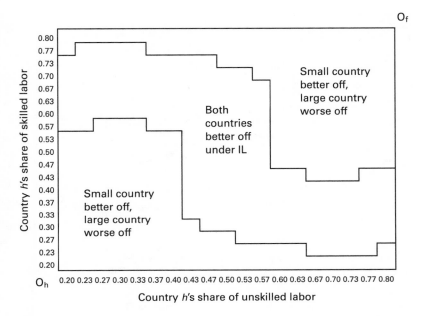

Figure 3.8
Change in welfare following investment liberalization

region where country h has a decrease in its share of plants in figure 3.5, panel A.

3.4   Some Relevant Data

We have tried very hard to find data that would allow us to examine some of the ideas in this chapter, however informally. We have not made much progress since, to the best of our knowledge, no comprehensive data set exists that would meet even basic requirements for formal econometric work. Nevertheless, there has been a good deal of recent work estimating and testing propositions from the knowledge capital model, and generally supporting evidence gives us some confidence for using this as serious theoretical model. Early work particularly supported the horizontal motive for multinational production, beginning first with Brainard (1997) and then later with Blonigen, Davies, and Head (2003) and Markusen and Maskus (2002). Finding support for parts of the theory relating to vertical firms has been slower in emerging, but now includes Carr, Markusen, and Maskus (2001, 2003), Davies (2004), and Braconier and Norbäck (2004, 2005).

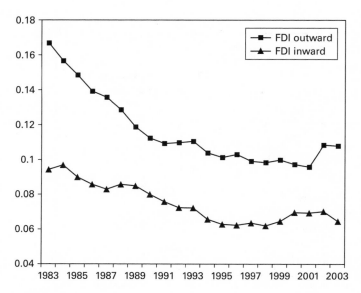

Figure 3.9
Herfindahl concentration indices for world inward and outward FDI

Thus, despite limited data for formal econometric work on the present paper, there is an emerging body of evidence that the theory model is relevant.[10]

We can present some other data from the *World Investment Report* of UNCTAD consistent with the ideas expressed in this paper. Figure 3.9 presents Herfindahl indices of concentration for world inward and outward stocks for the twenty-one-year period 1983 to 2003. Overall, the data on FDI and multinational firms indicate a higher concentration of headquarters than plants. The concentration was decreasing for both headquarters and plants during the 1980s. The concentration was stable during the 1990s, whereas the newest data suggest an increase in concentration of outward investment and a decrease in inward investment.

The inward investments have seen a rather stable decrease in concentration in the period. The decrease in concentration from the early 1980s to the early 1990s was partly due to an increase in the number of countries receiving FDI. The number of countries with an FDI stock of more than $10 million increased from around 140 in 1990 to around 180 in 1995.[11] The flattening of the curve from the mid-1990s is due to a very large increase in FDI in China.

Table 3.1
Herfindahl concentration of parents and affiliates (count data)

	Parents	Affiliates
All countries	0.072	0.229
All countries minus China	0.072	0.067
All countries − 31 Chinese provinces	0.071	0.048

The concentration of outward investment decreased a lot during the 1980s, when Japan and other large countries entered the scene as foreign investors. The U.S. share of total outward FDI (stock) decreased from 38 percent in 1980 to 24 percent in 1990. No new major players entered during the 1990s, which led to a stabled concentration with a slightly increasing trend.

If we make the assumption that outward investment is roughly related to the number of parent firms in a country and further assume that inward investment is a crude proxy for foreign affiliates, then these data are at least consistent with our model and with the outcomes shown in Figures 3.3 and 3.4. The data are consistent with the idea that headquarters are concentrated in skilled-labor-abundant countries (this has been verified in much other empirical work) but that affiliates (plants in our model) tend to be much more widely dispersed. The latter in turn is consistent with horizontal models and motives in particular, a phenomenon that has also received strong empirical support.

The UNCTAD report (2004) also gives count data on parent firms and foreign affiliates operating in each country. We have also calculated Herfindahl concentration indices on parent and affiliate shares across countries. These are shown in table 3.1. The data on parent corporations and foreign affiliates do not confirm the higher concentration of headquarters than plants if taken at face value. Calculations show that plants are about three times more concentrated that headquarters. However, these data are highly biased by China. China had about 45 percent of the world's foreign affiliates in 2002 but only about 6.1 percent of the world's inward FDI stock in 2002. There is thus a dramatic difference between the count data and the value data with respect to China. If both numbers are accurate, it suggests that China is host to a great many very small foreign affiliates. In any case, the second row of table 3.1 also presents the concentration statistics with China deleted from the data set.

China's FDI should also be seen in relation to its size. China accounts for almost 30 percent of the developing world's population. Thus, many OECD parent countries are going to have plants, perhaps many firms having multiple plants, in China. Thus, the fact that China is so large in a multicountry world is going to give a big upward push to affiliate concentration but not to parent concentration.

China's figures are also inflated by the round-tripping (some domestic investments are counted as FDI) of FDI through Hong Kong (China), which some estimates suggest may account for as much as 30 percent of total FDI to China (World Bank 2004). It is possible to break the Chinese data up in the thirty-one Chinese provinces, which makes the data much more comparable with other countries. The average population in a province is about 44 million people. Including the provinces reduces the concentration of the world plants significantly but has very little effect on the concentration of headquarters. Results are shown in the third row of table 3.1. By using this approach of treating Chinese provinces as additional countries in the full world data set, headquarters (parents) are now significantly more concentrated than plants (affiliates). Interestingly, the concentration index for outward FDI in figure 3.9 was 54 percent higher than the concentration index for inward investment in 1992 (0.108/0.070), while the concentration index for parents in table 3.1 using the Chinese provinces as additional countries was 48 percent higher than the concentration index for affiliates in 1992 (0.071/0.048).

These results are at least consistent with our model and with the importance of horizontal firms in particular (again, there is much existing evidence to that effect already). This is an important finding for the geography literature, which often emphasizes the instability of a symmetric equilibrium with similar countries. The introduction of horizontal multinationals in particular eliminates this instability property, as shown in Ekholm and Forslid (2001), Baybaudi-Massilia (2000), in this chapter in Figure 3.5, and for vertical multinationals by Gao (1999).

3.5   Summary and Conclusions

Much of the recent literature on location decision with increasing returns to scale and imperfect competition has concentrated on integrated single-plant national firms and the effects of trade-cost changes. Here we shift the focus to multinational firms and the effects of reductions in investment barriers. A firm is composed of two activities, a headquarters and a plant. In addition to the option of being a single-plant firm with headquarters and plant in the same location, referred to as a national firm, we allow two additional options: the firm may choose to have plants in both countries, referred to as a horizontal multinational, or have a single plant but locate the headquarters and plant in different countries, referred to as a vertical multinational. We model investment liberalization in a very simple way.

Initially either type of multinational is simply banned, meaning that a plant in one country cannot be controlled by a headquarters in another country. Thus only national firms headquartered in either country are permitted initially. As suggested by the geography literature, both relative size and relative endowments are determinants of revealed comparative advantage. An equilibrium in which countries differ in size but have similar relative endowments is unstable with respect to factor migration, meaning that such migration would cause the size difference to grow.

Investment liberalization leads to a concentration of headquarters in the skilled-labor-abundant country. With investment permitted, the optimal location of headquarters depends on only equilibrium factor prices. The location of plants is more complicated, depending on both factor prices and market size, with the latter of particular importance.

We define a Herfindahl concentration index for plants and headquarters, which is the sum of the squared market shares over the two countries. Over a broad area of parameter space, we find that investment liberalization leads to an increased concentration of headquarters but a decreased concentration of plants. This is especially robust when the countries are of similar size. When size is similar and investment is banned, national firms exist in both countries but are concentrated in the skilled-labor-abundant or larger country (the latter is referred to as a *home market effect*). Liberalization moves headquarters toward the skilled-labor-abundant or large country, thus moving the shares further away from 0.5 and increasing concentration. But the entering firms are generally two-plant horizontal firms, so liberalization moves the shares of plants closer to 0.5, decreasing concentration.

A section on the factor-market consequences of investment liberalization follows. Our results indicate that investment liberalization moves countries toward factor-price equalization, but incompletely so. A factor-price-equalization set exists, so migration incentives are removed by investment liberalization for countries similar in size and in relative endowments. In a generally more complex model, we thus obtain similar findings on migration incentives and the concentration of headquarters versus plants to those found in Gao (1999), Ekholm and Forslid (2001), and Raybaudi-Massilia (2000). Simply put, the introduction of endogenous multinationals in general decreases the agglomeration of production and the tendency for symmetric equilibria to be unstable with respect to migration (the exception is that headquarters become more concentrated).

The chapter concludes by considering some data on inward versus outward investment and the concentration of parent firms versus foreign affiliates. While not very suitable for formal econometric work, the data are at least consistent with the general thrust of Markusen's knowledge-capital model and the results of this chapter. We should also emphasize again that a great deal of empirical work over the past five years has affirmed the importance of horizontal multinationals and that the consequences of this observation for the new geography models are profound: horizontal firms arising between similar countries under moderate trade costs destroy the instability of symmetric equilibria that occurs under the same circumstance in the standard national-firm core-periphery model.

Notes

Data on the Chinese provinces was culled from several sources: OECD. (2001). Regional Disparities and Trade and Investment Liberalization in China. Paris: Territorial Development Service. OECD-China Conference "Foreign Investment in China's Regional Development: Prospect and Policy Challenges," 11–12 October 2001, Xi'an, China.

1. As we will note at several points throughout the chapter, a number of our results are not new, but have been previously identified in Barry (1996), Gao (1999), Raybaudi-Massilia (2000), and Ekholm and Forslid (2001). We feel that one contribution of this chapter is a more general approach to the problem that nests these earlier contributions as special cases.

2. In order to avoid confusion later, we should note here that there is no "capital" in the model in the usual macroeconomic sense. Multinational firms supply the services of "knowledge-based" or "intangible" assets to plants abroad and repatriate markup revenues. This is what is meant by "investment" in this chapter. Banning investment means that no firm headquartered in country i can own a plant in country j.

3. Egger et al. (2005) use a model very similar to ours, drawn from Markusen (1997, 2002), but focus on the role of trade costs and factor mobility given the existence of multinationals. In other words, they assume liberalized investment and concentrate on trade cost changes, while we assume fixed trade costs and consider investment liberalization.

4. Various versions of these results were identified by Barry (1996), Gao (1999), Raybaudi-Massilia (2000), and Ekholm and Forslid (2001).

5. "Real wages" will be properly defined as nominal values divided by the consumer price index (the unit expenditure function).

6. Evidence supporting the assumption that multinational branch plants are more skilled labor intensive than the overall economy (at least for developing economies) is inferred from Feenstra and Hanson (1996a, 1996b, 1997), and Aiken, Harrison, and Lipsey (1996). Slaughter (2000), gives data on the labor force composition of U.S. multinationals' home operations versus their affiliates abroad, but no comparable data are available for the overall economy. See also Braconier, Norbäck, and Urban (2005a, 2005b).

7. The model is calibrated such that unskilled labor has a much larger share of GDP than unskilled labor, so the locus of equal incomes is much steeper than the NW-SE diagonal.

8. At this point, following an important observation of one referee, we should pause and emphasize that the world Edgeworth box is really a series of two-country models, not a true multicountry world. In reality, a firm faces may host countries and may choose one country in the EU, for example, on the basis of cost (as in a vertical investment), to serve the whole EU (essentially a horizontal investment). There is thus a major gap between the theory and empirical estimation in this regard. It is a poor defense to say that we are following the tradition of almost all trade and geography modeling, but at least our approach does permit a precise comparison of our results to the new economic geography. Ekholm, Forslid, and Markusen (2007) make some progress in constructing a multi-region model and taking it to the data.

9. This could be thought of as technical or institutional advances (e.g., legal changes that allow foreign investment, enforce property, rights and contracts) that permit fragmentation or, alternatively, the technical and managerial costs of fragmentation going from a prohibitive value to zero.

10. We repeat an important caveat mentioned by one of our referees, which is that there remains an important disconnect between the existing body of theory, which is overwhelmingly two-country models, and the multicountry data. The latter reflects export platform production for sale in third countries (other than home and host), which cannot occur in two-country models. Ekholm, Forslid, and Markusen (2007) is one attempt to deal with this issue.

11. A change of the threshold to $100 million would imply a rather stable number of firms through the period.

References

Aiken, Brian, Ann Harrison, and Robert E. Lipsey. (1996). Wages and Foreign Ownership: A Comparative Study of Mexico, Venezuela, and the United States. *Journal of International Economics* 40, 345–371.

Baldwin, Richard E., Rikard Forslid, Philippe Martin, Gianmarco Ottaviano, and Frederik Robert-Nicoud. (2003). *Economic Geography and Public Policy*. Princeton: Princeton University Press.

Barry, Frank. (1996). Peripherality in Economic Geography and Modern Growth Theory: Evidence from Ireland's Adjustment to Free Trade. *World Economy* 19(3), 345–365.

Blonigen, Bruce A., Ronald B. Davies, and Keith Head. (2003). Estimating the Knowledge-Capital Model of the Multinational Enterprise: Comment. *American Economic Review* 93, 980–994.

Braconier, Henrik, Per-Johan Norbaeck, and Dieter Urban. (2005a). Multinational Enterprises and Wage Costs: Vertical FDI Revisited. *Journal of International Economics* 67(2), 446–470.

Braconier, Henrik, Per-Johan Norbaeck, and Dieter Urban. (2005b). Reconciling the Evidence of the Knowledge Capital Model. *Review of International Economics* 13(4), 770–786.

Brakman, Steven, Harry Garretsen, and Charles Van Marrewijk. (2001). *An Introduction to Geographical Economics: Trade, Location, and Growth*. Cambridge: Cambridge University Press.

Brainard, S. Lael. (1997). An Empirical Assessment of the Proximity-Concentration Tradeoff between Multinational Sales and Trade. *American Economic Review* 87, 520–544.

Carr, David L., James R. Markusen, and Keith E. Maskus. (2001). Estimating the Knowledge-Capital Model of the Multinational Enterprise. *American Economic Review* 91, 693–708.

Carr, David L., James R. Markusen, and Keith Maskus. (2003). Estimating the Knowledge-Capital Model of the Multinational Enterprise: Reply. *American Economic Review* 93, 995–1001.

Davies, Ronald B. (2004). Hunting High and Low for Vertical FDI. University of Oregon working paper, forthcoming *Review of International Economics*.

Egger, Peter, Stefan Gruber, Mario Larch, and Michael Pfaffermayr. (2005). Knowledge-Capital Meets New Economic Geography. Working paper 1432, CESifo.

Ekholm, Karolina, and Rikard Forslid. (2001). Trade and Location with Horizontal and Vertical Multi-Region Firms. *Scandinavian Journal of Economics* 103, 101–118.

Ekholm, Karolina, Rikard Forslid, and James R. Markusen. (2007). Export-Platform Foreign Direct Investment. *Journal of the European Economic Association* 4, 776–795.

Feenstra, Robert C., and Gordon H. Hanson. (1996a). Foreign Investment, Outsourcing, and Relative Wages. In R. C. Feenstra, G. M. Grossman, and D. A. Irwin (eds.), *The Political Economy of Trade Policy: Papers in Honor of Jagdish Bhagwati*. Cambridge, Mass.: MIT Press.

Feenstra, Robert C., and Gordon H. Hanson. (1996b). Globalization, Outsourcing, and Wage Inequality. *American Economic Review* 86, 240–245.

Feenstra, Robert C., and Gordon H. Hanson. (1997). Foreign Direct Investment and Relative Wages: Evidence from Mexico's Maquiladoras. *Journal of International Economics* 42, 371–393.

Fujita, Masahisa, Paul Krugman, and Anthony J. Venables. (1999). *The Spatial Economy: Cities, Regions, and International Trade*. Cambridge, Mass.: MIT Press.

Gao, Ting. (1999). Economic Geography and the Department of Vertical Multinational Production. *Journal of International Economics* 48, 301–320.

Markusen, James R. (1997). Trade versus Investment Liberalization. Working paper no. 6231, National Bureau of Economic Research.

Markusen, James R. (2002). *Multinational Firms and the Theory of International Trade*. Cambridge, Mass.: MIT Press.

Markusen, James R., and Keith E. Maskus. (2002). Discriminating among Alternative Theories of the Multinational Enterprise. *Review of International Economics* 10, 694–707.

Raybaudi-Massilia, Marzia. (2000). Economic Geography and Multinational Enterprises. *Review of International Economics* 8, 1–19.

Slaughter, Matthew J. (2000). Production Transfer within Multinational Enterprises and American Wages. *Journal of International Economics* 50, 449–472.

UNCTAD. (2004). *World Investment Report 2004.* New York: United Nations.

World Bank. (2004). *FDI Trends: Public Policy for the Private Sector.* Washington, D.C.: World Bank. September.

4

Outsourcing, Contracts, and Innovation Networks

Alireza Naghavi and
Gianmarco Ottaviano

4.1 Introduction

A substantial growth in the outsourcing of activities in industrial countries is the most recent form of a greater division of labor (Feenstra 1998). When corporations began selling their factories and relocating manufacturing in the 1980s and 1990s to boost efficiency and focus on specialization, most insisted that important R&D would remain in-house. Today leading multinationals are turning toward a new approach to innovation, one that employs global networks of partners.

Dell, Hewlett-Packard, Motorola, and Philips, among others, have started buying complete designs of some digital devices from Asian developers, modifying them to their own specifications, and using their own brand names. Dell, for example, does little of its own design for notebook PCs, digital TVs, or other products. Hewlett-Packard contributes key technology and some design to all its products but relies on outside partners to codevelop everything from servers to printers. Motorola buys complete designs for its cheapest phones but controls all of the development of high-end handsets. Asian contract manufacturers and independent design houses have become key players in nearly every technological device, from laptops and high-definition TVs to MP3 music players and digital cameras. While the electronics sector is the most significant example of search for offshore help with innovation, the concept is spreading to nearly every sector of the economy. Boeing, for instance, is working with India's HCL Technologies to codevelop software for everything from navigation systems and landing gear to the cockpit controls. Pharmaceuticals as GlaxoSmith-Kline and Eli Lilly are teaming up with Asian biotech research companies in a bid to cut the average $500 million cost of bringing a new drug to market. Procter & Gamble also wants half of its new product ideas to be generated from outside by 2010, compared with 20 percent now (Engardio and Einhorn 2005).

The growing importance of outsourcing has generated an intense debate on the costs and benefits of industrial fragmentation. Within the international trade literature, a recent strand of research tries to investigate the phenomenon of outsourcing as the result of a trade-off between the governance costs of complex vertical organizations and the contractual costs of networks of independent specialized upstream and downstream producers. Such networks are tainted by problems of contractual incompleteness stemming from the lack of ex post verifiability by third parties as the quality of deliverables is too costly to observe by courts. Related models can be classified in terms of their relative focus on two decisions: the "ownership decision" on whether production should be in-house or outsourced and the "location decision" on where to place production. The ownership decision is the focus of, for example, McLaren (2000) and Grossman and Helpman (2002) for a closed economy and Antras (2003), Grossman and Helpman (2003), and Feenstra and Hanson (2005) for an open economy. The location decision is analyzed by Grossman and Helpman (2005). Both decisions appear in Antras and Helpman (2004) as determinants of firm organizational form.[1]

While all these studies focus on the static effects of outsourcing, we investigate instead its dynamic effects. Our aim is to shed light on the driving forces behind the new approach to innovation based on global networks of partners. In so doing, we model an industry in which R&D is performed by independent research labs and outsourcing production requires complementary upstream and downstream inventions. In the presence of search friction and incomplete outsourcing contracts, we show that the ex post bargaining power of upstream and downstream parties at the production stage feeds back to R&D incentives, thus affecting the emergence and the performance of networks of labs specialized in complementary inventions.

In our model, R&D is always outsourced, and independent labs choose whether to invent integrated upstream and downstream production processes or to focus on specialized upstream or downstream innovation. Lai, Riezman, and Wang (2005) endogenize the decision to outsource R&D rather than perform it in-house by emphasizing the trade-off between the costs of information leakage and the benefits of specialization. In Acemoglu, Aghion, and Zilibotti (2005), R&D is always performed in-house, and firms closer to the technology frontier have a stronger incentive to outsource production in order to concentrate on more valuable R&D. Our model thus complements both contributions. This is achieved by introducing innovation and growth in the static outsourcing model of Grossman and Helpman (2002), who study the industrial organization of a sector in which the varieties of a horizontally differentiated good are produced by monopolistically competitive firms. Production has two stages: intermediate supply and final assembly. Firms choose whether to enter as intermediate suppliers, final assemblers, or vertically integrated firms by paying the corresponding organization-specific fixed costs. Vertical integration bears additional costs due to more complex governance and limited specialization. Specialized suppliers face, instead, additional costs of searching and contracting with complementary partners. Contracts themselves are incomplete due to input characteristics that are unverifiable by third parties, which leads to bargaining between intermediate suppliers and final assemblers after the former have produced their inputs. In Grossman and Helpman (2002) unobservable intermediate input quality is an issue insofar as only high-quality inputs can be processed, whereas low-quality inputs are useless even though supplied at zero cost.[2] The fear of being held up during the bargaining process causes the intermediate suppliers to underproduce, and this reduces the joint surplus of specialized firms with respect to vertically integrated ones. Accordingly, the choices of firms in terms of organizational modes depend on the balance between the costs of the two types of industrial structure.

Grossman and Helpman (2002) show that the bargaining power of partners plays a key role in the fragmentation of production. Outsourcing is preferred when specialized final assemblers have a good chance of finding specialized intermediate suppliers; when product differentiation is weak so that the profit portion of the revenues of vertically integrated firms is small relative to the share appropriated by final assemblers through bargaining in an outsourcing deal; when vertical revenues are relatively small due to large gains from specialization and mild intermediate underproduction thanks to strong supplier bargaining power; and when the entry costs for specialized assembly are relatively small compared with those for vertically integrated production. The matching probability of firms entering as specialized assemblers itself depends negatively on their relative costs of entry and positively on their relative profit margin with respect to intermediate suppliers. The result is a relationship between the incentives to outsource and supplier bargaining power that has an inverted-U shape. Intuitively, when their bargaining power is very weak, intermediate suppliers have little incentive to produce, so intermediates are very costly. When intermediate bargaining power is very strong, few final assemblers are attracted to the industry, so intermediate suppliers have little chance of finding partners.

To the static setup of Grossman and Helpman (2002) we add dynamic product innovation. Whatever their organizational choice, firms need blueprints for production to enter the market. These are invented by perfectly competitive labs. They are protected by infinitely lived patents and come in three organization-specific types depending on whether they are designed for vertical integration, intermediate supply, or final assembly. We show that for specific parameter values, the steady state of the dynamic model is isomorphic to the static equilibrium of Grossman and Helpman (2002) once their fixed entry costs are interpreted as the marginal costs of innovation.[3] Our analysis therefore complements their work by providing microfounded transitionary dynamics. This has three interesting implications. First, explicit dynamics allow a formal stability analysis and qualify the conditions for the existence of multiple equilibria.[4] Second, they introduce new microeconomic parameters that are shown to affect the steady-state outcomes. Third, they allow characterizing the path and speed of convergence to steady state after the economy is hit by some shock.[5]

Some parameters have the same impact independent of the industrial organization of firms. Weaker product differentiation reduces product development due to thinner profit margins. Also, faster depreciation has a negative impact on product development. Both discourage innovation and divert labor away from the latter. Stronger time preference slows product development by biasing intertemporal decisions toward consumption. Higher costs of innovation have a negative impact on product development, whereas a larger economy supports the creation of a proportionately larger number of product varieties.

The relationship between the incentives to outsource and the bargaining power of intermediate suppliers has the same inverted-U shape as in Grossman and Helpman (2002), and for the same reasons. Accordingly, outsourcing is sustainable in an industry equilibrium only if supplier bargaining power is neither too weak nor too strong. When the outsourcing mode is selected, supplier bargaining power plays a crucial role for innovation. In particular, product development is maximized when supplier bargaining power does not take extreme values.

The rest of the chapter is organized as follows. Section 4.2 presents the model. Section 4.3 determines the equilibrium of the dynamic model. Section 4.4 concludes.

4.2 A Model of Product Innovation

To study the organizational choice between vertical integration and outsourcing in a dynamic environment, we merge the organization model with incomplete contracts by Grossman and Helpman (2002) and the innovation model with horizontal product differentiation by Grossman and Helpman (1991).

4.2.1 Demand

There are L infinitely lived households that share the same preferences defined over the consumption of a horizontally differentiated good C. The utility function is assumed to be instantaneously Cobb-Douglas and intertemporally constant elasticity of substitution (CES) with unit elasticity of intertemporal substitution:

$$U = \int_0^\infty e^{-\rho t} \ln C(t)\, dt,$$

where $\rho > 0$ is the rate of time preference and

$$C(t) = \left[\int_0^{n(t)} c(i,t)^\alpha \, di \right]^{1/\alpha}$$

is a CES quantity index in which $c(i,t)$ is the consumption of variety i, $n(t)$ is the mass ("number") of varieties produced, and α is an inverse measure of the degree of product differentiation between varieties. In particular, if σ is defined as the constant own- and cross-price elasticity of demand, then $\alpha = 1 - 1/\sigma$. Households have perfect foresight, and they can borrow and lend freely in a perfect capital market at instantaneous interest rate $R(t)$.

Given the chosen functional forms, multistage budgeting can be used to solve the utility maximization problem. This allows the households' decisions to be modeled as a two-stage sequence. In the first stage, they allocate their income flow in each period between savings and expenditures. This yields a time path of total expenditures $E(t)$ that obeys the Euler equation of a standard Ramsey problem:

$$\frac{\dot{E}(t)}{E(t)} = R(t) - \rho, \tag{4.1}$$

where we have used the fact that the intertemporal elasticity of substitution equals unity. By definition, $E(t) = P(t)C(t)$ where $P(t)$ is the exact price index associated with the quantity index $C(t)$:

$$P(t) \equiv \left[\int_0^{n(t)} p(i,t)^{\alpha/(1-\alpha)} \, di \right]^{(1-\alpha)/\alpha}. \tag{4.2}$$

In the second stage, households allocate their expenditures across all varieties, which yields instantaneous demand functions for each variety:

$$c(i,t) = A(t)p(i,t)^{-1/(1-\alpha)}, \quad i \in [0, n(t)], \tag{4.3}$$

where $p(i,t)$ is the price of variety i and

$$A(t) = \frac{E(t)}{P(t)^{-\alpha/(1-\alpha)}} \tag{4.4}$$

is aggregate demand. To simplify notation, from now on we leave the time dependence of variables implicit when this does not generate confusion.

4.2.2 Supply

The economy is endowed with two factors. Labor is inelastically supplied by households. Each household supplies one unit of labor, and we call L the number of households as well as the total endowment of labor. Labor is chosen as numeraire. The other factor is knowledge capital in the form of blueprints required for the production of differentiated varieties. These blueprints are protected by infinitely lived patents that depreciate at the constant rate δ.

There are two sectors: production and innovation (R&D). Innovation is performed by perfectly competitive labs that invent different types of blueprints for vertically integrated processes and fragmented ones. Each of the former processes requires a blueprint with marginal cost of invention equal to k_v. Each of the latter requires two blueprints: one for an intermediate component and one for final assembly with marginal R&D costs equal to k_m and k_s, respectively, where $k_s + k_m \leq k_v$.[6] We call v, m, and s the numbers of the three types of blueprints available at time t.

As to production, varieties are supplied by monopolistically competitive firms that buy the corresponding patents from R&D labs and hire an amount of labor proportionate to output. Therefore, each firm produces under increasing returns to scale as the price of its patent generates a fixed cost and the wage bill a variable cost. Depending on the patent it has chosen to buy, a firm can enter in three alternative modes: as a vertically integrated firm, as an intermediate supplier, or as a final assembler. The first needs λ units of labor per unit of final output; the second needs $1 \leq \lambda$ units of labor per unit of intermediate component; the third needs one unit of intermediate component per unit of final output. Accordingly, fragmented production is cheaper in terms of both fixed and marginal costs. The reason is lower R&D costs and productivity gains from specialization.

Fragmented production (henceforth referred to as outsourcing) faces additional costs that result from search frictions and incomplete contracting. After buying their patents, specialized entrants of each type must find a suitable partner in a matching process that may not always end in success. Moreover, intermediate suppliers also suffer hold-up problems due to contractual incompleteness. In particular, after matching, each intermediate supplier produces a relation-specific input. This input has no value outside the relation, and its quality is unverifiable by third parties.[7] This implies that the final assembler can refuse payment after the intermediate has been produced and the parties have to bargain on the division of the joint surplus that will materialize after final assembly. This gives rise to a holdup problem insofar as the production cost of the variety-specific input, which has no alternative use at the bargaining stage, is sunk. The transaction costs involved in ex post bargaining may then cause both parties to underinvest in their contractual relation, thus reducing their joint surplus.

Specifically, define $\dot{s} = ds/dt$ and $\dot{m} = dm/dt$ as the flows of new entrants as final assemblers and suppliers, respectively, that is, the numbers of new assembler and supplier blueprints invented at time t. Let $n(\dot{s}, \dot{m}) \leq \min(\dot{s}, \dot{m})$ be a constant-return-to-scale matching function that at time t determines the number of new supplier-assembler

matches given the number of entrants of each type $\dot{s}$ and $\dot{m}$. Then if
we define $r \equiv \dot{m}/\dot{s}$, $\eta(r) \equiv n(\dot{s}, \dot{m})/\dot{s}$ is the matching probability of an
assembler entrant, while $\eta(r)/r$ is the matching probability of a sup-
plier entrant. Accordingly, the relative abundance of the two types of
entrants determines their probabilities of being matched.

After a match is formed, each pair of firms bargains on the division
of their joint surplus, given by the prospective revenues of the corresponding variety. Since both parties cannot find a replacement, there
is bilateral monopoly so that they will eventually agree on a share that
makes both better off than if they had not met. We denote the bargaining weight of the intermediate input producer by ω.

To summarize, in each period t, the sequence of actions is the following. First, R&D takes place, and firms choose their mode of entry by
buying the corresponding patents. Second, prospective parties of an
outsourcing agreement search for partners, which could end in a suc-
cessful or an unsuccessful match. Unmatched entrants exit, and their
blueprints are destroyed. Third, each matched intermediate producer
manufactures the input needed by its partner. Fourth, parties bargain
over the division of total revenues from final sales, and inputs are
handed over to assemblers. Fifth, final assembly takes place, and the
final goods are sold to households, together with those supplied by
vertically integrated firms.

4.3   Organization and Product Variety

At time t the instantaneous equilibrium is found by solving the model
backward from final production to R&D for given numbers of each
type of blueprints: vertically integrated firms v, intermediate suppliers
m, and final assemblers s. For production and innovation to take place
at time 0, we assume that the economy is initially endowed with positive stocks of both vertically integrated and matched pairs of specialized blueprints: $v_0 > 0$ and $f_0 > 0$.[8]

4.3.1   Production

Varieties can be sold to final customers by two types of firms: vertically
integrated firms and final assemblers. A typical vertically integrated
firm faces a demand curve derived from equation 4.3 and a marginal
cost equal to λ. It chooses its scale by maximizing its operating profit,

$$\pi_v = p_v y_v - \lambda x_v, \tag{4.5}$$

where x_v is the amount of the intermediate input produced and $y_v = x_v$ is final output. Optimal final output and price are then given by

$$x_v = y_v = A\left(\frac{\alpha}{\lambda}\right)^{1/(1-\alpha)} \tag{4.6}$$

and

$$p_v = \frac{\lambda}{\alpha}. \tag{4.7}$$

Replacing these values in equation 4.5 results in operating profit equal to

$$\pi_v = (1 - \alpha)A\left(\frac{\alpha}{\lambda}\right)^{\alpha/(1-\alpha)}, \tag{4.8}$$

which is a decreasing function of the elasticity of substitution $1/(1 - \alpha)$ and of the marginal cost λ.

Turning to outsourcing, there is a one-to-one equilibrium relationship between the number of matched assemblers, the number of matched intermediate suppliers, and the number of outsourced varieties, which are all equal to f. The joint surplus of a matched pair of entrants is given by the revenues from the final sales of the corresponding variety $p_s y_s$. This is divided according to the bargaining weights of the parties. Accordingly, a share $(1 - \omega)$ goes to the final assembler:

$$\pi_s = (1 - \omega)p_s y_s. \tag{4.9}$$

The remaining $\omega p_s y_s$ goes to the intermediate supplier.

Moving one step backward, the intermediate producer must decide how much input x_m to produce, anticipating a share of revenues $\omega p_s y_s$ while bearing a cost of x_m units of labor. Therefore, the intermediate supplier maximizes

$$\pi_m = \omega p_s y_s - x_m, \tag{4.10}$$

which implies intermediate and final outputs equal to

$$x_m = y_s = A(\alpha\omega)^{1/(1-\alpha)} \tag{4.11}$$

with associated prices

$$p_m = \frac{1}{\omega}, \quad p_s = \frac{1}{\alpha\omega}. \tag{4.12}$$

Note that $p_v/p_s = \lambda\omega$, which is the ratio of the efficiency loss of vertical integration to that of outsourcing. The former stems from the lack of specialization, the latter from intermediate underproduction due to holdup fears. Using these results in equations 4.9 and 4.10 gives the operating profits of matched final assemblers and intermediate suppliers:

$$\pi_s = (1 - \omega)A(\alpha\omega)^{\alpha/(1-\alpha)} \tag{4.13}$$

and

$$\pi_m = (1 - \alpha)\omega A(\alpha\omega)^{\alpha/(1-\alpha)}. \tag{4.14}$$

Finally, when both vertically integrated firms and final assemblers are active, substituting equations 4.7 and 4.12 into 4.2 and 4.4 allows us to write aggregate demand as

$$A = \frac{E}{v\left(\frac{\alpha}{\lambda}\right)^{\alpha/(1-\alpha)} + f(\alpha\omega)^{\alpha/(1-\alpha)}}, \tag{4.15}$$

where v is the number of vertically integrated firms and f is the number of matched pairs of specialized producers that are active at time t.

4.3.2 Innovation
Going backward, we reach the entry stage. Here labs invent new blueprints at marginal costs k_v, k_m, and k_s depending on the organizational modes. Their output determines the laws of motion of v and f. For vertically integrated firms, we have

$$\dot{v} = \frac{L_v^I}{k_v} - \delta v, \tag{4.16}$$

where $\dot{v} \equiv dv/dt$, L_v^I is labor employed in inventing new blueprints for vertically integrated production, $1/k_v$ is its productivity, and δ is the depreciation rate. For specialized pairs, we have

$$\dot{f} = \eta(r)\dot{s} - \delta f \quad \text{with} \quad r \equiv \frac{\dot{m}}{\dot{s}}, \; \dot{s} = \frac{L_s^I}{k_s}, \; \dot{m} = \frac{L_m^I}{k_m}, \tag{4.17}$$

where $\dot{f} \equiv df/dt$, L_s^I, and L_m^I are labor employed in inventing new final assembler and intermediate supplier blueprints, while $1/k_s$ and $1/k_m$ are their respective productivities.

Labs pay their researchers by borrowing at the interest rate R while knowing that the resulting patents will generate instantaneous dividends equal to the expected profits of the corresponding firms. Since specialized entrants are not sure of being matched, equations 4.13 and 4.14 imply that the expected dividends of intermediate and final assembly patents are, respectively,

$$\pi_m^e = (1 - \alpha)\frac{\eta(r)}{r}\omega A(\alpha\omega)^{\alpha/(1-\alpha)} \tag{4.18}$$

and

$$\pi_s^e = \eta(r)(1 - \omega)A(\alpha\omega)^{\alpha/(1-\alpha)}. \tag{4.19}$$

Then if we call J_j the asset value of a patent for $j = v, s, m$, arbitrage in the capital market implies

$$R = \frac{\pi_j^e}{J_j} + \frac{\dot{J}_j}{J_j} - \delta, \tag{4.20}$$

where $\dot{J}_j \equiv dJ_j/dt$ is the capital gain.

Due to perfect competition in R&D, patents are priced at marginal cost, which requires

$$J_j = k_j.$$

The value of a patent is therefore constant through time so that $\dot{J}_j = 0$. When substituted into equation 4.20, these results give

$$R + \delta = \frac{\pi_v}{k_v} = \frac{\pi_s^e}{k_s} = \frac{\pi_m^e}{k_m}, \tag{4.21}$$

which pins down the interest rate in the Euler, equation 4.1.

Finally, the aggregate resource constraint (or full employment condition) closes the characterization of the instantaneous equilibrium. Since labor is used in innovation and in intermediate production by both vertically integrated and specialized producers, we have $L = L_v^I + L_s^I + L_m^I + v\lambda x_v + fx_m$. By equations 4.6, 4.11, 4.16, and 4.17, the condition can be rewritten as

$$L = k_v(\dot{v} + \delta v) + k_s\dot{s} + k_m\dot{m} + v\lambda A\left(\frac{\alpha}{\lambda}\right)^{1/(1-\alpha)} + fA(\alpha\omega)^{1/(1-\alpha)}. \tag{4.22}$$

4.3.3 Equilibrium

The first thing to notice is that in any instant t, there is never simultaneous invention of both vertically integrated and specialized blueprints. This would be the case if all equalities in equation 4.21 held at the same time. This is generally impossible. To see this, consider first that new outsourcing agreements are signed only if there is new creation of both intermediate supplier and final assembler blueprints, which requires

$$\frac{\pi_m^e}{k_m} = \frac{\pi_s^e}{k_s} \Leftrightarrow r = \bar{r} \equiv \frac{k_s}{k_m} \frac{(1-\alpha)\omega}{1-\omega}, \tag{4.23}$$

where we have used equations 4.18 and 4.19. Thus, the two types of specialized blueprints have to be invented in fixed proportion. Second, if vertically integrated patents are simultaneously invented, it must be

$$\frac{\pi_v}{k_v} = \frac{\pi_s^e}{k_s} \Leftrightarrow \frac{(1-\alpha)\lambda^{-\alpha/(1-\alpha)}}{k_v} = \frac{\eta(\bar{r})(1-\omega)\omega^{\alpha/(1-\alpha)}}{k_s}.$$

Since both sides are constant, this equality is satisfied only for a zero-measure set of parameter values. Hence, in general, vertically integrated and specialized blueprints are not invented together in equilibrium. In particular, only the former are created when

$$\frac{(1-\alpha)\lambda^{-\alpha/(1-\alpha)}}{k_v} > \frac{\eta(\bar{r})(1-\omega)\omega^{\alpha/(1-\alpha)}}{k_s}, \tag{4.24}$$

and only the latter when the reverse is true.

Vertical Integration

When condition 4.24 holds, $L_s^I = L_m^I = 0$, so no new specialized blueprints are ever created: $\dot{s} = \dot{m} = 0$. As a result, the initial stocks of specialized blueprints are eroded by depreciation:

$$\dot{f} = -\delta f. \tag{4.25}$$

Then, using equations 4.6, 4.8, 4.15, and 4.21, the full employment condition, equation 4.22, and the Euler condition, equation 4.1, can be respectively rewritten as

$$L = k_v(\dot{v} + \delta v) + E \frac{v\lambda\left(\frac{\alpha}{\lambda}\right)^{1/(1-\alpha)} + f(\alpha\omega)^{1/(1-\alpha)}}{v\left(\frac{\alpha}{\lambda}\right)^{\alpha/(1-\alpha)} + f(\alpha\omega)^{\alpha/(1-\alpha)}} \tag{4.26}$$

and

$$\frac{\dot{E}}{E} = \frac{(1-\alpha)E}{k_v} \frac{\left(\frac{\alpha}{\lambda}\right)^{\alpha/(1-\alpha)}}{v\left(\frac{\alpha}{\lambda}\right)^{\alpha/(1-\alpha)} + f(\alpha\omega)^{\alpha/(1-\alpha)}} - \rho - \delta. \tag{4.27}$$

Equations 4.25, 4.26, and 4.27 form a three-dimensional dynamic system that has a unique steady state in E, v, f, and is saddle-path stable (see the appendix). The steady-state values can be obtained by solving the system after setting $\dot{E} = \dot{v} = \dot{f} = 0$:

$$E_v^* = \frac{\rho+\delta}{\delta+\alpha\rho}L, \quad v_v^* = \frac{1-\alpha}{\delta+\alpha\rho}\frac{L}{k_v}, \quad f_v^* = 0. \tag{4.28}$$

Due to depreciation, the steady-state mass of vertically integrated firms is maintained through ongoing innovation. When all firms are destroyed instantaneously ($\delta = 1$), these results are the same as in the dynamic model of Grossman and Helpman (1991). In addition, when there is no time discounting ($\rho = 0$), they are the same as in the static model by Grossman and Helpman (2002).

Outsourcing
When condition 4.24 does not hold, $L_v^I = 0$, so no vertically integrated blueprints are ever created, implying that their initial stock is depleted by depreciation:

$$\dot{v} = -\delta v. \tag{4.29}$$

Using equations 4.13, 4.14, 4.15, 4.17, 4.21, and 4.23, the full employment condition, 4.22, and the Euler condition, 4.1, can be respectively rewritten as

$$L = \frac{k_s + k_m\bar{r}}{\eta(\bar{r})}(\dot{f} + \delta f) + E\frac{v\lambda\left(\frac{\alpha}{\lambda}\right)^{1/(1-\alpha)} + f(\alpha\omega)^{1/(1-\alpha)}}{v\left(\frac{\alpha}{\lambda}\right)^{\alpha/(1-\alpha)} + f(\alpha\omega)^{\alpha/(1-\alpha)}} \tag{4.30}$$

and

$$\frac{\dot{E}}{E} = \frac{\eta(\bar{r})(1-\omega)E}{k_s} \frac{\left(\frac{\alpha}{\lambda}\right)^{\alpha/(1-\alpha)}}{v\left(\frac{\alpha}{\lambda}\right)^{\alpha/(1-\alpha)} + f(\alpha\omega)^{\alpha/(1-\alpha)}} - \rho - \delta. \tag{4.31}$$

This dynamic system 4.29-4.30-4.31 has a unique steady state, and it is saddle-path stable (see the appendix).[9] The associated level of expenditures and numbers of firms can be obtained by solving the system after setting $\dot{E} = \dot{f} = \dot{v} = 0$:

$$E^* = \frac{\rho + \delta}{\delta + \omega\alpha\rho}L, \quad f^* = \eta(\bar{r})\frac{1 - \omega}{\delta + \omega\alpha\rho}\frac{L}{k_s}, \quad v^* = 0. \tag{4.32}$$

Note that the number of active outsourcing pairs f_s^* depends on the matching probability of assembler entrants $\eta(\bar{r})$. Again, due to depreciation, the steady-state masses of firms are maintained through ongoing innovation. Given equation 4.23, imposing $\dot{f} = 0$ and $r = \bar{r}$ in equation 4.17 allows us to determine the flows of assembler and intermediate entrants in each period:

$$\dot{s}^* = \frac{\delta(1 - \omega)}{\delta + \omega\alpha\rho}\frac{L}{k_s}, \quad \dot{m}^* = \frac{\delta\omega(1 - \alpha)}{\delta + \omega\alpha\rho}\frac{L}{k_m}. \tag{4.33}$$

Note that the static equilibrium in Grossman Helpman (2002) corresponds to the steady state of our model when $\rho = 0$ (no time discounting) and $\delta = 1$ (all firms die every period).

4.3.4 Comparative Statics

Economic intuition on the driving forces behind the choice of the organizational mode is boosted by remembering that $\alpha = (1 - 1/\sigma)$ and rewriting equation 4.24 as

$$\underbrace{\frac{1}{\eta(\bar{r})}}_{\text{probability } v/s} \underbrace{\frac{1/\sigma}{1 - \omega}}_{\text{profit share } v/s} \underbrace{\left(\frac{\lambda}{1/\omega}\right)^{1-\sigma}}_{\text{revenues } v/s} > \underbrace{\frac{k_v}{k_s}}_{\text{R\&D cost } v/s} \tag{4.34}$$

with

$$\left.\frac{d\eta(r)}{dr}\right|_{r=\bar{r}} > 0, \quad \bar{r} = \underbrace{\frac{k_s}{k_m}}_{\text{R\&D cost } s/m} \underbrace{\frac{1/\sigma}{1/\omega - 1}}_{\text{margin } s/m}. \tag{4.35}$$

$$\frac{\bar{r}}{\eta(\bar{r})}\frac{k_m}{k_s}\frac{1/\omega - 1}{1/\sigma}\frac{1/\sigma}{1 - \omega}\left(\frac{\lambda}{1/\omega}\right)^{1-\sigma} > \frac{k_v}{k_s} \quad \omega(\lambda\omega)^{\sigma-1}\eta(\bar{r})/\bar{r} < k_m/k_v.$$

If condition 4.34 holds, all entrants choose vertical integration. Of course, this is the case when the relative benefits of vertical integration dominate the relative costs. The left-hand side of equation 4.34 shows that the former come from three sources: the fact that specialized final assemblers face matching uncertainty whereas vertically integrated firms do not $(1/\eta(\bar{r}))$, the relative profit margin $((1/\sigma)/(1-\omega))$, and the relative total revenues $((\lambda\omega)^{1-\sigma})$. The right-hand side shows instead that the relative costs of vertical integration derive from the costs of innovation (k_v/k_s). Then vertical integration is chosen when specialized final assemblers have low chances of finding specialized intermediate suppliers (small $\eta(\bar{r})$); when product differentiation is strong, so that the profit share of revenues of vertically integrated firms is large (large $1/\sigma$) relative to the share appropriated by final assemblers through bargaining (small $1-\omega$); when vertically integrated revenues are relatively large due to small gains from specialization (small λ) and severe intermediate underproduction caused by weak supplier bargaining power (small ω); and when the blueprints for vertically integrated production are relatively cheap compared with those for specialized assembly (small k_v/k_s). Expressions 4.35 highlight the fact that the matching probability of specialized assemblers itself depends on the relative R&D costs (k_s/k_m) and the relative profit margin of final assemblers and intermediate suppliers $((1/\sigma)/(1/\omega-1))$. When their R&D costs are relatively small and the profit margin is relatively large, the entrants are mostly final assemblers, reducing their probability $\eta(\bar{r})$ of being matched. This makes condition 4.34 easier to fulfill.

All parameters have unambiguous impacts on the propensity to vertical integration except σ and ω. Larger σ unambiguously fosters outsourcing provided that $\lambda\omega > 1$. Otherwise that happens only if σ is small enough. This can be understood by plugging $\bar{r}$ from equation 4.35 in 4.34 and rewriting the resulting condition as $\omega(\lambda\omega)^{\sigma-1}\eta(\bar{r})/\bar{r} < k_m/k_v$. As larger σ decreases $\bar{r}$, it always raises the matching probability of intermediate suppliers $\eta(\bar{r})/\bar{r}$. On the other hand, larger σ amplifies the revenue advantage of final assemblers $(\lambda\omega)^{\sigma-1}$ if their relative marginal costs are lower $(\lambda\omega > 1)$ and their revenue disadvantage if their relative marginal costs are higher $(\lambda\omega < 1)$. This is because larger σ makes demand more sensitive to small price differences. In the former case, both effects work in the direction of fostering outsourcing. In the latter, the relative revenue effect favors vertical integration, the more so the larger is σ.

As to ω, stronger supplier bargaining power also has two opposite effects: it promotes intermediate production but at the same time reduces the matching probability of intermediate suppliers. While the former effect fosters outsourcing, the latter hampers it. Favorable scenarios for outsourcing strike a balance between the two effects. This happens for values of ω that are neither too small nor too large. Too see this, use equation 4.24 to derive the following condition for outsourcing to dominate vertical integration:

$$\gamma \equiv \frac{\eta(\bar{r})(1 - \omega)k_v}{(1 - \alpha)k_s}(\omega\lambda)^{\alpha/(1-\alpha)} > 1.$$

Then, recalling the value of $\bar{r}$ from equation 4.23, γ is an increasing function of ω if and only if

$$\varepsilon_\eta > \frac{\omega - \alpha}{1 - \alpha},$$

where ε_η is the elasticity of $\eta(r)$ with respect to r. Given our assumptions of the matching function, we have $0 < \varepsilon_\eta < 1$, and therefore γ is increasing (decreasing) in ω when this is very small (large). This implies a relationship between the incentives to outsource and the bargaining power of intermediate suppliers that has an inverted-U shape.

All results so far mirror those in Grossman and Helpman (2002). Parameters specific to our dynamic setting play a role when we turn to steady-state outcomes. Most parameters have the same impact under both vertical integration and outsourcing. Larger elasticity of substitution (larger σ, i.e., larger α) reduces both expenditures and variety. The reason is thinner profit margins, which discourage innovation and force firms to employ more workers to cover their fixed R&D costs through large-scale production. Faster depreciation (larger δ) also negatively affects both expenditures and variety as it reduces the incentives to innovate and diverts labor from alternative use. Differently, stronger time preference (larger ρ) has a negative impact on product variety but a positive one on expenditures since it biases intertemporal decisions toward consumption and away from saving. Finally, higher costs of innovation (larger k_v, k_s, or k_m) have no impact on expenditures and a negative impact on product variety, whereas a larger economy (larger L) supports both higher expenditures and more product varieties.

The bargaining weight ω is, of course, peculiar to outsourcing. Larger ω is associated with smaller expenditures. Its impact on product variety is instead ambiguous depending on the specific functional form of $\eta(.)$. Given equation 4.32, f^* is an increasing function of ω if and only if

$$\varepsilon_\eta > \frac{\delta\omega + \omega\alpha\rho}{\delta + \omega\alpha\rho}.$$

Since $0 < \varepsilon_\eta < 1$, this condition holds for $\omega = 0$ and is violated for $\omega = 1$. Hence, product development is higher for values of ω that are neither too small nor too large. This is because larger ω encourages more intermediate entry (larger $\bar{r}$) and thus increases the matching probability of assemblers (larger $\eta(\bar{r})$). On the other hand, it reduces their share of surplus once matched. Finally, larger ω always leads to faster convergence to steady state (see the appendix).

4.4 Conclusion

We have proposed a theoretical framework to shed light on some aspects of the new approach to innovation that relies on increasingly global networks of partners. In particular, conditional on the outsourcing of innovation occurring, we have studied how alternative organizational forms in production arise and how these affect the incentives to innovate.

The underlying idea is that the outsourcing of production brings about gains in terms of both lower costs of R&D and higher benefits of specialization in upstream and downstream production. It is, however, associated with larger transaction costs due to incomplete contracts and holdup problems. We have shown that the bargaining power of upstream and downstream parties at the production stage feeds back to R&D incentives, thus affecting innovation. The reason is that specialized production also requires specialized R&D, whose returns depend on the bargaining outcomes. Product development is best served by contracts in which the bargaining power of upstream suppliers is neither too weak nor too strong.

The proposed framework combines the new features of outsourcing contracts as in Grossman and Helpman (2002) with the well-known model of growth under horizontal differentiation as in Grossman and Helpman (1991). While one might have guessed that the combination would be too complex to analyze, we have shown that this is not the case. Indeed, as discussed by Naghavi and Ottaviano (2006a, 2006b), the framework is simple enough to be extended to model endogenous growth and study how the organizational choices of firms affect the long-run growth rate of the economy even in the presence of heterogenous firms. These are interesting directions for future research.

Appendix: Stability of Steady States

We show that in section 4.3.3 the steady states with vertical integration and outsourcing are both saddle-path stable. Consider the former case. The corresponding dynamic system is formed by equations 4.27, 4.26, and 4.25. The Jacobian matrix evaluated at equation 4.28 is

$$
D_v \equiv \begin{bmatrix}
\delta + \rho & -\frac{(\delta+\rho)^2 k_v}{1-\alpha} & -\frac{(\delta+\rho)^2 k_v}{1-\alpha}(\lambda\omega)^{\alpha/(1-\alpha)} \\
-\frac{\alpha}{k_v} & -\delta & \frac{(\delta+\rho)\alpha(1-\omega)}{1-\alpha}(\lambda\omega)^{\alpha/(1-\alpha)} \\
0 & 0 & -\delta
\end{bmatrix}
$$

with eigenvalues

$$
\lambda_{1,2}^v = \frac{\rho}{2} \pm \frac{\rho}{2}\sqrt{1 + 4\frac{(\delta+\rho)(\delta+\alpha\rho)}{\rho^2(1-\alpha)}}; \quad \lambda_3^v = -\delta.
$$

Consider now the outsourcing case. The associated dynamic system is formed by equations 4.31, 4.29, and 4.30. The Jacobian matrix evaluated at steady state in equation 4.32 is given by

$$
D \equiv \begin{bmatrix}
\delta + \rho & -\frac{(\delta+\rho)^2 k_s}{\eta(\bar{r})(1-\omega)(\lambda\omega)^{\alpha/(1-\alpha)}} & -\frac{(\delta+\rho)^2 k_s}{\eta(\bar{r})(1-\omega)} \\
0 & -\delta & 0 \\
-\frac{\eta(\bar{r})\alpha\omega(1-\omega)}{k_s(1-\alpha\omega)} & -\frac{(\delta+\rho)\alpha(1-\omega)}{(1-\alpha\omega)(\lambda\omega)^{\alpha/(1-\alpha)}} & -\delta
\end{bmatrix}.
$$

The associated eigenvalues are independent from $\eta(\bar{r})$:

$$
\lambda_{1,2} = \frac{\rho}{2} \pm \frac{\rho}{2}\sqrt{1 + 4\frac{(\delta+\rho)(\delta+\omega\alpha\rho)}{\rho^2(1-\alpha\omega)}}; \quad \lambda_3 = -\delta.
$$

Then, all the rest given, the speed of convergence to steady state is increasing in ω.

Notes

We are indebted to Elhanan Helpman, two anonymous referees, and seminar participants at the PSE-CEPR workshop, "Globalization and Contracts," in Paris as well as at the CESIFO workshop, "Globalization and the Multinational Enterprise," in Venice for helpful comments.

1. See Helpman (2006) for an overview of recent models of firm involvement in foreign activities and Gattai (2005) for a survey of additional applications of the theory of the firm to international trade issues.

2. Marin and Verdier (2003) as well as Antras (2003) argue that within a vertically integrated firm, the agreements among stakeholders are also incomplete. This approach differs from the transaction-cost approach adopted by Grossman and Helpman (2002, 2003, 2005) in the wake of Williamson (1985). It is, instead in line with the property rights theory proposed by Grossman and Hart (1986) and further developed by Hart and Moore (1990), according to which holdup problems arise also within integrated firms with their relevance depending on the allocation of property rights between stakeholders.

3. Specifically, when all firms are destroyed instantaneously, our results are the same as in the dynamic model by Grossman and Helpman (1991). In addition, when there is no time discounting, they are the same as in the static model by Grossman and Helpman (2002).

4. Our analysis is performed under the assumption of constant-returns-to-scale matching. Grossman and Helpman (2002) also consider the case of increasing returns to scale and show how matching externalities may generate multiple stable steady states. We do not cover this case but note that with explicit transitionary dynamics and multiple stable steady states, history ("initial conditions") or expectations ("initial beliefs") would determine the steady state that is eventually reached, depending on the speed of adjustment and the strength of the externalities (Ottaviano 2001).

5. The stability analysis is presented in the appendix, which reports the eigenvalues of the dynamic systems. Together with the steady-state values in the main text, the eigenvalues allow one to derive the (unreported) adjustment paths following standard techniques.

6. This assumption captures the idea that the coordination of research teams is more complex when their aim is to create vertically integrated blueprints. In other words, the governance costs of R&D labs are higher for vertically integrated than for specialized blueprints. In equilibrium, such assumption will prevent vertically integrated firms from buying inputs from specialized suppliers.

7. As in Grossman and Helpman (2002, 2003, 2005), unobservable input quality is an issue to the extent that only high-quality inputs can be processed, whereas low-quality inputs are useless even though freely supplied.

8. The zero-measure case with $v_0 > 0$ and $f_0 = 0$ is discussed in section 4.3.3 for comparison with the static setup.

9. In the static model by Grossman and Helpman (2002), the outcome such that all firms are vertically integrated remains an equilibrium even when condition 4.24 is violated. In particular, it is a self-fulfilling expectation equilibrium supported by the common belief that no specialized firm will ever enter the market. As this implies zero matching probability, no specialized firm will indeed enter, thus making the common belief self-fulfilling. This equilibrium is, however, unstable: any specialized entry would make all firms abandon vertical integration. In our dynamic model, the positive initial stock $f_0 > 0$ rules out the possibility of such a self-fulfilling equilibrium. This would be viable only in the zero-measure case where $f_0 = 0$ and $v_0 > 0$.

References

Acemoglu, D., P. Aghion, and F. Zilibotti. (2006). Distance to Frontier, Selection, and Economic Growth. *Journal of the European Economic Association* 4, 37–74.

Antras, P. (2003). Firms, Contracts, and Trade Structure. *Quarterly Journal of Economics* 118, 1375–1418.

Antras, P., and E. Helpman. (2004). Global Sourcing. *Journal of Political Economy* 112, 552–580.

Engardio, P., and B. Einhorn. (2005). Outsourcing Innovation. *Business Week*, March 21.

Feenstra, R. (1998). Integration of Trade and Disintegration of Production in the Global Economy. *Journal of Economic Perspectives* 12, 31–50.

Feenstra, R., and G. Hanson. (2005). Ownership and Control in Outsourcing to China: Estimating the Property-Rights Theory of the Firm. *Quarterly Journal of Economics* 120, 729–761.

Gattai, V. (2005). From the Theory of the Firm to FDI and Internalization: A Survey. *FEEM Nota di Lavoro*, 51.05.

Grossman, S., and O. Hart. (1986). The Costs and Benefits of Ownership: A Theory of Vertical and Lateral Integration. *Journal of Political Economy* 94, 691–719.

Grossman, G., and E. Helpman. (1991). *Innovation and Growth in the Global Economy.* Cambridge Mass.: MIT Press.

Grossman, G., and E. Helpman. (2002). Integration vs. Outsourcing in Industry Equilibrium. *Quarterly Journal of Economics* 117, 85–120.

Grossman, G., and E. Helpman. (2003). Outsourcing versus FDI in Industry Equilibrium. *Journal of European Economic Association* 1, 317–327.

Grossman, G., and E. Helpman. (2005). Outsourcing in a Global Economy. *Review of Economic Studies* 72, 135–159.

Hart, O., and J. Moore. (1990). Property Rights and the Nature of the Firm. *Journal of Political Economy* 98, 1119–1158.

Helpman, E. (2006). Trade, FDI, and the Organization of Firms. *Journal of Economic Literature* 44, 589–630.

Lai, E., R. Riezman, and P. Wang. (2005). Outsourcing of Innovation. Mimeo., University of Iowa.

McLaren, J. (2000). Globalisation and Vertical Structure. *American Economic Review* 90, 1239–1254.

Marin, D., and T. Verdier. (2003). Globalization and the "New Enterprise." *Journal of the European Economic Association* 1, 337–344.

Naghavi, A., and G. Ottaviano. (2006a). Outsourcing, Complementary Innovations and Growth. Discussion Paper no. 5925, Centre for Economic Policy Research.

Naghavi, A., and G. Ottaviano. (2006b). On the Industry Dynamics of Offshoring. Mimeo., Università di Bologna.

Ottaviano, G. (2001). Monopolistic Competition, Trade, and Endogenous Spatial Fluctuations. *Regional Science and Urban Economics* 31, 51–77.

Williamson, O. E. (1985). *The Economic Institutions of Capitalism.* New York: Free Press.

5

Agglomeration and Government Spending

Steven Brakman, Harry Garretsen, and Charles van Marrewijk

5.1 Introduction

Tax harmonization is high on the political agenda of the European Union (EU) countries. It is widely believed that with the arrival of the Economic and Monetary Union (EMU) and with globalization in general, the EU countries are forced to harmonize taxes. The standard reasoning is that in the absence of a policy of tax harmonization, full-fledged economic integration in the EU will lead to a race to the bottom. For the EU, Sinn (1990) has aptly summarized this line of reasoning. A race to the bottom would mean that in a truly common market in the EU, the mobile factors of production (in particular, high-skilled labor and capital) will locate in the country with the lowest tax rate, with the result that all EU countries are forced to adopt this tax rate. In other words, economic integration could go along with fierce tax competition among the EU countries. This is thought to be harmful because it would imply a suboptimal provision of public goods. To avoid this unwanted outcome, a policy of tax harmonization is deemed necessary. However, taxes are only part of the story: location-specific government expenditures, which affect the quality of a country's social and economic infrastructure, also determine the attractiveness of a location.

The recent new economic geography literature leads potentially to very different conclusions with respect to tax competition and harmonization (Baldwin et al. 2003; Neary 2001). In a much-debated paper, Baldwin and Krugman (2004) show that there is no need for a race to the bottom to begin with and that a policy of tax harmonization could make all countries worse off. The main idea is that economic integration could lead to a core-periphery outcome, with an agglomeration rent for the production factors located in the core, reflecting the fact that the production factors earn more (in real terms) in the core than in the periphery. The rent can be taxed, and this allows the core countries to have a higher tax rate than the peripheral countries (see also Andersson and Forslid 2003). Tax competition thus does not need to lead to a race to the bottom, which is important because it corresponds to the observed lack of a race to the bottom in reality.

Although the contributions of Baldwin and Krugman (2004) and Andersson and Forslid (2003) challenge the standard views about the race to the bottom, their treatment of the government sector is rather rudimentary, emphasizing taxes and not the productive effects of public expenditures on the economy, which is also used as a policy instrument in order to increase the attractiveness of a region.[1] Furthermore, these studies concentrate on the agglomeration equilibrium and analyze the relationship between the agglomeration rent and the tax gap between core and periphery. In doing so, the focus is on the conditions under which the agglomeration equilibrium is stable (that is, the sustain, and not the break, analysis in new economic geography (NEG) terminology is central).

Public regional expenditure, however, is potentially very important. During the European Council meeting of the EU in Lisbon in March 2000, for example, the EU member states agreed on a benchmarking method to determine the competitiveness of the EU economies using no fewer than fifty-four indicators, with emphasis on the quality of the social and economic infrastructure. Keen and Marchand (1997) use a simpler model in which agglomeration economies play no role and explore a government's choice of type of public expenditures (public input to production versus public consumption good) and show that similar incentives as discussed below lead to a bias in favor of public inputs. Similarly, Brülhart and Trionfetti (2004) show that (biased) public expenditures can influence a country's specialization pattern.

When the effects of agglomeration are thought to be important, tax and spending policies represent two opposing forces. All other things remaining the same, higher taxes stimulate spreading even though the existence of an agglomeration rent may prevent the spreading from actually taking place. Similarly, an increase in public spending stimulates agglomeration if this spending enhances the attractiveness of the location for the mobile factors of production.[2] But all things do not remain the same in the sense that higher taxes typically also imply higher public spending, and vice versa. The extent to which a larger government sector (meaning higher public spending and taxes) really leads to a better quality of the country's infrastructure is an issue that has troubled EU policymakers for a long time.

In this chapter, we extend the Baldwin and Krugman (2004) and Andersson and Forslid (2003) approach in three ways. First, we allow public spending to affect the cost of production, which has an impact on the location decisions of firms and workers. Second, we take into account that the public sector competes with the private sector on the labor market so that public spending takes up net resources. Third, we focus on the symmetric equilibrium, as opposed to the core-periphery or agglomeration equilibrium (as in Baldwin and Krugman 2004), and thereby on the impact of the provision of public goods on the symmetric equilibrium. This chapter focuses on the interdependencies between taxes and government spending from a production cost perspective (see Brakman, Garretsen, and van Marrewijk 2002 for a discussion of the relation between government spending and consumption externalities). At this stage, it is important to note what we do not do. We do not analyze locational competition in which optimizing governments compete, often in a Nash setting, for mobile factors of production. This would require a discussion of what it is that governments optimize and in what type of game they are involved (cooperative or noncooperative). These important issues require a separate work.

The chapter is organized as follows. Section 5.2 briefly presents some stylized facts for the EU about cross-country differences in corporate rate income taxation, public spending, location indicators, and the corresponding differences in location decisions. Section 5.3 presents the two-region new economic geography model, the so-called Forslid-Ottaviano model, with the addition of a more elaborate government sector. In section 5.4 we analyze the impact of the (symmetric) introduction of public goods on the key variables in our model. Section 5.5 conducts a break analysis. That is, for a given level of public goods, we analyze when the symmetric equilibrium becomes unstable. The outcome is also compared with the benchmark of no public goods provision. In section 5.6 we present some simulations to illustrate how the introduction of public goods may affect the equilibrium distribution of the footloose factor of production (capital) between the two countries. Section 5.7 summarizes and concludes. Our main finding is that the introduction of our version of public goods fosters agglomeration.

5.2   Stylized Facts about Taxation and Public Spending in the EU

A race to the bottom in the EU is not inevitable. We concentrate on the taxation of capital because in our model, we assume that capital is mobile and labor is not. This is in accordance with the often observed higher degree of capital mobility as compared to labor mobility. For the EU countries, table 5.1 shows the development of corporate income taxes for the period 1990–1999, an era of increasing economic integration. These tax rates differ from the nominal tax rates as they take into account the implications of differences in tax base, allowances for depreciation, and others that exist between EU countries. The reported data are based on financial accounts of individual firms.

Table 5.1 offers no conclusive evidence, but a number of findings are worth pointing out:

• The large countries of the EU (Germany, the United Kingdom, France, and Italy) clearly have an above-average tax rate.[3]

Table 5.1
Effective corporate income tax rates across the EU, 1990–1999 (%)

	1990	1991	1992	1993	1994	1995	1996	1997	1998	1999
Austria	18	22	14	16	20	17	24	25	21	24
Belgium	17	16	22	23	23	24	23	22	21	17
Denmark	33	32	30	30	32	32	31	31	32	31
Finland	45	37	34	24	26	27	28	28	28	28
France	33	33	33	33	33	36	35	38	38	38
Germany	48	49	49	44	41	41	41	40	40	41
Greece	11	11	24	29	29	31	33	35	35	35
Ireland	20	22	19	20	17	22	21	21	24	22
Italy	38	41	47	50	44	46	45	43	44	40
Netherlands	31	32	32	31	31	31	32	31	31	30
Portugal	17	20	27	25	20	23	22	21	24	25
Spain	27	28	29	27	25	24	26	26	26	29
Sweden	31	32	30	19	28	27	28	28	28	28
United Kingdom	33	31	31	30	30	30	30	29	29	29
Average	28.7	29	30.2	27.7	28.4	29.3	29.9	29.8	30	29.8
Weighted average[a]	35.5	36.1	37.3	35.3	34.1	35	35.1	34.8	34.9	34.6
SD	10.6	9.8	9.1	9.0	7.4	7.5	6.8	6.7	6.8	6.5

Note: Data for Luxembourg are not available.
[a] Weighted by a country's GDP.
Source: CPB (2001, 27).

• The smaller and "peripheral" countries (Greece, Portugal, and Spain) started out with a below-average tax rate, but their corporate income tax rates clearly increased during the 1990s. Ireland is a notable exception.

• The average EU corporate income tax rate is fairly constant through time; in any case, it shows no discernible downward trend.

• The standard deviation strongly decreased from 1990 to 1999, so there is some tax rate convergence, but not toward the lowest rate.

These four observations offer some preliminary support for the lack of a race to the bottom. Core/large countries persistently have higher tax rates, and small/peripheral countries even display some catching up in terms of their tax rates.[4] Measuring the effective corporate income tax burden for firms is, however, not an easy task, and the findings shown in table 5.1 are not undisputed. It is clear that for almost every Organization for Economic Cooperation and Development (OECD) country, statutory income tax rates have come down from the 1980s onward. With respect to effective tax rates, the seminal study by Devereux, Griffith, and Klemm (2002) concludes that effective marginal rates have remained rather stable, whereas effective average tax rates have come down. Even if corporate income tax rates have decreased, the tax base has invariably been broadened, with the result that for most countries, tax revenues on corporate income as a percentage of GDP have been more or less stable since 1965 (Devereux et al. 2002, 487). Be that as it may, these findings are in line with those in table 5.1 to the extent that they are both at odds with the predictions that follow from the standard tax competition literature and pose questions as to the relevance of the race-to-the-bottom hypothesis.[5] In related empirical work, and taking the NEG literature into account, Krogstrup (2004) and Garretsen and Peeters (2006) find that capital mobility puts (at most) a limited downward pressure on corporate tax rates but also that core or more centrally located countries typically have a higher corporate tax rate.

Next, we turn to government spending (table 5.2). Baldwin and Krugman (2004) explain the lack of a race to the bottom for taxation in the EU by the fact that despite higher tax rates, the after-tax income in the core EU countries is still larger than in the more peripheral EU countries due to a positive agglomeration rent. These rents are the result of positive pecuniary externalities. By looking only at taxation, government policy either has no impact at all on the location of

Table 5.2
General government final consumption expenditure (% of GDP)

	1960	1965	1970	1975	1980	1985	1990	1995	2000	2003
Austria	13.4	13.8	15.2	17.8	18.5	19.6	18.9	20.4	19.2	18.7
Belgium	15.6	16.1	16.9	21.2	23	22.9	20.3	21.4	21.2	22.8
Denmark	13.6	17	20.9	25.3	27.3	25.9	25.6	25.8	25.3	26.5
Finland	12.2	14	14.8	17.5	18.4	20.6	21.6	22.8	20.6	22.1
France	16.7	16.9	17.3	19.5	21.5	23.7	22.3	23.9	23.2	24.3
Germany				21.7	21.7	21.3	19.7	19.8	19	19.3
Greece	10.1	10.1	10.9	12.8	13.5	16.6	15.1	15.3	15.7	15.5
Ireland	13.3	14.5	15.6	19.8	21.2	19.8	16.4	16.4	13.9	15.1[a]
Italy	14.3	17	15.5	16.5	16.9	18.6	20.2	17.9	18.3	19.5
Netherlands	16.3	18.8	19.9	23.8	25.3	24.3	23.5	24	22.7	24.5[a]
Portugal	9.8	11.1	12.8	13.9	13.5	14.4	16.2	18.6	20.5	21.1[a]
Spain	9.0	9.0	10.1	11.2	14	15.6	16.7	18.1	17.6	17.9
Sweden	16.4	18.3	22.2	24.6	29.8	27.9	27.4	27.2	26.6	28.3
United Kingdom	16.5	17.1	18	22.3	21.5	20.9	19.8	19.6	18.7	21.1
Average	13.6	14.9	16.2	19.1	20.4	20.9	20.3	20.8	20.2	21.2
SD	2.6	3.0	3.5	4.3	4.8	3.7	3.5	3.4	3.4	3.7
Minimum	9.0	9.0	10.1	11.2	13.5	14.4	15.1	15.3	13.9	15.1
Maximum	16.7	18.8	22.2	25.3	29.8	27.9	27.4	27.2	26.6	28.3

Note: Sequential maximum for France, Netherlands, Sweden, Denmark, Sweden, Denmark, and Sweden; sequential minimum for Spain, Greece, Spain, Portugal, Greece, Portugal, Greece, Ireland, and Greece.
[a] Data for 2002.
Source: World Bank CD-ROM (2005).

economic activity as long as the tax rate is not too high or, if the tax rate exceeds a specific threshold, the agglomeration equilibrium can no longer be sustained. A core country can thus afford a higher tax rate, but in essence taxation is a potential spreading force. Government policies then, in principle, do not contribute to the agglomeration forces. However, we stress that public spending is an essential part of the story and that government policies can increase the attractiveness of a country.[6]

Table 5.2 illustrates that with respect to government spending, the EU countries are not involved in a race to the bottom. For most EU countries, there is no downward trend in central government expenditures as a percentage of GDP. This is certainly true for the core EU countries: Germany, France and the United Kingdom. Furthermore, in some of the peripheral EU countries, there is an increase in this expen-

Table 5.3
Preferred locations in northwest Europe

Regions	Reasons for preference
Niedersachsen (Germany)	Close to Hannover.
Nordrhein Westfalen (Germany)	Enough space, good accessibility.
Saarland (Germany)	Near highways leading to Ruhrgebiet. Subsidies to start businesses. Enough space, and low land prices.
Picardie (France)	Near Paris (airport); good accessibility, low land prices.
Champagne (France)	Good infrastructure; always had a strong position (path dependency).
Netherlands	Good accessibility; near airport (Schiphol). Good infrastructure (connections to Germany).

Source: Dutch Ministry of Economic Affairs of *leading companies in North-West Europe* (1999, 36).

diture ratio. Again, there are marked cross-country differences but no evidence of a race to the bottom.

Benchmarking has been a popular method recently among EU policymakers to compare the relative location advantages of the EU countries and regions for the mobile factors of production. If we take northwest Europe as an example, the Dutch Ministry of Economic Affairs has identified the regions in table 5.3 as having the most attractive location characteristics. The table indicates that the attractiveness is to some extent thought to be the result of past regional public spending. The table lists just a few reasons that some regions are preferred locations, but nevertheless suggests that location decisions can be affected by regional government spending on, for example, infrastructure and not only by the levels of taxation. This last point also comes across from an UNCTAD survey on location and foreign direct investment (UNCTAD 1996). Large companies like Samsung and Daimler-Chrysler stated that apart from taxes and subsidies, the social and economic infrastructures (transports) are key determinants for their location decisions. To show this point formally, we turn to the model.

5.3   The Model

We extend the analytically solvable model developed by Forslid (1999), Ottaviano (2001), and Forslid and Ottaviano (2001, 2003), henceforth referred to as the Forslid-Ottaviano model, by including a more detailed analysis of the government sector, incorporating government spending effects, the efficiency of government production, and competition between the government and the private sector on the labor market. The reason to use this analytically solvable model is twofold. First, in the discussion of tax competition, the main issue is that mobile and immobile factors of production react differently to taxation. We will call the immobile factor labor and the mobile factor capital. In the European context, this corresponds to the fact that labor is less mobile than capital. As argued by Ottaviano (2001), it is realistic to assume that the manufacturing or modern sector uses both skilled and unskilled labor to produce its output.[7] The ability to distinguish between mobile and immobile factors in the manufacturing sector is also why Baldwin and Krugman (2004) and Andersson and Forslid (2003) take this model as the starting point in their analyses of tax competition and economic integration. A second reason to use the model is that it can be solved analytically, which enables us to derive some analytical results.

There are two regions ($j = 1, 2$). Each region has L_j workers and K_j capital.[8] Capital can be thought of as human or knowledge capital. Workers are geographically immobile, whereas capital is mobile. Henceforth we make the following assumption: the two regions are identical with respect to the immobile factor of production, that is, $L_1 = L_2 = 0.5$.

All agents have the same preferences, depending on the consumption of food F and manufactures M, a composite of n different varieties c_i:

$$U = M^\delta F^{(1-\delta)}; \quad 0 < \delta < 1 \tag{5.1}$$

$$M = \left(\sum_{i=1}^{n} c_i^{(\sigma-1)/\sigma} \right)^{\sigma/(\sigma-1)}; \quad \sigma > 1, \tag{5.2}$$

where δ is the share of income spent on manufactures and σ is the elasticity of substitution between different varieties of manufactures. The production of food, which is freely traded at zero transport costs, takes place under constant returns to scale and requires only workers. A suitable choice of units ensures that one unit of labor produces one unit of food. Labor is used in food production and in the variable cost part of production in the manufacturing sector. Using food as a numeraire and assuming free trade implies that its price, and hence the wage rate, can be set equal to one. This means that we have to determine only the return to capital, r.

Firms in the manufacturing industry use labor and capital to produce a variety of manufactures under increasing returns to scale. The fixed-cost component represents the knowledge-intensive part of the manufacturing production process, such as R&D, marketing, and management. Both the fixed- and variable-cost components of production depend on the quality of the infrastructure, education level, judicial system, police services, and others. All of these are related to the level of government spending Z_j. The reduction in costs is measured by the efficiency function $f_j(Z_j)$ with $f_j(0) = 1$, $f_j' \leq 0$. This distinguishes our model from that of Andersson and Forslid (2003) and Baldwin and Krugman (2004). Let r_j be the return to capital in region j; then the costs of producing x units of a manufacturing variety in region j are equal to (the choice of units, and the fact that the wage rate equals unity simplifies the notation below)

$$f_j(Z_j)[r_j + [(\sigma - 1)/\sigma]x]. \tag{5.3}$$

The production of public goods requires capital only under constant returns to scale. This is the second extension of our model: we assume that the production of public goods takes up net resources. It captures the idea that government production competes with private production and relates to the discussion about the optimal size of the government sector. Market clearing for capital in region j allows us to determine the number of varieties produced in region j:

$$n_j = (K_j - Z_j)/f_j(Z_j). \tag{5.4}$$

Note that this equation differs from the standard equation in the NEG literature that determines the number of varieties in the sense that the "fixed" costs are no longer fixed in our variant of the model. Equation 5.4 reflects the fact that the private and public sectors compete with each other on the labor market. Equilibrium in the public sector requires that the value of public spending is fully paid by taxes,

$$r_j Z_j = t_j Y_j, \tag{5.5}$$

where t_j is the uniform income tax rate that applies to both labor and capital.[9] Given the sector distribution of capital and the return to capital, choosing a level of public goods determines the tax rate, and vice versa. In addition, we assume that capital employed in the public sector earns the same return as in the private sector. This reflects the notion that the public sector has to pay competing wages in order to attract capital.

Standard monopolistic competition markup pricing gives

$$p_j = f_j(Z_j). \tag{5.6}$$

This pricing rule applies for locally produced and sold goods. Two observations with respect to this rule can be made. First, due to the production structure (see equation 5.3), the price p_j does not depend on wages. Second, we cannot choose units such that $p_j = 1$ because the marginal cost of production is a function of the level of public goods Z_j provided in region j. However, once we know the level of public goods provided, the local price level for manufacturing varieties is also determined.

Free entry and exit in the manufacturing sector ensure that profits are zero, which determines the equilibrium output per firm (see equation 5.7). Using our normalization of wages, the income in region j is given in equation 5.8:

$$x_j = \sigma r_j \tag{5.7}$$

$$Y_j = r_j K_j + L_j \tag{5.8}$$

Using Samuelson's (1952) iceberg transport costs T (the number of goods shipped from a region to ensure that one unit arrives in the other region) in the manufacturing sector, the price charged in the other region is T times as high as the mill price. It is convenient to define the "freeness-of-trade" parameter ϕ as a function of transport costs and the elasticity of substitution: $\phi \equiv T^{1-\sigma}$. It ranges between 0 and 1, where $\phi = 0$ represents autarky and $\phi = 1$ indicates free trade (no obstacles to the movement of manufacturing varieties of any kind whatsoever).

The manufacturing sector market clearing condition is standard and given by (note that we assume that civil servants have the same preferences as non–civil servants, so that the income term reflects total income)

$$p_j x_j = \frac{p_j^{1-\sigma} \delta Y_j}{P_j^{1-\sigma}} + \frac{\phi p_k^{1-\sigma} \delta Y_k}{P_k^{1-\sigma}} \tag{5.9}$$

$$P_j = (p_j^{1-\sigma} n_j + \phi p_k^{1-\sigma} n_k)^{1/(1-\sigma)}, \tag{5.10}$$

where P_j is the price index for manufactures in region j. The left-hand side of equation 5.9 gives the equilibrium (value of) output per firm and the right-hand side the associated demand coming from the home region and from the distant region, which explains the transport cost term. Using equations 5.6, 5.7, 5.9, and 5.10 gives

$$r_1 = \left(\frac{1}{f_1\sigma}\right)\left[\frac{f_1^{1-\sigma}\delta Y_1}{n_1 f_1^{1-\sigma} + \phi n_2 f_2^{1-\sigma}} + \frac{\phi f_2^{1-\sigma}\delta Y_2}{n_2 f_2^{1-\sigma} + \phi n_1 f_1^{1-\sigma}}\right] \tag{5.11}$$

$$r_2 = \left(\frac{1}{f_2\sigma}\right)\left[\frac{f_2^{1-\sigma}\delta Y_2}{n_2 f_2^{1-\sigma} + \phi n_1 f_1^{1-\sigma}} + \frac{\phi f_1^{1-\sigma}\delta Y_1}{n_1 f_1^{1-\sigma} + \phi n_2 f_2^{1-\sigma}}\right].$$

Henceforth, we let λ denote the share of capital in region 1. As shown in appendix 5A, the ratio of the rewards to capital is equal to

$$\frac{r_1}{r_2} = \frac{f_2\sigma[\phi n_1(1+\psi_1) + n_2(1+\phi^2\psi_2)] + (\phi^2-1)(1-\lambda)\delta}{f_1\sigma[\phi n_2(1+\psi_2) + n_1(1+\phi^2\psi_1)] + (\phi^2-1)\lambda\delta}.$$

$$\psi_j \equiv \frac{f_j^{1-\sigma}}{f_k^{1-\sigma}} \tag{5.12}$$

Once the functional form of the provision of public goods (see equation 5.3) is specified, in addition to a public policy rule determining the level of public goods, equation 5.12 can be explicitly written as a function of λ, the share of capital in region 1.

To round off the discussion of our model, we note that the location decision of capital involves not only the factor rewards r_1 and r_2 but also the respective price levels, tax rates, and the provision of public services. The incentive of capital to relocate is therefore determined by the ratio ρ of indirect utilities (or welfare):

$$\rho = \left(\frac{(1-t_1)r_1}{(1-t_2)r_2}\right)\left(\frac{P_2}{P_1}\right)^\delta. \tag{5.13}$$

This ratio is central to the analysis in the next sections. Apart from the case of complete agglomeration, capital has no incentive to relocate if welfare is the same in the two regions ($\rho = 1$), while capital moves from region 2 to region 1 if welfare is higher in region 1 ($\rho > 1$) and from region 1 to region 2 if welfare is lower in region 1 ($\rho < 1$). This completes our discussion of the model.

5.4   Analysis of the Symmetric Equilibrium for a Given Level of Public Goods

Extending the Forslid-Ottaviano model, in which the manufacturing sector uses both a mobile and an immobile production factor, not only allows us to analyze and illustrate locational competition but also enables us to derive some analytical results. In doing so, we focus attention on the analysis of the symmetric equilibrium, that is if both regions provide the same level of public goods and attract the same share of capital. This is another difference with, for instance, Baldwin and Krugman (2004), who build their analysis on the case of the agglomeration equilibrium, where all footloose economic activity is located in one country. Here, we ask a different question: What happens to the stability of the symmetric or no-agglomeration equilibrium once we allow for public goods? In particular, we want to know if agglomeration becomes more likely (see section 5.5).

Assumption 1

• The two regions have a constant and given level of public goods: $Z_1 = Z_2 = Z$.

• The influence of government spending on the cost of production in the two regions are identical: $f_1 = f_2 = f$.

Proposition 1 (spreading)   Under assumption 1, the impact of public goods on the symmetric equilibrium is summarized in table 5.4 (see appendix 5B).

The impact of the standard new economic geography parameters on the spreading equilibrium is not surprising: an increase in the freeness of trade parameter has no direct effect on most variables as measured relative to the numeraire, but of course reduces the price index (as more manufactured goods arrive at their destination) and thus increases real income and the real return to capital (and labor). As the freeness of trade increases beyond a certain level, the symmetric equilibrium will become unstable. An increase in the elasticity of substitution increases competition between varieties, which therefore reduces the return to capital and thus income. In addition, an increase in the ease with which consumers can substitute between different varieties reduces the price index.[10] An increase in the share of income spent on

Table 5.4
Symmetric equilibrium

Endogenous variable in symmetric equilibrium	Impact of rise in			
	σ	δ	ϕ	Z
$r = \dfrac{\delta}{\sigma(1 - 2Z) - \delta}$	−	+	0	+
$Y = \dfrac{\sigma(1 - 2Z)}{2[\sigma(1 - 2Z) - \delta]}$	−	+	0	+
$p = f(Z)$	0	0	0	−
$P = \left[\dfrac{(1 + \phi)(1 - 2Z)}{2}\right]^{1/(1-\sigma)} f(Z)^{\sigma/(\sigma-1)}$	−	0	−	?
$n = \dfrac{(1 - 2Z)}{2f(Z)}$	0	0	0	?
$t = \dfrac{2Z\delta}{(1 - 2Z)\sigma}$	−	+	0	+

manufactures increases the importance of capital relative to labor and thus increases the return to capital and income.

Increasing the provision of public goods reduces the cost of production (and thus the price) of an individual variety and (through the increased scarcity of capital) increases the return to capital and income. All of this comes at the cost of an increased tax rate because the government has to pay competitive returns to capital. Since the share of capital allocated to the production of manufactures decreases while at the same time the "waste" in terms of the fixed cost to produce varieties decreases, the net effect on the number of varieties produced and on the price index is unclear. Enlarging the government sector is therefore a mixed blessing, the wisdom of which depends on the particular circumstances. If the production of public goods has a large enough impact on reducing the costs of production, the improved efficiency of the economy is beneficial through a reduction in the price of a variety and the price index and through an increase in the number of varieties produced (love-of-variety effect; see Brakman, Garretsen, and Van Marrewijk 2001).

Note that under assumption 1, the terms ψ_j defined in equation 5.12 are equal to 1, which therefore simplifies to:

$$\frac{r_1}{r_2} = \frac{b_1(1 - \lambda) + b_2\lambda - b_3Z}{b_1\lambda + b_2(1 - \lambda) - b_3Z} \equiv h_2(\lambda|Z)$$

where

$$b_1 \equiv \sigma(1+\phi^2) - \delta(1-\phi^2); \quad b_2 \equiv 2\phi\sigma; \quad b_3 \equiv \sigma(1-\phi)^2. \qquad (5.12')$$

The function $h_2(\lambda|Z)$ is defined for future reference.[11] As the notation clarifies, the return to capital is a function of the share λ of capital located in region 1, given the level of public goods Z produced in each region. The direction of the impact of the provision of public goods on the ratio of rewards to capital is readily determined and gives us proposition 2:

Proposition 2 (magnification I)   If, for a given distribution of capital under assumption 1, region 1 has a higher reward to capital than region 2 in the absence of public goods, an equal provision of public goods in both regions magnifies the relatively higher reward to capital in region 1.

Similarly, using the above conditions, the relative price index P_2/P_1 simplifies to

$$\frac{P_2}{P_1} = \left(\frac{(1-\lambda) + \phi\lambda - (1+\phi)Z}{\lambda + \phi(1-\lambda) - (1+\phi)Z} \right)^{1/(1-\sigma)}. \qquad (5.14)$$

Again, the direction of the impact of the provision of public goods on the relative price ratio can be readily determined.

Proposition 3 (magnification II)   If, for a given distribution of capital under assumption 1, region 2 has a higher price index than region 1 in the absence of public goods, an equal provision of public goods in both regions magnifies the relatively higher price index of region 2.

Obviously, if a higher return to capital in a particular region (e.g., $r_1 > r_2$) is also associated with a higher price index in that region ($P_1 > P_2$), the combination of propositions 2 and 3 shows that the net effect on the real rate of return to capital of the introduction of public goods depends on the relative magnitude of the impact on the rate of return compared to the impact on the price index. In the core geographical economics model on which the Forslid-Ottaviano model is based, it is typically true that the region with a larger share of the mobile factor of production (say, region 1) would have a higher return to capital $(r_1 > r_2)$ as well as a lower price index $(P_1 < P_2)$, in which case the introduction of public goods would unambiguously foster agglomeration.

5.5 Break Analysis for a Given Level of Public Goods

Based on the propositions derived in the previous section and our simulation results that follow, the introduction of productive public goods increases the possibilities for active government intervention by fostering agglomeration of manufacturing production rather than spreading of manufacturing production. This section formally addresses this question by analyzing the stability of the symmetric spreading equilibrium. In particular, we will determine for which value of the freeness of trade parameter ϕ spreading of manufacturing production is no longer a stable equilibrium. First, we note that since there is an equal provision of public goods in both regions, the welfare ratio for capital given in equation 5.13 simplifies to

$$\rho(\lambda|Z) = \frac{(1-t_1)}{(1-t_2)} \frac{r_1}{r_2} \left(\frac{P_2}{P_1}\right)^\delta \equiv h_1(\lambda|Z)h_2(\lambda|Z)h_3(\lambda|Z),$$

where

$$h_1(\lambda|Z) \equiv \frac{(1-t_1)}{(1-t_2)}, \quad h_2(\lambda|Z) \equiv \frac{r_1}{r_2}, \quad h_3(\lambda|Z) \equiv \left(\frac{P_2}{P_1}\right)^\delta. \tag{5.13'}$$

At the symmetric equilibrium $\lambda = 0.5$, we have

$$h_1(0.5|Z) = h_2(0.5|Z) = h_3(0.5|Z) = 1$$

such that

$$\rho'(0.5|Z) = h_1'(0.5|Z) + h_2'(0.5|Z) + h_3'(0.5|Z). \tag{5.15}$$

Using this notation the break analysis (figure 5.1) consists of finding values of ϕ for which $\rho' = 0$. As shown in appendix 5C, for the real rental rate, this implies solving equation 5.16:

$$\frac{4\delta(1-\phi)}{(\sigma-1)(1+\phi)(1-2Z)} - \frac{4(\sigma(1+\phi^2) - \delta(1-\phi^2) - 2\phi\sigma)}{[\sigma(1+\phi^2) - \delta(1-\phi^2) + 2\phi\sigma - 2\sigma(1-\phi)^2 Z]}$$

$$= 0. \tag{5.16}$$

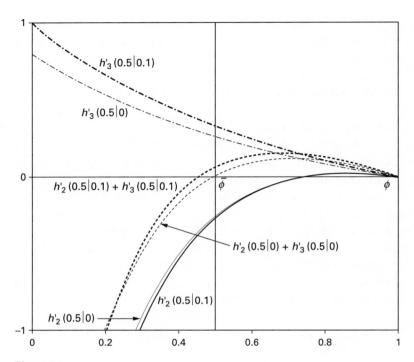

Figure 5.1
Break analysis ($\sigma = 4, \delta = 0.6$)

Let $\bar{\phi}$ be the solution to equation 5.16 if there are no public goods provided, that is, if $Z = 0$ (see appendix 5C). We can determine the impact
of the introduction of public goods on the break condition at the mar-
gin, that is, the solution evaluated at $Z = 0$, $\lambda = 0.5$, and $\phi = \bar{\phi}$. Appendix 5C shows that at the margin, the break condition for the freeness of
trade parameter falls if, and only if, condition 5.17 holds:

$$\bar{\phi}(\delta\bar{\phi} + 4\sigma) > \delta. \tag{5.17}$$

Proposition 4 (break point) Under assumption 1, the introduction of
an equal provision of public goods in both regions at the margin
reduces the freeness of trade index for the break point if, and only if,
condition 5.17 holds.

Proposition 4 is illustrated if condition 5.17 holds in figure 5.1, showing that the break point is reached for a lower value of the freeness-of-
trade parameter ϕ if there are public goods ($Z = 0.1$) than in the

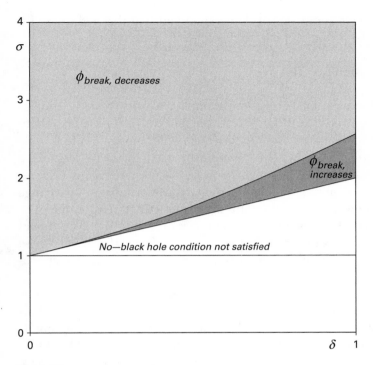

Figure 5.2
Marginal impact of introducing public goods on break-point

absence of public goods $(Z = 0)$. Since condition 5.17 is rather weak and holds for a wide range of parameter combinations (δ, σ), the introduction of public goods usually leads to a fall in the freeness of trade break point, tending to reduce the stability of the spreading equilibrium, as illustrated in figure 5.2. For Europe, for example, this suggests that incorporating the impact of the provision of public goods on the stability of the economic process, the process of continued economic integration (EU enlargement), which increases the freeness-of-trade parameter ϕ, is more likely to lead to instability of the spreading equilibrium or, equivalently, more likely to result in core-periphery outcomes. Figure 5.1 also illustrates why this is the case: $h'_3 > 0$, and this indicates that the additional provision of public goods represents a negative externality as it reduces the number of available varieties. This implies that for lower values of the freeness-of-trade index, the incentive to move to a (marginal) larger region (more varieties) is reached sooner than without public goods. The next section illustrates our findings by showing a few simulation results. It shows again that the introduction of public goods stimulates agglomeration and that this is the case for all intermediate values of the freeness-of-trade parameter ϕ.

5.6   Simulation Results

Before we show some simulation examples, we first have to address the following question: What is a reasonable choice for the tax rate to use in our simulations? We apply the following motivation to be able to answer this question. The government maximizes $(1 - t)r$, taking into consideration that r is a function of the tax rate t, and assumes that the change in remuneration is directly proportional to the change in capital productivity in the manufacturing sector (thus ignoring price index effects). The first-order condition implies that the government sets the income tax rate such that $1/(1 - t) = r'/r = -f'/f$. If we choose $f(Z) = \exp(\eta Z)$, we have $1/(1 - t) = \eta$, which we use in the simulations below.

First note that figure 5.3 illustrates, for $Z_1 = Z_2 = 0$ (no public goods), that around the break point, the symmetric equilibrium is borderline stable (the break point occurs at $\phi = 0.359$). Introducing public goods (the line with squares) in both countries ($Z_1 = Z_2 = 0.1$) has a strong effect on the stability of the symmetric equilibrium in the sense

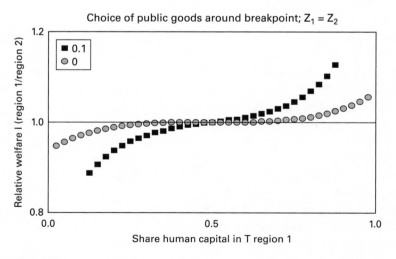

Figure 5.3

Introduction of Public Goods around Breakpoint

Parameter settings: $\eta_i = 1$ $(i = 1, 2)$; $\delta = 0.6$; $\sigma = 3$; $Z_i = 0.1$ (default 0); $L_i = 0.5$: φ-break for $Z = 0$ is 0.359

that it becomes unstable. This simulation result is in line with the analytical results from the previous section. In section 5.5 we showed that for a broad range of parameter values, in particular for a broad range of σ and δ (see condition 5.17 and figure 5.2), the introduction of public goods stimulates agglomeration by making the spreading equilibrium unstable at a higher level of trade costs (lower values for ϕ). It is only for a sufficiently low elasticity of substitution σ and a sufficiently high share of income spent on manufactures δ that this is not the case. To illustrate this, we ran the same simulation as in figure 5.3, but now with $\sigma = 2$ and $\delta = 0.8$ (not shown here), and just like figure 5.2 predicts, the introduction of public goods makes the stability of the spreading equilibrium stronger.

The analytical results derived in the previous section are based on the assumption that the two countries or regions are symmetric with regard to the provision of public goods: $Z_1 = Z_2$. Figure 5.4 shows a simulation where we dropped this assumption. In figure 5.4 we compare the situation where the provision of public goods in country 1 is the same as in country 2, $Z_1 = 0.05$, and the situation when the provision of public goods is higher, $Z_1 = 0.07$.

If the two countries have the same level of public goods (line with circles), we end up with a stable symmetric equilibrium where both

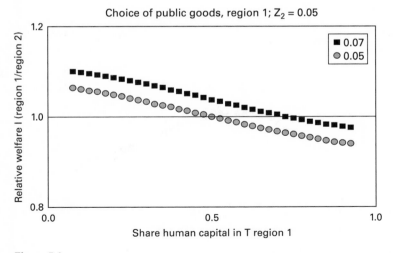

Figure 5.4
Asymmetric provision of public goods
Parameter settings: $\eta_i = 1$ $(i = 1, 2)$; $\delta = 0.6$; $\sigma = 4$; $\varphi = 0.4$; $Z_2 = 0.05$; $Z_1 = 0.05$ or 0.07; $L_i = 0.5$

countries thus have the same share of capital of 0.5. For the case where $Z_1 > Z_2$ (line with squares), country 1 ends up with a higher share of capital λ than country 2. The stable equilibrium now is one of partial agglomeration: $\lambda_1 > \lambda_2$. This simulation result suggests that for countries to attract a larger share of the mobile production factor, they need to make sure that they provide more public goods. This is interesting because a relatively higher level of the provision of public goods is associated with higher tax levels. The positive effects of public goods dominate in this case.

One might be tempted to conclude that tax competition would lead to a race to the top with respect to taxation and public expenditures, where in the end, all of a country's productive resources are directed toward the public goods sector. This is, however, not what our model predicts. A relatively higher level of public goods provision might be effective, as figure 5.4 shows (in terms of attracting a more than a proportional share of capital), but a country can easily push this argument too far. This is illustrated in figure 5.5, which gives the simulation results for the case where country 1 spends far more on public goods than country 2, but more public goods may imply that country 1's share of capital will be lower compared to the case with less public goods. In figure 5.5, country 2 does not provide public goods at all

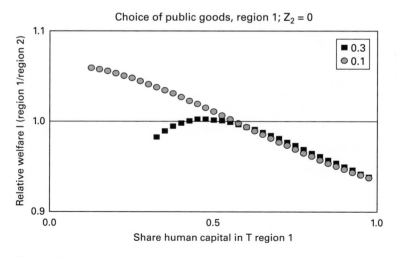

Figure 5.5
Pushing the Public Goods Argument too Far ...
Parameter settings: $\eta_i = 0.1$ $(i = 1, 2)$; $\delta = 0.6$, $\sigma = 4$; $\varphi = 0.4$; $Z_2 = 0$; $Z_1 = 0.1$ or 0.3; $L_i = 0.5$

$(Z_2 = 0)$, and, in line with figure 5.4, a moderate level of public goods provision by country 1 $(Z_1 = 0.1)$ makes country 1 better off to the extent that it ends up with more than its proportionate share of capital in equilibrium: $\lambda_1 > 0.5$ (see the line with circles). When, however, country 1 decides to increase the production of public goods, the resulting equilibrium is such that there is no longer partial agglomeration in favor of country 1. Stronger still, its share of capital could even drop below 0.5, as figure 5.5 illustrates for $Z_1 = 0.3$ (line with squares).

As in all other NEG models (partial) agglomeration is the result of the balance between spreading and agglomerating forces. In the present NEG model the production of public goods has negative effects that may outweigh the benefits of public goods. The relative welfare ρ for capital in country 1 is, for instance, negatively affected by an increased tax rate or the reduction of the number of varieties of the manufacturing good, both of which result when the level of public goods is increased. This important cautionary note as to the benefits of a relative increase in the level of public goods by, here, country 1 is reinforced if we would also allow for another asymmetry between the two countries, a country-specific efficiency of public goods production $f_i(Z) = \exp(-\eta_i Z)$ by making η_i country specific (see Brakman et al. 2002).

5.7   Summary and Conclusions

Recent advances in the theory of trade and location have shown that economic integration does not need to lead to a race to the bottom with respect to taxation. This important result challenges the standard views about tax competition, but the treatment of the government sector is still rather rudimentary. The emphasis is almost exclusively on taxes and their distributional consequences. This is rather one-sided because taxes are a means to an end, and tax-financed public spending can also be used as an instrument of locational competition. Countries try to increase their attractiveness as a location by investing in location-specific infrastructure. When the effects of agglomeration are thought to be important, tax and spending policies represent two opposing forces. All other things remaining the same, higher taxes stimulate spreading even though the existence of an agglomeration rent may prevent the spreading from actually taking place. Similarly, an increase in public spending stimulates agglomeration if this spending enhances the attractiveness of the location for the mobile factors of production.

But all things do not remain the same, in the sense that higher taxes typically also imply higher public spending and vice versa.

In this chapter, we extend recent work in the new economic geography literature on tax competition by Baldwin and Krugman (2004) and Andersson and Forslid (2003) in three ways. First, we allow public spending to affect the cost of production, and this has an impact on the location decisions of firms and workers. Second, we take into account that the public sector has to compete with the private sector on the labor market so that public spending takes up net resources. Third, we focus on the symmetric equilibrium, as opposed to the agglomeration equilibrium, and the impact of the provision of public goods on the symmetric equilibrium.

The main contribution of this chapter is that it takes the interdependency between taxes and spending as a starting point. This means that by restricting locational competition to tax competition only, one neglects that the provision of public goods also determines (positively or negatively) the attractiveness of locations for footloose economic activity and thereby determines the equilibrium with respect to the distribution of footloose factors of production across space. Our conclusions are based on simulation results as well as analytical results. In general, the results indicate that starting from an initial symmetric equilibrium, the introduction of public goods stimulates agglomeration and that, compared to the no-public-goods case, the symmetric equilibrium becomes unstable for lower degrees of economic integration (higher trade costs). Our simulations not only back up our analytical results, but by allowing an asymmetric provision of public goods between the two countries, they additionally show that there is a limit up to which an increase in public goods provision stimulates (partial) agglomeration.

Appendix 5A: Derivation of Equation 5.12

Using the income equations 5.8, equations 5.11 can be written as

$$r_1 = \left(\frac{1}{f_1\sigma}\right)\left[\frac{f_1^{1-\sigma}\delta(r_1K_1 + L_1)}{n_1f_1^{1-\sigma} + \phi n_2 f_2^{1-\sigma}} + \frac{\phi f_2^{1-\sigma}(r_2K_2 + L_2)}{n_2 f_2^{1-\sigma} + \phi n_1 f_1^{1-\sigma}}\right]$$

$$r_2 = \left(\frac{1}{f_2\sigma}\right)\left[\frac{f_2^{1-\sigma}\delta(r_2K_2 + L_2)}{n_2f_2^{1-\sigma} + \phi n_1 f_1^{1-\sigma}} + \frac{\phi f_1^{1-\sigma}(r_1K_1 + L_1)}{n_1 f_1^{1-\sigma} + \phi n_2 f_2^{1-\sigma}}\right].$$

Two linear equations in the unknowns r_1 and r_2 that can be solved analytically:

$$\begin{aligned} r_1 &= a_{11}r_1 + a_{12}r_2 + d_1 \\ r_2 &= a_{21}r_1 + a_{22}r_2 + d_2 \end{aligned} \Rightarrow \begin{bmatrix} r_1 \\ r_2 \end{bmatrix}$$

$$= \frac{1}{(1-a_{11})(1-a_{22}) - a_{12}a_{21}} \begin{bmatrix} (1-a_{22})d_1 + a_{12}d_2 \\ a_{21}d_1 + (1-a_{11})d_2 \end{bmatrix}$$

where

$$a_{11} = \left(\frac{1}{f_1\sigma}\right)\bar{h}_1 K_1 \qquad\qquad a_{12} = \left(\frac{1}{f_1\sigma}\right)\phi\bar{h}_2 K_2$$

$$a_{21} = \left(\frac{1}{f_2\sigma}\right)\phi\bar{h}_1 K_1 \qquad\qquad a_{22} = \left(\frac{1}{f_2\sigma}\right)\bar{h}_2 K_2$$

$$d_1 = \left(\frac{1}{f_1\sigma}\right)(\bar{h}_1 L_1 + \phi\bar{h}_2 L_2) \qquad d_2 = \left(\frac{1}{f_2\sigma}\right)(\phi\bar{h}_1 L_1 + \bar{h}_2 L_2)$$

$$\bar{h}_j \equiv \left(\frac{f_j^{1-\sigma}\delta}{n_j f_j^{1-\sigma} + \phi n_k f_k^{1-\sigma}}\right).$$

For $K = 1$, $K_1 = \lambda$, $L_1 = L_2 = 1/2$, the derivation of r_i is now straightforward:

$$r_1 = \frac{\frac{1 - \frac{\bar{h}_2(1-\lambda)}{\sigma f_2}}{2\sigma f_1}(\bar{h}_1 + \phi\bar{h}_2) + \frac{\phi\bar{h}_2(1-\lambda)(\bar{h}_2 + \phi\bar{h}_1)}{2\sigma^2 f_1 f_2}}{\left(1 - \frac{\bar{h}_1\lambda}{\sigma f_1}\right)\left(1 - \frac{\bar{h}_2(1-\lambda)}{\sigma f_2}\right) - \frac{\phi^2\bar{h}_1\bar{h}_2\lambda(1-\lambda)}{\sigma^2 f_1 f_2}},$$

and similarly for r_2. Using the definitions of $\bar{h}_j$ and defining ψ_j gives equation 5.14:

$$\frac{r_1}{r_2} = \frac{f_2\sigma[\phi n_1(1+\psi_1) + n_2(1+\phi^2\psi_2)] + (\phi^2-1)(1-\lambda)\delta}{f_1\sigma[\phi n_2(1+\psi_2) + n_1(1+\phi^2\psi_1)] + (\phi^2-1)\lambda\delta};$$

$$\psi_j \equiv f_j^{1-\sigma}/f_k^{1-\sigma}, \; j \neq k.$$

In the absence of a government sector, that is, if $f_1 = f_2 = 1$ (such that $\psi_1 = \psi_2 = 1$) and $n_1 = \lambda$; $n_2 = 1 - \lambda$, this expression simplifies to the Forslid-Ottaviano model:

$$\frac{r_1}{r_2} = \frac{\sigma[2\phi\lambda + (1-\lambda)(1+\phi^2)] + (\phi^2-1)(1-\lambda)\delta}{\sigma[2\phi(1-\lambda) + \lambda(1+\phi^2)] + (\phi^2-1)\lambda\delta}.$$

Appendix 5B: Derivation of Table 5.4

At the symmetric equilibrium we have $\lambda = 0.5$; $f_1 = f_2 = f$; $\bar{h}_1 = \bar{h}_2 = \bar{h}$; $n_1 = n_2 = n$. Use this in appendix A to calculate the rental rate:

$$r_1|_{\lambda=0.5} = \frac{(1+\phi)\bar{h}}{2\sigma f - (1+\phi)\bar{h}}; \quad \bar{h} = \frac{\delta}{(1+\phi)n}.$$

Since $n = (1/2 - Z)/f$ we get

$$r_1|_{\lambda=0.5} = r_2|_{\lambda=0.5} \equiv r = \frac{\delta}{\sigma(1-2Z)-\delta},$$

such that $Y_1 = Y_2 \equiv \frac{r}{2} + \frac{1}{2} = \sigma(1-2Z)/(2[\sigma(1-2Z)-\delta])$ and $t_1 = t_2 \equiv t = rZ/Y = 2Z\delta/(1-2Z)\sigma$. These results allow us to calculate the impact of changes of policy parameters on the endogenous variables of the model. The results are summarized in table 5.4.

Appendix 5C: Derivation of Equations 5.16 and 5.17

The function h_1 transfers the pretax return to the posttax return:

$$h_1(\lambda|Z) \equiv \frac{1 - t_1(\lambda|Z)}{1 - t_2(\lambda|Z)}.$$

At the point of symmetry, $t_1 = t_2 = t$, $h_1(0.5|Z) = 1$, and $t_1'(0.5|Z) = -t_2'(0.5|Z)$, such that the derivative of h_1 simplifies to $h_1'(0.5|Z) = -[2/(1-t)]t_1'(0.5|Z)$. We therefore have to determine the impact of a change in the distribution of capital on the tax rate. Since $Y_1 = r_1 K_1 + L_1$ and $r_1 Z = t_1 Y_1$ in the symmetric equilibrium,

$$t_1'(0.5|Z) = t_1 \left[\frac{r_1'(0.5|Z)}{2r_1 Y_1} - \frac{r_1}{Y_1} \right].$$

Evaluating this expression at the margin at which no public goods are provided (such that the tax rate $t_1 = 0$) shows that $t_1'(0.5|Z)$ is identically 0, such that $h_1'(0.5|0)$ is identically 0 and at the margin the posttax break-point analysis coincides with the pretax break-point analysis (note that this will simplify the break analysis below).

The function h_2 gives the relative return on capital. Using assumption 1, the ratio of rewards to capital r_1/r_2 is given in equation 5.12'. It is obvious that $h_2(0.5|Z) = 1$. Taking the derivative of the function h_2 and evaluating it at the symmetric equilibrium gives

$$h_2'(\lambda|Z) = \frac{-(b_1 - b_2)(b_1 + b_2 - 2b_3 Z)}{[b_1 \lambda + b_2(1 - \lambda) - b_3 Z]^2}, \quad h_2'(0.5|Z) = \frac{-4(b_1 - b_2)}{[b_1 + b_2 - 2b_3 Z]}.$$

The function h_3 gives the relative price index effect in the utility function:

$$h_3(\lambda|Z) \equiv \left(\frac{P_2}{P_1}\right)^\delta = \left(\frac{(1 - \lambda) + \phi\lambda - (1 + \phi)Z}{\lambda + \phi(1 - \lambda) - (1 + \phi)Z}\right)^{\delta/(1-\sigma)}.$$

It is obvious that $h_3(0.5) = 1$. Taking the derivative of h_3 and evaluating it at the symmetric equilibrium gives

$$h_3(0.5|Z) = \frac{4\delta(1 - \phi)}{(\sigma - 1)(1 + \phi)(1 - 2Z)}.$$

Combining these results above implies that the break condition is equation 5.16 in the text. If there are no public goods, that is, if $Z = 0$, the solution for the freeness-of-trade parameter, $\bar{\phi}$ say, that solves equation 5.16 is given by (see Forslid 1999, equation 13, or Forslid and Ottaviano 2001, equation 15)

$$\phi_{break}|_{Z=0} \equiv \bar{\phi} = \frac{(\sigma - \delta)(\sigma - 1 - \delta)}{(\sigma + \delta)(\sigma + \delta - 1)}.$$

We can determine the impact of the introduction of public goods at the margin by differentiating condition 5.16 with respect to Z and evaluating the result at $Z = 0$, $\lambda = 0.5$, and $\phi = \bar{\phi}$:

$$\frac{\partial h_2'(0.5|0)}{\partial Z}\bigg|_{\phi=\bar{\phi}} + \frac{\partial h_3'(0.5|0)}{\partial Z}\bigg|_{\phi=\bar{\phi}}. \tag{5.18}$$

It can be shown that as a function of ϕ, equation 5.18 always cuts the horizontal axis from below if $\delta < \sigma - 1$, which corresponds to the standard no-black-hole condition.[12] The break point will be reached for a smaller value of the freeness-of-trade index ϕ if equation 5.18 is positive, and for a larger value if equation 5A.1 is negative. This is illustrated in figure 5.1. Straightforward, but tedious, calculations show that equation 5.18 is positive if and only if condition 5.17 in the text holds.

Notes

A first and rather different version of this chapter was published as CESifo working paper no. 775 (Brakman, Garretsen, and Van Marrewijk 2002). We thank Ron Davies, Jim Markusen, Gianmarco Ottaviano, Jolanda Peeters, Marc Schramm, Jan Egbert Sturm, Albert de Vaal, participants of the 2002 EEA conference in Venice, participants of the 2005 CESifo summer conference in Venice, and our referees, Ruud de Mooij and Rikard Forslid, for their useful comments. Please send correspondence to Charles van Marrewijk (vanmarrewijk@few.eur.nl), Department of Economics, Erasmus University Rotterdam, PO Box 1738, 3000 DR Rotterdam, the Netherlands.

1. Baldwin and Forslid (2002) is one of the first NEG papers to date that also deals with the role of public goods alongside taxes.

2. We do not address the difficult question about the most likely outcome of location competition between governments. In the absence of ideal market conditions, international welfare maximization is not guaranteed (see Sinn 2004).

3. These four countries are also the core countries in the sense that their share in total EU manufacturing production is about 75 percent. This share remained fairly constant through the 1990s.

4. Note that we do not claim that there is no tax competition at all in the EU. Sinn (2004), for instance, shows that the average tax burden for subsidiaries of U.S. companies in the EU decreased strongly in the various EU countries between 1986 and 1992.

5. The data used in Devereux et al. (2002) do not cover all EU countries. For the actual data set used in this study and various measures of the corporate income tax rates and tax revenues, see http://www.ifs.org.uk/publications.php?publication_id=3210.

6. To some extent, as shown below, the issue here is the difference between pure and pecuniary externalities. The former are absent in the standard geographical economics model.

7. In the literature, one finds various labels: skilled versus unskilled, human capital versus capital, labor versus capital. The precise label is not important for us as long as one production factor is internationally mobile and the other is not.

8. The main point here is to include a mobile and an immobile factor of production. The labeling of these two factors (unskilled versus skilled labor or labor versus capital) is not material as long as the mobile factor (be it skilled labor or capital) spends its income in the region where it is used for production; see in particular Forslid (1999, 11) for a discussion of the importance of this assumption.

9. Differentiating between labor and capital income taxation raises the complication why to tax the mobile factor at all (see also Sinn 2004).

10. The net effect on welfare cannot be discussed as a change in the elasticity of substitution affects the utility function itself. This also holds for a change in the share of income spent on manufactures.

11. This expression readily simplifies to the Forslid-Ottaviano model if there are no public goods (see Ottaviano 2001, equation 5.10).

12. This condition is somewhat less restrictive than the no-black-hole condition in Fujita, Krugman, and Venables (1999). See also the appendix in Ottaviano (2001).

References

Anderson, F., and R. Forslid. (2003). Tax Competition and Economic Geography, *Journal of Public Economic Theory* 5, 279–303.

Baldwin, R., R. Forslid, P. Martin, G. Ottaviano, and F. Robert-Nicoud. (2003). *Economic Geography and Public Policy*. Princeton: Princeton University Press.

Baldwin, R., and P. Krugman. (2004). Agglomeration, Integration and Tax Harmonization. *European Economic Review* 48, 1–23.

Brakman, S., H. Garretsen, and C. Van Marrewijk. (2001). *An Introduction to Geographical Economics*. Cambridge: Cambridge University Press.

Brakman, S., H. Garretsen, and C. Van Marrewijk. (2002). Location Competition and Agglomeration: The Role of Government Spending. Working Paper Series, no. 775, CESifo.

Brülhart, M., and F. Trionfetti. (2004). Public Expenditure, International Specialisation, and Agglomeration. *European Economic Review* 48, 851–881.

CPB Netherlands Bureau for Economic Policy Analysis. (2001). *Capital Income Taxation in Europe, Trends and Trade-Offs*. The Hague: SDU Uitgevers.

Devereux, M., R. Griffith, and A. Klemm. (2002). Corporate Income Tax, Reforms and Tax Competition. *Economic Policy* 35, 451–495.

Forslid, R. (1999). Agglomeration with Human and Physical Capital: An Analytically Solvable Case. Discussion paper 2102, Centre for Economic Policy Research, London.

Forslid, R., and G. Ottaviano. (2001). Trade and Location: Two Analytically Solvable Cases. Mimeo.

Forslid, R., and G. Ottaviano. (2003). An Analytically Solvable Core-Periphery Model. *Journal of Economic Geography* 3, 229–240.

Garretsen, H., and J. Peeters. (2006). Capital Mobility, Agglomeration, and Corporate Tax Rates: Is the Race to the Bottom for Real? De Nederlandsche Bank Working paper 113, DNB, Amsterdam.

Keen, M., and M. Marchand. (1997). Fiscal Competition and the Pattern of Public Spending. *Journal of Public Economics* 66, 33–53.

Krogstrup, S. (2004). Are Corporate Tax Burdens Racing to the Bottom in the European Union? Economic Policy Research Unit Working paper series 2004-04, ERPU.

Neary, J. P. (2001). Of Hype and Hyperbolas: Introducing the New Economic Geography. *Journal of Economic Literature* 39, 536–561.

Netherlands Ministry of Economic Affairs. (1999). *Location Patterns of Leading Companies in North-West Europe*. Den Haag: Ministry of Economic Affairs.

Ottaviano, G. (2001). Monopolistic Competition, Trade, and Endogenous Spatial Fluctuations. *Regional Science and Urban Economics* 31, 51–77.

Samuelson, P. A. (1952). Spatial Price Equilibrium and Linear Programming. *American Economic Review* 42, 283–303.

Sinn, H.-W. (1990). Tax Harmonization and Tax Competition in Europe. *European Economic Review* 34, 489–504.

Sinn, H.-W. (2004). The New Systems Competition. *Perspektiven der Wirtschaftspolitik* 5, 23–38.

UNCTAD. (1996). *Incentives and Foreign Direct Investment*. New York: United Nations.

World Bank CD-ROM. (2005). World Statisties. Washington D.C.: World Bank.

6

Transfer Pricing and Enforcement Policy in Oligopolistic Markets

Oscar Amerighi

6.1 Introduction

Nowadays a large share of international trade occurs within multinational enterprises (MNEs), and manipulation of the transfer prices they use for internal transactions can shift a huge amount of taxable profits between countries. The empirical evidence almost unambiguously suggests that MNEs are able to reduce their worldwide tax payments by shifting profits from highly taxed to more lightly taxed jurisdictions.[1] Most of the empirical work is concerned with profit shifting from the United States to low-tax countries (or tax havens), and it relies mainly on statistical relationships between country tax rates and affiliate profitabilities or tax liabilities.[2] Clausing (2003) is a notable exception in that she analyzes U.S. data on intrafirm transfer prices to understand in what direction and to what extent these prices differ from those charged in outside markets due to tax rate differentials.[3]

International tax rules attempt to moderate these tax arbitrage activities through the principle that transactions within MNEs should be valued at their arm's-length price, that is, the price that would be paid by unrelated parties for similar transactions (OECD 1995).[4] The same concern emerges from the U.S. regulations on transfer pricing, whose main objectives are to "ensure that taxpayers clearly reflect income attributable to controlled transactions, and to prevent the avoidance of taxes with respect to such transactions" (U.S. Department of the Treasury 1994, 34990). However, although tax authorities of Organization for Economic Cooperation and Development (OECD) countries are usually supposed to follow the standard guidelines for transfer pricing, Bartelsman and Beetsma (2003) show that profit-shifting opportunities for MNEs do exist among OECD countries, including the United States. Moreover, they provide evidence that the degree of enforcement of the

Table 6.1
Formal enforcement of transfer pricing rules by country

Country	Explicit TP rules	Formal TP documentation rules	TP specific penalties
Australia	7/83	9/95	7/83
Austria	—	—	—
Belgium	7/99	7/99	—
Canada	—	1/99	1/99
Denmark	1/99	1/99	—
Finland	1/31	—	—
France	9/85	4/96	4/96
Germany	2/83	—	—
Italy	12/86	—	—
Japan	4/86	—	—
Netherlands	—	—	—
Portugal	—	—	—
Spain	1/96	—	—
Sweden	—	—	—
United Kingdom	7/99	7/99	7/99
United States	1/28	1/94	1/94

Note: Numbers indicate the month and year when the TP-related policies were introduced.
Source: Ernst & Young (2000), cited in Bartelsman and Beetsma (2003, 2230) and Peralta, Wauthy, and Ypersele (2003, 3).

arm's-length principle differs across these countries. Table 6.1 summarizes the information about transfer pricing (TP) enforcement policies for the countries involved in their empirical analysis.[5]

My purpose here is to think about international taxation of MNEs and enforcement of the arm's-length principle. These issues look increasingly important in a world where economic integration proceeds at a very rapid pace and the relevance of MNEs and intrafirm trade is undoubtedly rising.[6] My work is essentially related to the literature that studies transfer pricing and tax competition in the presence of MNEs. For instance, Elitzur and Mintz (1996) model the trade-off for an MNE between the minimization of its worldwide tax payments and the incentives provided to the managing partner of a foreign subsidiary. They find that corporate tax rates are too high from a global welfare maximization perspective. Haufler and Schjelderup (2000) develop a tax competition model with investment and transfer pricing decisions by an MNE operating in two small countries. They show that the optimal policy is to accept some distortions of the investment decision—an incomplete deduction for the cost of capital—in order to reduce the incentive for the MNE to shift profits out of the country. Mansori and Weichenrieder (2001) and Raimondos-Møller and Scharf (2002) study competition in transfer pricing regulations between two governments. In both models, the noncooperative outcome implies an excessive taxation of the MNE because of a partial double taxation of its profits. However, none of these studies explicitly accounts for the impact that the degree of enforcement of the arm's-length principle may have on the corporate profit tax rate set by the government, and none of them analyzes the effects of economic integration on the two policy instruments and the product market equilibrium.

In such a sense, the analysis that I carry out here is close to and relies heavily on Kind, Midelfart Knarvik, and Schjelderup (2001, 2002, 2004, 2005) and is also based on the contributions by Peralta, Wauthy, and van Ypersele (2003, 2006). In particular, Kind et al. (2002) study the effects of economic integration on equilibrium taxes. They develop a symmetric two-country model with two MNEs, whose location is given, and where the corporate tax base is partly owned by residents in a third country (i.e., the rest of the world). The MNEs compete on quantities in the two markets and have to incur some costs in order to conceal transfer price manipulation. Such costs are reflected by an exogenous parameter, and they are tax deductible, meaning that tax authorities may not even know that they are related to transfer pricing. Trade liberalization is shown to reduce equilibrium taxes if MNEs are owned by third-country residents, but it increases them if MNEs are owned by home-country residents. Furthermore, increased international ownership leads to higher equilibrium tax rates. Peralta et al. (2003) instead set up a model where two almost symmetric countries compete for both the location of a single MNE and the taxation of its profits. The MNE acts as a monopolist in the two markets and is required to follow the arm's-length principle. Governments can decide between being strict or lenient on this requirement: such an enforcement policy is costless and essentially determined by the government's reputation. As a result, transfer price manipulation implies a non–tax-deductible cost for the MNE. Moreover, since the same tax rate applies to domestic firms as well, each government faces a trade-off between the benefit of attracting the MNE and the fiscal cost of hosting it. In such a framework, a country can optimally decide not to enforce the transfer pricing rule in order to attract the MNE, while setting high profit taxes on domestic firms. The other country, in turn, does not enjoy the benefits from the location of the MNE but taxes its profits.

I modify the model by Kind et al. (2002) in two main respects: (1) I add an extra fiscal policy variable, the level of enforcement of the arm's-length principle, which is costly to the enforcing government; and (2) I let transfer price manipulation costs be a function of the enforcement level and make these costs non–tax deductible. In my model, the government of each country is thus endowed with two policy instruments: the corporate profit tax rate and the transfer pricing enforcement policy. The latter identifies the government's efforts and resources invested in forcing the domestic MNE to adhere to the arm's-length principle. As in Peralta et al. (2003, 2006), the choice of such a policy is endogenous and might reflect government's attitude toward MNEs. To account for the possible interaction between the two fiscal policies and to analyze the effects of increased economic integration on both of them, I solve a three-stage game where governments choose first the enforcement level and then the corporate profit tax rate. In the last stage, the headquarters of the two MNEs set transfer prices to their foreign subsidiaries and compete on quantities in the two markets.

I show that as governments increase the level of enforcement to discourage transfer pricing, equilibrium tax rates increase as well. Moreover, increased economic integration may lead to higher equilibrium tax rates and stronger enforcement. Namely, a larger third-country ownership of MNEs leads to a *race to the top* in both policies between the two countries. On the contrary, when MNEs are not fully owned by domestic residents, trade liberalization initially implies a *race to the bottom*, but as trade becomes free enough, a further decrease in trade costs increases both corporate tax rates and enforcement policies.

The rest of the chapter is organized as follows. In section 6.2, I outline the model. Section 6.3 illustrates the transfer pricing and quantity decisions by MNEs when faced with the two policy instruments. In sections 6.4 and 6.5, I derive the symmetric equilibrium tax rate and transfer pricing enforcement policy levels. Furthermore, I analyze and discuss the effects of increased economic integration on the two policy instruments. In section 6.6, I summarize the main results and provide a conclusion.

6.2   The Model

We consider a partial equilibrium model with two countries, i and j, which are identical in all respects, and two identical horizontally integrated MNEs. The location choices of MNEs are exogenously given such that multinational enterprise MNE_i (resp., MNE_j) has headquarters in country i (j) and a foreign subsidiary in country j (i).

The production process within each MNE is divided into production of intermediate and final goods, implying marginal costs c^I and c^F, respectively. Without loss of generality, we postulate that all intermediate goods are produced at the headquarters and final production takes place locally. Therefore, part of the production of intermediate goods is further processed by the parent company and then sold in the domestic market, while the rest is exported to the foreign subsidiary for final processing and sale abroad. To make our point, we normalize to zero both marginal production costs so that $c^I = c^F = 0$. The marginal cost of the exporting parent company, c^I, plays the role of the arm's-length price that the OECD recommends for the pricing of intra-firm transactions. As shall become clear, the key to our argument is that while both countries are supposed to follow the arm's-length principle, they can endogenously choose the corresponding level of enforcement.

The foreign subsidiary of, say, MNE_i is charged a transfer price, q_i, for each unit of the intermediate good it buys from its headquarters. Since $c^I = 0$ by assumption, the transfer price is higher (lower) than the arm's-length price when $q_i > 0$ ($q_i < 0$). The subsidiary also has to pay a per unit trade cost, $\tau \geq 0$, which may reflect different types of barriers to international trade (e.g., transport costs and differing product standards), but does not include any kind of revenue-generating tariffs imposed by governments.

The products of the MNEs are perfect substitutes in demand in both markets. That is, the two MNEs produce homogeneous goods and face the same inverse demand function,

$$p_i = 1 - x_{ii} - x_{ji}, \tag{6.1}$$

where $p_i > 0$ is the price to consumers in country i, while x_{ii} and x_{ji} denote MNE_i's home sales and MNE_j's exports to country i, respectively.[7]

We let π_{ii} and π_{ij} denote before-tax profits for MNE_i's parent company and foreign subsidiary, with the first subscript indicating the headquarters' location and the second the country where profits are

derived. Due to our specifications, MNE_i's domestic and foreign before-tax profits are given by

$$\pi_{ii} = p_i x_{ii} + q_i x_{ij} \tag{6.2}$$

$$\pi_{ij} = (p_j - \tau - q_i)x_{ij}. \tag{6.3}$$

We assume that international corporate taxation follows the *source*
principle, meaning that each country imposes a tax on the profits generated within its borders.[8] Furthermore, we postulate that tax authorities cannot directly observe the true production cost of the parent
company, so that transfer prices may be manipulated in response to international tax differentials to shift taxable profits across countries.

To limit this profit-shifting incentive and formalize the evidence by
Bartelsman and Beetsma (2003), we argue that governments are concerned about such a tax-avoiding strategy and try to induce domestic
MNEs to meet the objective of national tax authorities. In particular,
the government of, say, country i chooses a nonnegative level of enforcement, $\delta_i \in [0, \infty)$, of the arm's-length principle and requires MNE_i
to charge a transfer price equal to the marginal production cost of the
exporting parent company.[9]

On the one hand, implementing such a policy entails a cost to the
government, $C_i(\delta_i) = \frac{d}{2}\delta_i^2$, $d > 0$, which rises more than proportionally
with the enforcement level. Intuitively, governments need to allocate
resources to control the transfer-pricing behavior of MNEs, and the enforcement cost function is intended to reflect both the direct cost of this
policy (e.g., the fact that tax authorities pay wages to people monitor-
ing and controlling the accounts of MNEs) and its implicit opportunity
cost. Since governments do not enjoy an infinity of resources (they face
a budget constraint to respect), any amount of money spent to enforce
the arm's-length principle cannot be spent for other purposes. For example, if a government decides to allocate a given amount of money
for this policy, it forgoes the opportunity to use that same money in
order to improve the national health system, control levels of environ-
mental pollution, or something else.[10]

On the other hand, a higher level of enforcement of the arm's-length
principle by country i's government makes it costlier for MNE_i to manipulate the transfer price on its intrafirm trade. Since the objective of
tax authorities is to induce the MNE to set a transfer price as close as
possible to the true production cost of the intrafirm traded good, over-

invoicing and underinvoicing will be equally expensive for MNE_i, and manipulation costs will be higher the larger is the difference between q_i and c^I. Moreover, these costs will be proportional to the volume of intrafirm exports.[11] Namely, we let MNE_i's transfer price manipulation costs take the following form,

$$TPM_i(\delta_i, q_i - c^I, x_{ij}) = \delta_i q_i^2 x_{ij},$$

and we assume that they are not tax deductible. The idea is that governments are aware of the effect of their enforcement policies on these costs and know that MNEs need to hire tax consultants, lawyers, or accountants to keep track of their transfer-pricing decisions and to show that they are consistent with the arm's-length principle.[12] Therefore, MNE_i's objective function can be written as

$$\Pi_i = (1 - t_i)\pi_{ii} + (1 - t_j)\pi_{ij} - \delta_i q_i^2 x_{ij}, \tag{6.4}$$

where t_i and t_j denote corporate profit tax rates imposed by country i and country j, respectively.

Turning to the government's objective function, we denote by $\alpha \in [0, 1]$ the share of each MNE owned by domestic residents, while the residual $(1 - \alpha)$ is owned by residents of a third country. Hence, welfare in country i can be expressed as[13]

$$W_i = CS_i + T_i + \alpha \Pi_i - C_i(\delta_i),$$

where $CS_i = \frac{1}{2}(x_{ii} + x_{ji})^2$ represents consumer surplus and $T_i = t_i(\pi_{ii} + \pi_{ji})$ is tax revenue.

To emphasize the different effects on the welfare of the two policies and the MNEs' ownership structure, we can rearrange the government's objective function as

$$W_i = CS_i + \underbrace{\alpha(\pi_{ii} + \pi_{ij})}_{(I)} - \underbrace{\alpha t_j \pi_{ij}}_{(II)} + \underbrace{t_i \pi_{ji} + (1 - \alpha) t_i \pi_{ii}}_{(III)} - \underbrace{\left(\alpha \delta_i q_i^2 x_{ij} + \frac{d}{2}\delta_i^2\right)}_{(IV)}$$

$$\tag{6.5}$$

where:

(I) The profit ownership effect shows that welfare increases with MNE_i's before-tax profits and with the share of such profits accruing to domestic residents

(II) The foreign tax exporting effect indicates that country j has the ability to tax MNE_i's profits—by taxing its subsidiary—thereby reducing the amount available to country i residents; this effect decreases welfare in country i and is stronger the larger is the domestic ownership share of MNE_i

(III) The home tax exporting effect increases welfare, since country i is able to shift the burden of taxation onto foreigners by taxing both MNE_j's foreign subsidiary profits and the share of MNE_i's parent company profits accruing to third-country residents

(IV) The enforcement policy effect shows that the costs, in terms of welfare, of such a policy are increasing in the share of MNE_i owned by domestic residents

Given this scenario, we solve a three-stage game characterized by the following order of moves:

Stage 1: The two governments simultaneously set the level of enforcement of the arm's-length principle, $\delta_i, \delta_j \in [0, \infty)$.

Stage 2: The two governments simultaneously choose corporate profit tax rates, $t_i, t_j \in [0, 1]$.

Stage 3: The headquarters of the MNEs set transfer prices to their foreign subsidiaries and compete on quantities in the two markets.

This timing is consistent with Kind et al. (2002), where δ is an exogenous parameter that reflects how costly it is for MNEs to manipulate transfer prices. In their model, the two countries simultaneously choose their tax rates for a given δ, and at the final stage, Cournot competition between the two MNEs takes place. The same timing characterizes the model by Peralta et al. (2003) as well, where the sequence of decisions I have described implies that one country's enforcement policy is essentially determined by its government's reputation. Thus, it can be considered a long-term policy variable.[14]

6.3   Transfer Pricing and Quantity Decisions

I solve the three-stage game by backward induction. In the third stage, MNE_i maximizes its objective function, equation 6.4, with respect to its home sales, exports, and transfer price (x_{ii}, x_{ij}, and q_i), taking the quantities supplied and the transfer price charged by MNE_j, the tax rates, and the enforcement policies of both countries as given.[15]

6.3.1   Equilibrium Transfer Price

I use equations 6.1, 6.2, and 6.3, and differentiate equation 6.4 with respect to q_i, which gives

$$q_i(t_i, t_j, \delta_i) = \frac{t_j - t_i}{2\delta_i}. \tag{6.6}$$

Note that the equilibrium transfer price depends only on the tax rates set by the two governments and the enforcement policy of the domestic country.

Equation 6.6 illustrates the *profit-shifting* incentive to manipulate the transfer price. If, say, $t_i > t_j$, MNE_i is induced to underinvoice its exports ($q_i < 0$) and shift profits to country j. Similarly, an incentive for overinvoicing ($q_i > 0$) and profit shifting to country i arises when $t_i < t_j$. Nevertheless, this profit-shifting incentive is limited by country i's enforcement policy, δ_i. Intuitively, this policy should act in the same direction as the tax policy. Indeed, if country i is the high-tax country, MNE_i is induced to charge a negative transfer price, thereby shifting profits to country j. Hence, country i should set a higher enforcement level—compared to the case where it is the low-tax country—to minimize as much as possible the negative effect that transfer pricing may have on the profits declared by MNE_i's parent company. On the contrary, if both countries levy the same corporate profit tax rate ($t_i = t_j$), no profit-shifting motive exists, and MNE_i optimally sets its transfer price equal to the arm's-length price: $q_i^* = c^l = 0$.[16]

To further investigate the previous argument, I derive the effects on the equilibrium transfer price of a marginal change in tax rates and in country i's enforcement policy:

$$\frac{\partial q_i}{\partial t_i} = -\frac{\partial q_i}{\partial t_j} = -\frac{1}{2\delta_i} < 0 \tag{6.7}$$

$$\frac{\partial q_i}{\partial \delta_i} = \frac{t_i - t_j}{2\delta_i^2}. \tag{6.8}$$

Equation 6.7 shows that as long as $\delta_i > 0$, a marginal increase in t_i induces MNE_i to lower its transfer price and shift profits out of country i. But the reduction in q_i turns out to be lower the higher is the level of δ_i. On the contrary, a marginal increase in t_j determines an increase in q_i so that MNE_i shifts a larger amount of profits into country i. But the rise in q_i turns out to be higher the lower is the level of δ_i. Both situations suggest that the enforcement policy of country i should work in the same direction as its tax policy in order to keep more profits within its borders.

Equation 6.8 confirms the last statement. If country i is the low-tax country, MNE_i is induced to overinvoice its exports to country j. As $\partial q_i/\partial \delta_i < 0$, a marginal increase in δ_i decreases q_i and MNE_i declares a lower amount of profits in country i. Hence, δ_i should be set as low as possible. But if country i is the high-tax country, MNE_i is induced to underinvoice its exports to country j. In this case, $\partial q_i/\partial \delta_i > 0$, and country i should set δ_i as high as possible because the higher δ_i, the closer to the arm's-length price the transfer price q_i is, and the smaller the amount of profits that MNE_i is willing to declare in country j.

6.3.2 Equilibrium Home Sales and Exports

Differentiating MNE_i's objective function (see equation 6.4) with respect to x_{ii} and x_{ij}, we get the following first-order conditions,

$$\frac{\partial \Pi_i}{\partial x_{ii}} = 1 - 2x_{ii} - x_{ji} = 0, \tag{6.9}$$

$$\frac{\partial \Pi_i}{\partial x_{ij}} = (1 - t_i)q_i + (1 - t_j)(1 - 2x_{ij} - x_{jj} - \tau - q_i) - \delta_i q_i^2 = 0, \tag{6.10}$$

which, together with the symmetric expressions for MNE_j, implicitly define the best response functions of the two MNEs to a change in the quantities supplied on the two markets. Note that quantities are strategic substitutes ($\partial x_{ii}/\partial x_{ji} < 0$ and $\partial x_{jj}/\partial x_{ij} < 0$).

Solving equations 6.9 and 6.10 simultaneously for the two MNEs and using the equilibrium transfer price, equation 6.6, we obtain equilibrium home sales and exports by MNE_i and MNE_j:

$$x_{ii} = \frac{1+\tau}{3} - \frac{(t_j - t_i)^2}{12\delta_j(1 - t_i)}, \quad x_{jj} = \frac{1+\tau}{3} - \frac{(t_j - t_i)^2}{12\delta_i(1 - t_j)} \tag{6.11}$$

$$\underbrace{x_{ij} = \frac{1-2\tau}{3} + \frac{(t_j - t_i)^2}{6\delta_i(1 - t_j)}}_{MNE_i}, \quad \underbrace{x_{ji} = \frac{1-2\tau}{3} + \frac{(t_j - t_i)^2}{6\delta_j(1 - t_i)}}_{MNE_j}. \tag{6.12}$$

When the two countries set symmetric corporate profit tax rates ($t_i = t_j$), equilibrium quantities reduce to

$$x_{ii}^* = x_{jj}^* = \frac{1+\tau}{3}, \quad x_{ij}^* = x_{ji}^* = \frac{1-2\tau}{3}, \tag{6.13}$$

and since the two MNEs are induced to set the same transfer price $q_i^* = q_j^* = 0$, their symmetric equilibrium before-tax profits are given by

$$\pi_{ii}^* = \pi_{jj}^* = \frac{(1+\tau)^2}{9}, \quad \pi_{ij}^* = \pi_{ji}^* = \frac{(1-2\tau)^2}{9}. \tag{6.14}$$

Equation 6.13 suggests that sufficiently high trade costs, $\tau \geq \frac{1}{2}$, would lead to negative exports for both MNEs. Thus, in order to have international trade in our model, we need to assume that $\tau \in [0, \frac{1}{2})$ in what follows. Furthermore, we easily see from equations 6.11 and 6.12 that a decrease in trade costs reduces domestic sales and simultaneously increases exports by both MNEs, thereby inducing more competition on the two markets.

Export Incentive and Enforcement Policy

According to the expressions for equilibrium quantities, 6.11 and 6.12, home sales by the two MNEs are affected by the enforcement policy of the foreign country, while they are independent of the domestic enforcement policy. On the contrary, exports depend on only the latter. Namely, differentiating equations 6.11 and 6.12 with respect to δ_i, we have, as long as $t_i \neq t_j$,

$$\underbrace{\frac{\partial x_{ii}}{\partial \delta_i} = \frac{\partial x_{ji}}{\partial \delta_i} = 0,}_{\text{Country } i\text{'s market}} \quad \underbrace{\frac{\partial x_{ij}}{\partial \delta_i} < 0, \quad \frac{\partial x_{jj}}{\partial \delta_i} > 0,}_{\text{Country } j\text{'s market}}$$

implying that a marginal increase in δ_i has no impact on home sales by MNE_i but leads to a decrease in its exports to country j. At the same time, it induces MNE_j to increase its home sales in country j, leaving unaffected its exports to country i. In other words, country i's enforcement policy affects the quantities sold in country j's market through its negative impact on exports by MNE_i.

To account for this observation, we need to put forward the *export incentive* faced by MNE_i. Substituting for the equilibrium transfer price 6.6, MNE_i's first-order condition, 6.10, can be rewritten as

$$\frac{\partial \Pi_i}{\partial x_{ij}} = (1 - t_i) \left(\frac{t_j - t_i}{2\delta_i} \right) + (1 - t_j) \left[1 - 2x_{ij} - x_{jj} - \tau - \left(\frac{t_j - t_i}{2\delta_i} \right) \right]$$

$$- \frac{(t_j - t_i)^2}{4\delta_i}. \tag{6.15}$$

If, regardless of a tax rate differential $(t_i \neq t_j)$, MNE_i does not manipulate the transfer price and sets $q_i^* = 0$, it follows from equation 6.10 that $1 - 2x_{ij} - x_{jj} - \tau = 0$. Inserting the last expression into equation 6.15, we obtain

$$\frac{\partial \Pi_i}{\partial x_{ij}} = \frac{(t_j - t_i)^2}{4\delta_i} > 0.$$

Since it is optimal for MNE_i to increase its exports until the marginal profit from exports is nil, we can argue that MNE_i will export more when there is room for manipulating the transfer price $(t_i \neq t_j)$ than in the case of symmetric tax rates.

Such an export incentive, as well as the profit-shifting incentive already defined, turns out to be decreasing in the level of country i's enforcement policy. This is precisely the reason that, even in the presence of a tax rate differential, an increase in δ_i induces MNE_i to decrease its exports to country j. Finally, consider what happens in country j's market. Since the two competing MNEs set their quantities simultaneously, MNE_j cannot observe MNE_i's actual behavior before setting its own quantity. It can, however, anticipate such a behavior by observing the enforcement policy level that country i has previously chosen. Hence, if δ_i increases, MNE_j can anticipate that MNE_i will reduce its exports to country j, and since quantities are strategic substitutes, its optimal response will be to increase its home sales.

Strategic Effect of Corporate Profit Tax Rates

In order to investigate how a change in country i's tax rate affects home sales and exports by the two MNEs, we derive the following expressions,

$$\frac{\partial x_{ii}}{\partial t_i} = \frac{(t_j - t_i)(2 - t_i - t_j)}{12\delta_j(1 - t_i)^2}, \quad \frac{\partial x_{ij}}{\partial t_i} = \frac{t_i - t_j}{3\delta_i(1 - t_j)} \tag{6.16}$$

$$\underbrace{\frac{\partial x_{ji}}{\partial t_i} = \frac{(t_i - t_j)(2 - t_i - t_j)}{6\delta_j(1 - t_i)^2}}_{\text{Country } i\text{'s market}}, \quad \underbrace{\frac{\partial x_{jj}}{\partial t_i} = \frac{t_j - t_i}{6\delta_i(1 - t_j)}}_{\text{Country } j\text{'s market}}, \tag{6.17}$$

whose sign depends on only the difference between t_i and t_j as long as $\delta_i, \delta_j > 0$ and $t_i, t_j \neq 1$. In particular, if $t_i = t_j$, home sales and exports by the two MNEs are independent of the actual tax rates. Thus, a marginal increase in one of the tax rates starting from a symmetric equilibrium will not have any effect on supplied quantities. This will prove a useful property when deriving the equilibrium tax rate at the second stage.

Suppose now that $t_i \neq t_j$. We observe from equation 6.16 that as long as $t_i < t_j$, a marginal increase in country i's tax rate induces MNE_i to increase its home sales and reduce its exports to country j. Furthermore, equation 6.17 suggests that MNE_j will respond to such a marginal increase in t_i by raising its home sales and decreasing its exports to country i. To account for these effects, we must recall that the two MNEs compete on the quantities knowing the tax rates that the two countries have previously set and that quantities are strategic substitutes. That is, we need to consider the *strategic effect of tax rates* on supplied quantities. When $t_i < t_j$, MNE_i is willing to overinvoice its exports and shift profits to country i, where the parent company resides. But a marginal increase in t_i will lower both the gain from manipulating the transfer price (profit-shifting incentive) and the marginal profit of exports (export incentive). Thus, it will be optimal for MNE_i to decrease its exports to country j and increase its home sales. Given that tax rates are set before quantity competition, MNE_j can anticipate MNE_i's decisions, and since quantities are strategic substitutes, its optimal response will be to increase its home sales and decrease its exports to country i.

On the contrary, if $t_i > t_j$, a marginal increase in country i's tax rate will have opposite effects on supplied quantities: MNE_i will be induced to decrease its home sales and increase its exports to country j, while MNE_j will reduce its home sales and increase its exports to country i. In this case, we know that MNE_i is willing to underinvoice its exports and shift profits to country j, where the foreign subsidiary resides. Moreover, a marginal increase in t_i will increase even further its profit-shifting and export incentives. Hence, MNE_i will behave more aggressively in country j and less aggressively in country i. As before, since MNE_j can anticipate MNE_i's behavior by observing tax rates, its best response will be to lower its home sales and raise its exports to country i.[17]

6.4   Tax Competition

At the second stage, the welfare maximization problem of the two countries is symmetric: each government sets its corporate profit tax rate in order to maximize national welfare, taking the tax rate of the other country and both enforcement policies as given. In particular, country i's government maximizes its welfare function, equation 6.5, with respect to t_i, taking country j's tax rate, t_j, as well as δ_i and δ_j, as given. The corresponding first-order condition is given by

$$\frac{\partial W_i}{\partial t_i} = \frac{\partial CS_i}{\partial t_i} + \alpha\left(\frac{\partial \pi_{ii}}{\partial t_i} + \frac{\partial \pi_{ij}}{\partial t_i}\right) - \alpha t_j \frac{\partial \pi_{ij}}{\partial t_i} + \pi_{ji} + t_i \frac{\partial \pi_{ji}}{\partial t_i} + (1 - \alpha)\pi_{ii}$$

$$+ (1 - \alpha)t_i \frac{\partial \pi_{ii}}{\partial t_i} - \alpha\left(\delta_i q_i^2 \frac{\partial x_{ij}}{\partial t_i} + 2\delta_i q_i x_{ij} \frac{\partial q_i}{\partial t_i}\right) = 0,$$

and we can easily show that the total effect of country i's tax rate on national welfare can be decomposed into three different effects:

$$\frac{\partial W_i}{\partial t_i} = \underbrace{\pi_{ji} + (1 - \alpha)\pi_{ii}}_{Direct} + \underbrace{[(1 - \alpha)t_i + \alpha(t_j - 2\delta_i q_i)]x_{ij} \frac{\partial q_i}{\partial t_i} - t_i x_{ji} \frac{\partial q_j}{\partial t_i}}_{TP}$$

$$+ \left\{x_{ii} + (1 - t_i)x_{ji} + (1 - 2x_{ii} - x_{ji})[\alpha + (1 - \alpha)t_i]\right\} \frac{\partial x_{ii}}{\partial t_i}$$

$$+ \left\{\alpha(1 - t_j)(1 - 2x_{ij} - x_{jj} - \tau) + q_i t_i + \alpha q_i(t_j - t_i - \delta_i q_i)\right\} \frac{\partial x_{ij}}{\partial t_i}$$

$$+ \left\{x_{ji} + (1 - \alpha)(1 - t_i)x_{ii} + t_i(1 - 2x_{ji} - x_{ii} - \tau - q_j)\right\} \frac{\partial x_{ji}}{\partial t_i}$$

$$- \alpha(1 - t_j)x_{ij} \frac{\partial x_{jj}}{\partial t_i} = 0,$$

where *Direct* and *TP* denote, respectively, the *direct effect* on tax revenue (for constant transfer price and supplied quantities) and the *profit-shifting effect* through transfer pricing, while the remaining terms represent the strategic effect of t_i on supplied quantities.

6.4.1 Symmetric Tax Rates and Enforcement Policies

In any symmetric equilibrium in tax rates $(t_i = t_j)$, the two MNEs will find it optimal not to manipulate the transfer price and set $q_i^* = q_j^* = 0$. Moreover, their home sales and exports are independent of the actual tax rates. This means that the strategic effect on supplied quantities is equal to zero so that country i's tax rate affects national welfare only through the other two effects.[18] Hence, to keep our analysis as simple as possible, we assume that there exists a symmetric equilibrium in tax rates and define $t^* \equiv t_i = t_j$ in any such equilibrium. We must stress that at this stage, we do not need to require enforcement policies to be equal. In other words, the two countries do not necessarily have to choose the same level of enforcement of the arm's-length principle (at the first stage) for a symmetric equilibrium in tax rates to—possibly— arise (at the second stage).

Evaluating the government's first-order condition at $t_i = t_j$ gives

$$\frac{\partial W_i}{\partial t_i}\bigg|_{t_i=t_j} = \underbrace{\pi_{ji}^* + (1-\alpha)\pi_{ii}^*}_{Direct} + \underbrace{t^*\left(x_{ij}^*\frac{\partial q_i}{\partial t_i} - x_{ji}^*\frac{\partial q_j}{\partial t_i}\right)}_{TP} = 0, \tag{6.18}$$

and we substitute for equations 6.7, 6.13, 6.14, and $\partial q_j/\partial t_i = 1/2\delta_j$ to get

$$t^*(\delta_i,\delta_j,\alpha,\tau) = \frac{2\delta_i\delta_j[5\tau^2 - 2\tau + 2 - \alpha(1+\tau)^2]}{3(\delta_i+\delta_j)(1-2\tau)}. \tag{6.19}$$

The symmetric equilibrium tax rate depends on the enforcement policies of the two countries (δ_i and δ_j), on the ownership structure of MNEs (α) and on trade costs (τ). Such an optimal tax rate is equal to zero when one of the two countries decides not to enforce the arm's-length principle, while it turns out to be positive as long as both δ_i and δ_j are positive.

The symmetric solution to the government's problem allows us to analyze the effects that enforcement policies may have on corporate profit tax rates. Differentiating equation 6.19 with respect to δ_i and δ_j, we obtain

$$\frac{\partial t^*}{\partial \delta_i} > 0, \quad \frac{\partial t^*}{\partial \delta_j} > 0, \quad \frac{\partial t^*}{\partial \delta_i \partial \delta_j} > 0,$$

so that we can state:

Proposition 1   An increase in the enforcement level of the arm's-length principle by one of the two countries, or by both of them, increases the symmetric equilibrium tax rate.

The proof is in appendix 6A.

A stronger enforcement of the arm's-length principle will induce governments to increase the symmetric equilibrium tax rate, meaning that the two fiscal policy instruments at the government's disposal turn out to be complementary. Such a result can be explained as follows. The decision of a country's government to strengthen the enforcement level is based on the presumption that MNEs will have to bear higher costs to manipulate transfer prices in order to avoid taxes on their worldwide profits. As a consequence, tax authorities expect MNEs to declare profits that are closer to those actually earned in each jurisdiction. If, in addition, the two countries impose the same corporate profit tax rate, no profit-shifting motive exists and a higher enforcement level makes it possible for governments to improve national welfare by taxing MNEs more heavily without losing tax revenue. However, since enforcing the arm's-length principle is costly, it cannot be optimal from each country's government perspective to spend an infinite amount of resources on that policy.

The following quotation from the Economist (Gimme Shelter, 2000), which we borrow from Peralta et al. (2003), nicely illustrates our theoretical framework and seems to suggest that the way that national governments are taking to limit cross-country profit shifting is that of a stronger enforcement of the arm's-length principle: "In theory the transfer price is supposed to be the same as the market price between two independent firms. . . . So multinationals spend a fortune on economists and accountants to justify the transfer prices that suit their tax needs. Increasingly, firms try to restructure their operations to get their tax bill down as far as possible. . . . But tax authorities are increasingly looking out for such wheezes. In America, in particular, the taxman has been putting the squeeze on companies, which have responded by allowing more of their taxable profits to arise there to keep him happy. This is prompting other countries to get tougher, too."

6.4.2 Effects of Economic Integration

In our framework, economic integration may be interpreted as either a more dispersed (or internationalized) ownership structure of the two MNEs or trade liberalization. The former is represented by a decrease in the share of the domestic MNE owned by domestic residents (α) and by a corresponding increase in the ownership by third-country residents, while the latter is captured by a decrease in trade costs (τ).[19]

We first consider the effect on t^* of a change in the ownership structure of MNEs. Differentiating equation 6.19 with respect to α, we find that

$$\frac{\partial t^*}{\partial \alpha} < 0,$$

which allows us to state:

Proposition 2 A more internationalized ownership structure of MNEs (i.e., a lower α) increases the symmetric equilibrium tax rate.

See appendix 6A for the proof.

Intuitively, the larger is the share of the domestic MNE owned by residents in the rest of the world (or the lower is the domestic ownership share), the stronger is the incentive for governments to raise corporate tax rates, thereby shifting more of the tax burden onto foreigners.[20]

The effects of trade liberalization on t^* depend on the ownership structure of MNEs. In order to disentangle the main forces driving our results, we analyze the two extreme cases where MNEs are fully owned by either domestic or third-country residents.

With full domestic ownership ($\alpha = 1$), country i's government first-order condition (equation 6.18) reduces to

$$\frac{\partial W_i}{\partial t_i}\bigg|_{t_i=t_j} = \underbrace{\pi_{ji}^*}_{\text{Direct}} + \underbrace{t^*\left(x_{ij}^* \frac{\partial q_i}{\partial t_i} - x_{ji}^* \frac{\partial q_j}{\partial t_i}\right)}_{TP} = 0.$$

A higher tax rate allows country i to tax more heavily the profits of MNE_j's subsidiary but it also leads to more profit shifting through transfer price manipulation. On the one hand, MNE_i is induced to decrease the transfer price charged to its subsidiary in country j ($\partial q_i/\partial t_i < 0$), thus increasing the profits of the latter and allowing country j to export more of its tax burden to country i's residents. On the other hand, MNE_j is induced to increase the transfer price for its subsidiary in country i ($\partial q_j/\partial t_i > 0$), thereby decreasing the subsidiary profits and reducing the scope for country i to tax foreigners.

Substituting for the symmetric equilibrium values of before-tax profits and exports and using equation 6.7, we obtain

$$\frac{\partial W_i}{\partial t_i}\bigg|_{t_i=t_j} = \underbrace{\frac{(1-2\tau)^2}{9}}_{\text{Direct}} - \underbrace{t^* \frac{(\delta_i + \delta_j)(1-2\tau)}{6\delta_i\delta_j}}_{TP} = 0.$$

Trade liberalization increases the profits of MNE_j's subsidiary in country i (*tax base expansion*), so that for given transfer prices, more of the domestic tax burden can be exported to foreigners. However, a decrease in trade costs, for constant enforcement policies, leads to more profit shifting (*tax base loss*). The idea is that lower trade costs induce MNEs to increase their export volume; moreover, as t_i marginally increases with respect to t_j, both MNEs will gain by manipulating transfer prices on such intrafirm trade.

We easily prove that trade liberalization will increase the symmetric equilibrium tax rate.[21] This means that in the case of full domestic ownership, the positive direct effect on welfare of raising t_i when τ falls dominates the negative profit shifting effect.

With full third-country ownership ($\alpha = 0$), country i again faces a trade-off between the incentive to shift taxes onto foreigners and a potential loss of tax revenue due to profit shifting. The only difference is that the direct effect now consists of both MNE_j's subsidiary and MNE_i's parent company equilibrium profits, which entirely accrue to third-country residents. Using equations 6.7, 6.13, and 6.14, the first-order condition becomes

$$\frac{\partial W_i}{\partial t_i}\bigg|_{t_i=t_j} = \underbrace{\frac{(1-2\tau)^2}{9} + \frac{(1+\tau)^2}{9}}_{Direct} - \underbrace{t^* \frac{(\delta_i + \delta_j)(1-2\tau)}{6\delta_i\delta_j}}_{TP} = 0.$$

As before, if t_i increases, trade liberalization leads to a tax base loss because of transfer price manipulation. Here, however, the impact of trade liberalization on the direct effect turns out to be positive just for low values of trade costs. The intuition behind this result is straightforward. Consider what happens when trade costs are prohibitive ($\tau = \frac{1}{2}$): MNE_j does not export to country i, so that its subsidiary earns no profits, while MNE_i's parent company can earn monopoly profits. As τ decreases, MNE_j will eventually enter country i's market, and its subsidiary will start earning positive profits; at the same time, MNE_i's parent company profits will reduce. Since monopoly profits are gradually replaced by lower total duopoly profits, the corporate tax base for country i's government shrinks (*tax base contraction*). Indeed, even if total duopoly profits rise again for lower values of τ, they will never reach the monopoly profit level in the absence of international trade. Therefore, if both MNEs are fully owned by third-country residents, trade liberalization will decrease the symmetric equilibrium tax rate, meaning that the direct effect on tax revenue is not positive enough to override the negative profit-shifting effect.

To account for the relationship between t^* and τ for values of $\alpha \in (0,1)$, we differentiate equation 6.19 with respect to τ and get

$$\frac{\partial t^*}{\partial \tau} = \frac{4\delta_i\delta_j[1 + 5\tau - 5\tau^2 - \alpha(1+\tau)(2-\tau)]}{3(\delta_i + \delta_j)(1-2\tau)^2},$$

whose sign depends on only the term in square brackets. In particular, for $\alpha \in \left(0, \frac{1}{2}\right]$, the symmetric equilibrium tax rate monotonically decreases as a result of trade liberalization, meaning that the negative transfer pricing effect is always stronger than the direct effect on tax revenue. On the contrary, for $\alpha \in \left(\frac{1}{2}, 1\right)$, we find a nonmonotonic relationship between t^* and τ. Intuitively, when trade costs are prohibitively high, the volume of intrafirm trade on which MNEs can manipulate transfer prices is relatively small, and profit shifting is negligible; if, moreover, third-country residents own a minimal share of the two MNEs, any positive tax rate will represent a pure tax on foreigners. Hence, t^* should be set as high as possible. However, as τ decreases, the corporate tax base becomes more sensitive to tax changes (since the scope for transfer price manipulation increases), and it will be optimal to decrease t^*. When trade costs become low enough, the tax base expansion turns out to be more important for governments than the tax base loss due to transfer pricing, so that a further decrease in τ will slightly increase t^*.

In the following proposition, we summarize our findings about the impact of trade liberalization on the symmetric equilibrium tax rate:

Proposition 3 The effects of trade liberalization on the symmetric equilibrium tax rate depend on the ownership structure of the two MNEs:

1. If both MNEs are fully owned by domestic residents ($\alpha = 1$), a decrease in trade costs increases t^*.

2. If both MNEs are fully owned by third-country residents ($\alpha = 0$), a decrease in trade costs decreases t^*.

3. If the ownership structure of MNEs is such that $\alpha \in \left(0, \frac{1}{2}\right]$, that is, third-country residents hold the majority of shares, a decrease in trade costs decreases t^*.

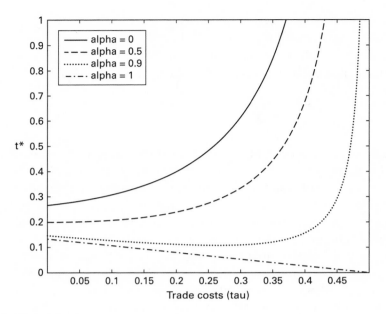

Figure 6.1
Effects of τ on t^* for $\delta_i = \delta_j$ and different values of α

4. If the ownership structure of MNEs is such that $\alpha \in \left(\frac{1}{2}, 1\right)$, that is, domestic residents hold the majority of shares, a decrease in trade costs increases t^* when trade costs are sufficiently low, that is for $\tau \in [0, \hat{\tau}]$. Otherwise, for $\tau \in \left(\hat{\tau}, \frac{1}{2}\right)$, a decrease in trade costs decreases t^*.

See appendix 6A for the proof.

Figures 6.1 and 6.2 illustrate the relationship between trade costs and the symmetric equilibrium tax rate for different values of α when the two countries choose the same level of enforcement ($\delta_i = \delta_j = 0.4$) and in the case of asymmetric enforcement policies ($\delta_i = 0.4, \delta_j = 0.3$), respectively. A comparison of the figures reveals that an increase in the enforcement level by one of the two countries (here, country j) increases t^* for any value of α. Furthermore, we observe that regardless of whether enforcement policies are symmetric, the symmetric equilibrium tax rate increases with the ownership share of third-country residents while the effects of trade liberalization depend on the ownership structure of MNEs. On the one hand, t^* decreases with τ when foreigners hold the whole or the majority of shares in both MNEs ($\alpha = 0$, $\alpha = 0.5$); on the other hand, t^* increases as τ falls when MNEs are en-

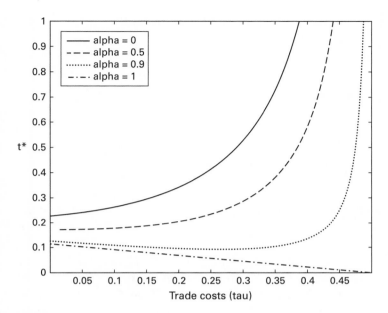

Figure 6.2
Effects of τ on t^* for $\delta_i \neq \delta_j$ and different values of α

tirely owned by domestic residents ($\alpha = 1$). Finally, the nonmonotonic relationship between t^* and τ for $\alpha = 0.9$ is consistent with result 4 in proposition 3.

6.5 Enforcement Policy Competition

At the first stage, each government chooses its level of enforcement of the arm's-length principle in order to maximize national welfare, taking the enforcement policy of the other country as given. Substituting for the symmetric equilibrium values of transfer price, home sales, exports, and before-tax profits, the government's objective function, equation 6.5, can be rewritten as

$$W_i^* = CS_i^* + \underbrace{\alpha(\pi_{ii}^* + \pi_{ij}^*)}_{(I)} - \underbrace{\alpha t^* \pi_{ij}^*}_{(II)} + \underbrace{t^* \pi_{ji}^* + (1 - \alpha)t^* \pi_{ii}^*}_{(III)}$$

$$- \underbrace{\left(\alpha \delta_i q_i^{*2} x_{ij}^* + \frac{d}{2} \delta_i^2 \right)}_{(IV)},$$

which, using equations 6.13, 6.14, and 6.19, reduces to

$$W_i^* = \frac{1}{18}(2 - \tau)^2 + \frac{(5\tau^2 - 2\tau + 2)[\alpha + (1 - \alpha)t^*]}{9} - \frac{d}{2}\delta_i^2,$$

so that the first-order condition for the government's maximization problem is given by

$$\frac{\partial W_i^*}{\partial \delta_i} = \underbrace{\frac{(1 - \alpha)(5\tau^2 - 2\tau + 2)}{9}\frac{\partial t^*}{\partial \delta_i}}_{Indirect} - \underbrace{d\delta_i}_{Implementation} = 0.$$

When setting its transfer pricing enforcement policy, country i must balance the positive impact of δ_i on the level of the symmetric equilibrium tax rate (*Indirect*) against a negative and direct effect reflected by the marginal cost of implementing δ_i itself (*Implementation*). It is evident that the direct effect does not vary with trade costs or the ownership structure parameter. Instead, the indirect effect on national welfare of increasing δ_i turns out to be positively related to trade costs, in the case of full third-country ownership ($\alpha = 0$), and decreasing in domestic ownership, for any value of trade costs. Hence, if the ownership share of foreigners in both MNEs increases, the benefits in terms of national welfare to enforce the arm's-length principle increase as well.

By solving the first-order conditions simultaneously for the two countries, we find a symmetric equilibrium in transfer pricing enforcement policies, $\delta^* \equiv \delta_i = \delta_j$, which can be characterized as follows:

Proposition 4   There exists a symmetric equilibrium level of enforcement of the arm's-length principle $\delta^*(\alpha, \tau)$, which depends on the ownership structure of MNEs and on trade costs.

See appendix 6B for the proof.

The symmetric equilibrium enforcement level turns out to be nonnegative for all possible values of α and τ. In particular, we can immediately observe that $\delta^*(1, \tau) = 0$, while $\delta^*(\alpha, \tau) > 0$, $\forall \alpha \in [0, 1)$, so that we can state:

Proposition 5   If both MNEs are fully owned by domestic residents ($\alpha = 1$), the two countries will find it optimal not to enforce the arm's-length principle. Otherwise both countries will optimally choose a positive level of enforcement.

The intuition for this result is simple. In the case of full domestic ownership, each country would incur the maximal costs in terms of national welfare to enforce the arm's-length principle. Indeed, any positive level of enforcement would have a negative impact because of its marginal implementation cost. On the contrary, when a minimal share of both MNEs is owned by foreigners, the enforcement policy has a positive impact on national welfare since it allows both countries to increase corporate profit tax rates and partly shift the burden of taxation onto foreigners.

To see how the ownership structure of MNEs affects the equilibrium enforcement policy, we derive the following expression,

$$\frac{\partial \delta^*}{\partial \alpha} = -\frac{(5\tau^2 - 2\tau + 2)[5\tau^2 - 2\tau + 2 + (1 + \tau^2)(1 - 2\alpha)]}{54d(1 - 2\tau)},$$

which is negative for all admissible values of α and τ. The positive effect of stronger enforcement is decreasing in α, while its marginal implementation cost is independent of such a parameter. Therefore, increased economic integration—in terms of larger international ownership of both MNEs—increases the equilibrium level of enforcement. This also confirms our previous result that the two countries optimally decide not to enforce the arm's-length principle in the case of full domestic ownership ($\alpha = 1$).

When the two MNEs are fully owned by residents of a third country ($\alpha = 0$), we easily show that the equilibrium level of enforcement decreases with trade liberalization. Indeed, a decrease in trade costs reduces the positive impact on national welfare of increasing the enforcement level while leaving unaffected the implementation cost of such a policy.

Figure 6.3 illustrates the relationship between trade costs and the symmetric equilibrium enforcement policy for values of $\alpha \in (0, 1)$ and $d = 1/27$. Trade liberalization initially leads to a decrease in δ^*, but when trade costs become sufficiently low, a further decrease in τ will increase δ^*. Such a nonmonotonic relationship is consistent with the impact of trade liberalization on t^* when domestic residents hold the majority of shares in both MNEs. We can also compute a threshold value for the ownership structure parameter, $\hat{\alpha}(\tau)$, above which trade liberalization leads the two countries to increase the level of enforcement of the arm's-length principle.

To conclude, our findings about the effects of increased economic integration on the equilibrium level of enforcement can be summarized as:

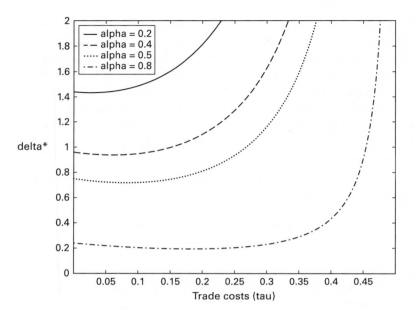

Figure 6.3
Effects of τ on δ^* for different values of α

Proposition 6 A more internationalized ownership structure of the two MNEs, that is, a lower α, increases δ^* for any level of trade costs. The effects of trade liberalization on δ^* instead depend on the ownership structure of MNEs:

1. If both MNEs are fully owned by third-country residents ($\alpha = 0$), a decrease in trade costs decreases δ^*.

2. If the ownership structure of both MNEs is such that $\alpha \in (0, 1)$, that is, the two MNEs are not fully owned by third-country or domestic residents, there exists a threshold value, $\hat{\alpha}(\tau)$, for α, above which trade liberalization increases δ^*. Instead, for $\alpha < \hat{\alpha}(\tau)$, trade liberalization decreases δ^*.

See appendix 6B for the proof.

6.6   Conclusion

In this chapter I have examined and discussed the outcome of a three-stage game where the governments of two symmetric countries set corporate profit tax rates and choose the level of enforcement of the arm's-length principle to maximize national welfare, taking into account the strategic choices of two MNEs competing on the quantities in the two markets. My purposes have been to study how enforcement policies affect the tax competition game and understand in what direction economic integration—in terms of lower trade costs or a more internationalized ownership structure of MNEs—influences the symmetric equilibrium levels of the two fiscal policy instruments.

In line with Kind et al. (2002), I have found that increased international ownership of MNEs unambiguously leads to higher corporate profit tax rates. Huizinga and Nicodeme (2006) offer empirical support for such a theoretical result by suggesting that corporate tax burdens in Europe are positively related to foreign ownership shares at the country level.[22] I have further shown that the effects of trade liberalization depend on the ownership structure of MNEs:

• If both MNEs are fully owned by third-country (domestic) residents, a decrease in trade costs decreases (increases) equilibrium tax rates.

• If both MNEs are partly owned by foreigners and partly by domestic residents, with the latter holding the majority of shares, trade liberalization increases equilibrium tax rates when trade costs become sufficiently low.

Therefore, increased economic integration may lead to either a *race to the bottom* or a *race to the top* in corporate profit tax rates between the two countries. While the former represents a good analogy with the standard results in the tax competition literature, the latter contrasts with the conventional conclusion that, due to tighter economic integration, tax competition between countries for a mobile tax base should imply a downward pressure on tax rates.[23]

My model also predicts that as governments strengthen the enforcement level of the arm's-length principle to control the transfer-pricing behavior of MNEs and to avoid cross-country profit shifting, equilibrium tax rates increase. Moreover, when MNEs are not fully owned by domestic residents, increased economic integration may determine a *race to the top* in transfer-pricing enforcement policies between the two countries. A larger international ownership share of MNEs monotonically increases the equilibrium level of enforcement, whereas trade liberalization initially has an opposite effect on this policy. But as trade becomes free enough and depending on the ownership structure of MNEs, a further decrease in trade costs may lead to an increase in the equilibrium enforcement policy. Instead, when MNEs are fully owned by domestic residents, it is optimal for both countries not to enforce the arm's-length principle. In such a case, any positive level of enforcement would uniquely have a negative impact on national welfare because of its marginal implementation cost.

To sum up, these results may be interpreted in the light of two different views of the economic integration process. On the one hand, if we look at increased economic integration just as a matter of internationalization of the ownership structure of MNEs, we have found that for any given level of trade costs, both equilibrium tax rates and enforcement policies will increase. Each country's government, by allocating more resources to control transfer pricing, is able to increase its corporate profit tax rate. Moreover, as the share of foreign ownership in the domestic MNE gets larger, increasing its tax rate allows each country to shift more of the tax burden to foreigners. Hence, such an internationalization phenomenon will lead to a *race to the top* in both policy instruments between countries.

On the other hand, if we consider economic integration only in terms of trade liberalization, we have proved that starting from a high level of trade costs and as long as MNEs are not fully owned by domestic residents, a *race to the bottom* in tax rates and enforcement policies will take place between the two countries. Then, when trade becomes free enough and depending on the ownership structure of MNEs, a further decrease in trade costs may increase the level of both policy instruments again. Indeed, the tax base expansion may be more important for each country's government than the tax base loss due to transfer pricing.

Most (if not all) of these results are driven by the symmetric country assumption and by the existence of a symmetric equilibrium in corporate tax rates. Therefore, as a task for future research, it looks important to analyze situations where countries (or MNEs) differ in some respects. For instance, I could imagine a setup with a single MNE and two countries. By letting production of the intermediate good take place just where the MNE's parent company is located and by further assuming that the MNE is fully owned by residents of that country, governments will find themselves in an asymmetric position relative to the MNE, and their objective functions will be substantially different. Indeed, due to the presence of trade costs, consumers living in the country hosting the MNE's subsidiary will have to pay a higher price for the final good than those living in the other country. In addition, all of the MNE's profits will accrue to people residing in the latter country. Hence, optimal corporate tax rates and enforcement policies might no longer be symmetric across countries. Alternatively, we could think about more complicated forms for the ownership structure of MNEs. In our model, country i's (country j's) residents do not hold any share of MNE_j (MNE_i). But things are likely to behave differently if we allow for (partial) international cross-ownership of MNEs.

Appendix 6A: Tax Competition

Symmetric Equilibrium Tax Rate

The symmetric outcome of the tax competition stage, $t^*(\delta_i, \delta_j, \alpha, \tau) \equiv t_i = t_j$, is a local Nash equilibrium under some parameter configurations. To prove this, we check that the government's second-order condition can be negative at $t_i = t_j$. We let

$$A \equiv x_{ii} + (1 - t_i)x_{ji} + (1 - 2x_{ii} - x_{ji})[\alpha + (1 - \alpha)t_i],$$

$$B \equiv \alpha(1 - t_j)(1 - 2x_{ij} - x_{jj} - \tau) + (1 - \alpha)q_i t_i + \alpha q_i(t_j - \delta_i q_i),$$

$$C \equiv x_{ji} + (1 - \alpha)(1 - t_i)x_{ii} + t_i(1 - 2x_{ji} - x_{ii} - \tau - q_j),$$

$$D \equiv \alpha(1 - t_j)x_{ij},$$

$$E \equiv (1 - \alpha)t_i + \alpha(t_j - 2\delta_i q_i),$$

and compute country i's government second-order condition as follows:

$$\frac{\partial^2 W_i}{\partial t_i^2} = \frac{\partial \pi_{ji}}{\partial t_i} + (1 - \alpha)\frac{\partial \pi_{ii}}{\partial t_i} + E\left(\frac{\partial x_{ij}}{\partial t_i}\frac{\partial q_i}{\partial t_i} + x_{ij}\frac{\partial^2 q_i}{\partial t_i^2}\right) + x_{ij}\frac{\partial q_i}{\partial t_i}\frac{\partial E}{\partial t_i}$$

$$- x_{ji}\frac{\partial q_j}{\partial t_i} - t_i\frac{\partial x_{ji}}{\partial t_i}\frac{\partial q_j}{\partial t_i} - t_i x_{ji}\frac{\partial^2 q_j}{\partial t_i^2} + A\frac{\partial^2 x_{ii}}{\partial t_i^2} + \frac{\partial x_{ii}}{\partial t_i}\frac{\partial A}{\partial t_i}$$

$$+ B\frac{\partial^2 x_{ij}}{\partial t_i^2} + \frac{\partial x_{ij}}{\partial t_i}\frac{\partial B}{\partial t_i} + C\frac{\partial^2 x_{ji}}{\partial t_i^2} + \frac{\partial x_{ji}}{\partial t_i}\frac{\partial C}{\partial t_i} - D\frac{\partial^2 x_{jj}}{\partial t_i^2} - \frac{\partial x_{jj}}{\partial t_i}\frac{\partial D}{\partial t_i},$$

where

$$\frac{\partial^2 x_{ji}}{\partial t_i^2} = -2\frac{\partial^2 x_{ii}}{\partial t_i^2} = \frac{(1 - t_j)^2}{3\delta_j(1 - t_i)^3}, \quad \frac{\partial^2 x_{ij}}{\partial t_i^2} = -2\frac{\partial^2 x_{jj}}{\partial t_i^2} = \frac{1}{3\delta_i(1 - t_j)},$$

$$\frac{\partial^2 q_i}{\partial t_i^2} = \frac{\partial^2 q_j}{\partial t_i^2} = 0, \quad \frac{\partial E}{\partial t_i} = 1 - \alpha - 2\alpha\delta_i\frac{\partial q_i}{\partial t_i}.$$

When $t_i = t_j \equiv t^*$, the strategic effect of corporate profit tax rates on supplied quantities is nil. Moreover, $q_i^* = q_j^* = 0$, $x_{ii}^* = x_{jj}^* = (1 + \tau)/3$, $x_{ij}^* = x_{ji}^* = (1 - 2\tau)/3$, and we also have that

$$\left.\frac{\partial \pi_{ji}}{\partial t_i}\right|_{t_i = t_j} = -x_{ji}^* \frac{\partial q_j}{\partial t_i}, \quad \left.\frac{\partial \pi_{ii}}{\partial t_i}\right|_{t_i = t_j} = x_{ij}^* \frac{\partial q_i}{\partial t_i},$$

$$A^* = \frac{2 - \tau - t^*(1 - 2\tau)}{3}, \quad B^* = 0,$$

$$C^* = \frac{1 - 2\tau + (1 - t^*)(1 - \alpha)(1 + \tau)}{3}, \quad D^* = \frac{(1 - 2\tau)(1 - t^*)\alpha}{3},$$

$$\left.\frac{\partial^2 x_{ii}}{\partial t_i^2}\right|_{t_i = t_j} = -\frac{1}{6\delta_j(1 - t^*)}, \quad \left.\frac{\partial^2 x_{jj}}{\partial t_i^2}\right|_{t_i = t_j} = -\frac{1}{6\delta_i(1 - t^*)}.$$

Therefore, substituting for $\partial q_i/\partial t_i = -1/2\delta_i$ and $\partial q_j/\partial t_i = 1/2\delta_j$ and evaluating the government's second-order condition at $t_i = t_j$ gives

$$\left.\frac{\partial^2 W_i}{\partial t_i^2}\right|_{t_i = t_j} = \underbrace{-\frac{1 - 2\tau}{3}\left(\frac{1}{\delta_j} + \frac{2 - \alpha}{2\delta_i}\right)}_{(a)} \underbrace{-\frac{1}{6(1 - t^*)}\left(\frac{A^* - 2C^*}{\delta_j} - \frac{D^*}{\delta_i}\right)}_{(b)}.$$

Since the first term on the right-hand side, (a), is always negative for any value of $\delta_i, \delta_j \in [0, \infty)$, $\alpha \in [0, 1]$, and $\tau \in [0, \frac{1}{2})$, and the second term, (b), can be either positive or negative, we can conclude that there exist parameter configurations such that

$$\left.\frac{\partial^2 W_i}{\partial t_i^2}\right|_{t_i = t_j} < 0,$$

implying that $t^*(\delta_i, \delta_j, \alpha, \tau) \equiv t_i = t_j$ is a local Nash equilibrium of the tax competition stage.

To show that such a symmetric equilibrium tax rate is positive for all possible values of $\alpha \in [0, 1]$ and $\tau \in [0, \frac{1}{2})$, as long as $\delta_i, \delta_j > 0$, we need to check the sign of the following expression,

$$f(\alpha, \tau) \equiv 5\tau^2 - 2\tau + 2 - \alpha(1 + \tau)^2,$$

which is strictly decreasing in α, since $\partial f(\alpha, \tau)/\partial \alpha = -(1 + \tau)^2 < 0$, $\forall \tau$. Then we can restrict our attention to the maximum value that α can take, $\alpha = 1$, which gives

$$f(1, \tau) = (2\tau - 1)^2 > 0, \quad \forall \tau \in \left[0, \frac{1}{2}\right).$$

Since $f(1, \tau) > 0$, $\forall \tau$, and $f(\alpha, \tau)$ is strictly decreasing in α, we can conclude that $f(\alpha, \tau) > 0$ for all $\alpha \in [0, 1]$, implying that $t^*(\delta_i, \delta_j, \alpha, \tau)$ is positive for all possible values of α and τ.

Proof of Proposition 1   The effects on t^* of a change in the level of enforcement of the arm's-length principle by country i, country j, or both countries are captured by

$$\frac{\partial t^*}{\partial \delta_i} = \frac{2\delta_j^2 [5\tau^2 - 2\tau + 2 - \alpha(1 + \tau)^2]}{3(1 - 2\tau)(\delta_i + \delta_j)^2} > 0, \quad \text{as long as } \delta_j > 0$$

$$\frac{\partial t^*}{\partial \delta_j} = \frac{2\delta_i^2 [5\tau^2 - 2\tau + 2 - \alpha(1 + \tau)^2]}{3(1 - 2\tau)(\delta_i + \delta_j)^2} > 0, \quad \text{as long as } \delta_i > 0$$

$$\frac{\partial t^*}{\partial \delta_i \partial \delta_j} = \frac{4\delta_i\delta_j [5\tau^2 - 2\tau + 2 - \alpha(1 + \tau)^2]}{3(1 - 2\tau)(\delta_i + \delta_j)^3} > 0, \quad \text{as long as } \delta_i, \delta_j > 0,$$

which allow us to conclude that an increase in the enforcement policy by one of the two, or by both, countries will increase t^*.

Proof of Proposition 2   The effect on t^* of a change in the ownership structure of MNEs is given by

$$\frac{\partial t^*}{\partial \alpha} = -\frac{2\delta_i\delta_j (1 + \tau)^2}{3(1 - 2\tau)(\delta_i + \delta_j)} < 0, \quad \text{as long as } \delta_i, \delta_j > 0,$$

so that we can argue that a lower α will increase t^*.

Trade Liberalization: Direct versus TP effect
In the case of full domestic ownership ($\alpha = 1$), direct and TP effects are given by $e(\tau) = (1 - 2\tau)^2/9$ and $g(\tau) = -t^*(\delta_i + \delta_j)(1 - 2\tau)/(6\delta_i\delta_j)$, respectively. Differentiating $e(\tau)$ with respect to τ, we find that

$$\frac{\partial e(\tau)}{\partial \tau} > 0 \Leftrightarrow \tau > \frac{1}{2}.$$

Hence, $\partial e(\tau)/\partial \tau < 0$, $\forall \tau \in [0, \frac{1}{2})$, meaning that the impact of trade liberalization on the direct effect is positive. By contrast, $\partial g(\tau)/\partial \tau > 0$,

$\forall \tau \in \left[0, \frac{1}{2}\right)$, implying that trade liberalization has a negative impact on the TP effect.

In the case of full third-country ownership ($\alpha = 0$), the TP effect and the impact on it of a decrease in trade costs are the same as above, while the direct effect is equal to $h(\tau) = (1 - 2\tau)^2/9 + (1 + \tau)^2/9$. Differentiating $h(\tau)$ with respect to τ, we find that

$$\frac{\partial h(\tau)}{\partial \tau} > 0 \Leftrightarrow \tau > \frac{1}{5}.$$

Furthermore, since $\partial^2 h(\tau)/\partial \tau^2 > 0$, we have that $h(\tau)$ is a strictly convex function that reaches its minimum value at $\tau = \frac{1}{5}$. Thus, trade liberalization has a nonmonotonic impact on the direct effect. For $\tau \in \left[0, \frac{1}{5}\right)$, $\partial h(\tau)/\partial \tau < 0$, meaning that such an impact is positive just for sufficiently low values of trade costs. Instead, $\partial h(\tau)/\partial \tau > 0$ for $\tau \in \left(\frac{1}{5}, \frac{1}{2}\right)$, implying that for higher values of trade costs, trade liberalization has a negative impact on the direct effect as well.

Proof of Proposition 3 In the case of full domestic ownership ($\alpha = 1$), the symmetric equilibrium tax rate is given by $t^*(\delta_i, \delta_j, 1, \tau) = 2\delta_i\delta_j(1 - 2\tau)/(3(\delta_i + \delta_j))$, and the effect on it of a change in trade costs is captured by

$$\frac{\partial t^*(\delta_i, \delta_j, 1, \tau)}{\partial \tau} = -\frac{4\delta_i\delta_j}{3(\delta_i + \delta_j)} \le 0.$$

In the case of full third-country ownership ($\alpha = 0$), the symmetric equilibrium tax rate is given by $t^*(\delta_i, \delta_j, 0, \tau) = 2\delta_i\delta_j(5\tau^2 - 2\tau + 2)/(3(\delta_i + \delta_j)(1 - 2\tau))$, and the effect on it of a change in trade costs is captured by

$$\frac{\partial t^*(\delta_i, \delta_j, 0, \tau)}{\partial \tau} = \frac{4\delta_i\delta_j(1 + 5\tau - 5\tau^2)}{3(\delta_i + \delta_j)(1 - 2\tau)^2} \ge 0.$$

The sign of $\partial t^*/\partial \tau$ for values of $\alpha \in (0, 1)$ depends on only the sign of $l(\alpha, \tau) \equiv 1 + 5\tau - 5\tau^2 - \alpha(1 + \tau)(2 - \tau)$. In particular, $l(\alpha, \tau) > 0$ for all values of τ satisfying $(5 - \alpha)\tau^2 - (5 - \alpha)\tau + 2\alpha - 1 < 0$, that is, for all $\tau \in (\hat{\tau}, \tilde{\tau})$, where

$$\hat{\tau} = \frac{1}{2} - \frac{3\sqrt{(5 - \alpha)(1 - \alpha)}}{2(5 - \alpha)}$$

and

$$\tilde{\tau} = \frac{1}{2} + \frac{3\sqrt{(5-\alpha)(1-\alpha)}}{2(5-\alpha)}.$$

Since $\alpha \in [0,1]$, we can easily check that $\tilde{\tau} \geq \frac{1}{2}$. Moreover, $\hat{\tau} > 0$ as long as $\alpha > \frac{1}{2}$. Therefore, we can conclude that:

• For $\alpha \leq \frac{1}{2}$, $\hat{\tau} \leq 0$ and $\tilde{\tau} \geq \frac{1}{2}$, implying that $l(\alpha, \tau) > 0$, $\forall \tau \in [0, \frac{1}{2})$; this, in turn, means that $\partial t^* / \partial \tau > 0$.

• For $\alpha > \frac{1}{2}$, $\hat{\tau} > 0$ and $\tilde{\tau} \geq \frac{1}{2}$. This implies that $l(\alpha, \tau)$ and $\partial t^* / \partial \tau$ are positive for $\tau \in (\hat{\tau}, \frac{1}{2})$, but they are negative for $\tau \in [0, \hat{\tau}]$.

Appendix 6B: Enforcement Policy Competition

Economic Integration and the Indirect Effect
The indirect effect on country i's national welfare of a change in the level of enforcement of the arm's-length principle is captured by

$$k(\alpha, \tau) = \frac{2\delta_j^2(1-\alpha)(5\tau^2 - 2\tau + 2)[5\tau^2 - 2\tau + 2 - \alpha(1+\tau)^2]}{27(1-2\tau)(\delta_i + \delta_j)^2}.$$

We easily find that $\partial k(\alpha, \tau) / \partial \alpha = -2\delta_j^2(5\tau^2 - 2\tau + 2)[5\tau^2 - 2\tau + 2 + (1 - 2\alpha)(1 + \tau)^2]/(27(1 - 2\tau)(\delta_i + \delta_j)^2) < 0$, as long as $\delta_j > 0$. With full third-country ownership ($\alpha = 0$), the indirect effect reduces to $k(0, \tau) = 2\delta_j^2(5\tau^2 - 2\tau + 2)^2/(27(1 - 2\tau)(\delta_i + \delta_j)^2)$, and the impact of a change in trade costs is given by $\partial k(0, \tau)/\partial \tau = 4\delta_j^2\tau(4 - 5\tau)(5\tau^2 - 2\tau + 2)/(9(1 - 2\tau)^2(\delta_i + \delta_j)^2) > 0$, $\forall \tau \in [0, \frac{1}{2})$.

Existence of the Symmetric Equilibrium in Enforcement Policies
To prove such a result, we first need to show that the objective function of country i (country j) identified in section 6.5 is concave in δ_i (δ_j). This amounts to checking the sign of the following second order-derivatives:

$$\frac{\partial^2 W_i^*}{\partial \delta_i^2} = -\frac{4(1-\alpha)(5\tau^2 - 2\tau + 2)[5\tau^2 - 2\tau + 2 - \alpha(1+\tau)^2]\delta_j^2}{27(1 - 2\tau)(\delta_i + \delta_j)^3} - d$$

$$\frac{\partial^2 W_j^*}{\partial \delta_j^2} = -\frac{4(1-\alpha)(5\tau^2 - 2\tau + 2)[5\tau^2 - 2\tau + 2 - \alpha(1+\tau)^2]\delta_i^2}{27(1 - 2\tau)(\delta_i + \delta_j)^3} - d.$$

Since $d > 0$ by assumption and the term in square brackets— $f(\alpha, \tau)$—is always positive, both derivatives turn out to be negative for all possible values of δ_i, δ_j, α, and τ. Hence, the objective function of country i (country j) is concave in its own argument.

We take the first-order conditions for the maximization problem of the two governments and substitute for $\partial t^*/\partial \delta_i$ and $\partial t^*/\partial \delta_j$. After some rearrangements, we get the following system,

$$
\begin{cases}
\dfrac{2(1-\alpha)(5\tau^2 - 2\tau + 2)[5\tau^2 - 2\tau + 2 - \alpha(1+\tau)^2]}{27d(1-2\tau)(\delta_i + \delta_j)^2} = \dfrac{\delta_i}{\delta_j^2} \\[4mm]
\dfrac{2(1-\alpha)(5\tau^2 - 2\tau + 2)[5\tau^2 - 2\tau + 2 - \alpha(1+\tau)^2]}{27d(1-2\tau)(\delta_i + \delta_j)^2} = \dfrac{\delta_j}{\delta_i^2},
\end{cases}
$$

which implies that $\delta_i/\delta_j^2 = \delta_j/\delta_i^2$; consequently,

$$\delta_i^3 = \delta_j^3 \Leftrightarrow \delta_i = \delta_j,$$

that is, there exists a symmetric equilibrium in transfer pricing enforcement policies, $\delta^*(\alpha, \tau) \equiv \delta_i = \delta_j = (1-\alpha)(5\tau^2 - 2\tau + 2)[5\tau^2 - 2\tau + 2 - \alpha(1+\tau)^2]/(54d(1-2\tau)) \geq 0$.

Proof of Proposition 6   To prove the negative relationship between α and δ^*, we need to show that the function $m(\alpha, \tau) \equiv 5\tau^2 - 2\tau + 2 + (1 + \tau^2)(1 - 2\alpha)$ is positive for all admissible values of α and τ. Since $\partial m(\alpha, \tau)/\partial \alpha = -2\tau^2 - 2 < 0$, $\forall \tau$, we have that $m(\alpha, \tau)$ is strictly decreasing in α. Then we focus on the maximum value that α can take, $\alpha = 1$, which gives $m(1, \tau) = 4\tau^2 - 2\tau + 1 > 0$, $\forall \tau \in [0, \frac{1}{2})$. Given that $m(1, \tau) > 0$ and $m(\alpha, \tau)$ is strictly decreasing in α, we conclude that $m(\alpha, \tau) > 0$ for all $\alpha \in [0, 1]$.

With full third-country ownership $(\alpha = 0)$, the symmetric equilibrium level of enforcement reduces $\delta^*(0, \tau) = (5\tau^2 - 2\tau + 2)^2/(54d(1 - 2\tau)) > 0$ and the effect on it of a change in trade costs is captured by

$$\frac{\partial \delta^*(0, \tau)}{\partial \tau} = \frac{\tau(4 - 5\tau)(5\tau^2 - 2\tau + 2)}{9d(1 - 2\tau)^2} > 0, \quad \forall \tau \in \left[0, \frac{1}{2}\right).$$

To analyze the relationship between τ and δ^* for values of $\alpha \in (0, 1)$, we need to check the sign of this expression:

$$\frac{\partial \delta^*(\alpha, \tau)}{\partial \tau} = \frac{1 - \alpha}{27d(1 - 2\tau)^2} \{(1 - 2\tau)(5\tau^2 - 2\tau + 2)[5\tau - 1 - \alpha(1 + \tau)]$$

$$+ (1 - 2\tau)(5\tau - 1)[5\tau^2 - 2\tau + 2 - \alpha(1 + \tau)^2]$$

$$+ (5\tau^2 - 2\tau + 2)[5\tau^2 - 2\tau + 2 - \alpha(1 + \tau)^2]\}.$$

Since $(1 - \alpha)/27d(1 - 2\tau)^2 > 0$ for all values of $\alpha \in (0, 1)$ and $\tau \in [0, \frac{1}{2})$, we have that $\partial \delta^*(\alpha, \tau)/\partial \tau > 0$ as long as the term in braces is positive. The last requirement is satisfied for all values of α such that

$$\alpha < \hat{\alpha}(\tau) \equiv \frac{\tau(5\tau^2 - 2\tau + 2)(4 - 5\tau)}{(1 + \tau)(1 + 3\tau^2 - 5\tau^3)},$$

where $\hat{\alpha}(\tau)$ represents the threshold value above which trade liberalization leads to an increase in the equilibrium enforcement policy. Furthermore, $\partial \hat{\alpha}(\tau)/\partial \tau > 0$, $\forall \tau \in [0, \frac{1}{2})$, meaning that as τ decreases, the threshold value for α decreases as well.

Notes

I am grateful to Giacomo Calzolari, Jean Hindriks, and Susana Peralta for helpful discussions and suggestions. I also wish to thank Antonio Minniti and Cecilia Vergari; seminar participants at the Fifth Doctoral Meetings in International Trade and International Finance (Paris, November 18–19, 2004), the CESifo Venice Summer Institute Workshop, "Recent Developments in International Trade: Globalization and the Multinational Enterprise" (San Servolo, July 18–19, 2005), and the University of Bologna (January 2006); as well as two anonymous referees, for useful comments. Financial support from Marco Polo grant, Department of Economics, University of Bologna, and CORE is gratefully acknowledged.

1. See Hines (1997, 1999) for comprehensive surveys of the empirical literature about tax-motivated transfer pricing and profit shifting by MNEs. Gresik (2001) and Gordon and Hines (2002) provide an overview of the theoretical literature on international taxation and its connections with empirical observations.

2. See, for example, Jenkins and Wright (1975), Grubert and Mutti (1991), Harris et al. (1993), Grubert, Goodspeed, and Swenson (1993), and Hines and Rice (1994).

3. Her estimates indicate that a tax rate 1 percent lower in the country of destination (origin) is associated with intrafirm export (import) prices 1.8 percent lower (2 percent higher) relative to non-intrafirm goods.

4. The OECD transfer-pricing guidelines were first issued in 1979 and are updated periodically. They maintain the arm's-length principle of treating related enterprises within a multinational group. Such a principle is also found in Article 9 of the OECD Model Tax Convention on Income and on Capital (OECD, 2003) and represents the framework for bilateral treaties between OECD countries and many non-OECD governments as well.

5. Most countries have explicit TP rules. A smaller group of countries uses formal TP documentation rules, meaning that tax authorities recommend taxpayers to maintain written documentation showing that the prices charged for intrafirm transactions are consistent with the arm's-length principle. And an even smaller set of countries imposes TP-specific penalties.

6. About 33 percent of world trade was intrafirm already in 1993 (Markusen 2002).

7. Substituting for equilibrium quantities in country i's market, we find that $p_i > 0$ if and only if $\delta_j > (t_j - t_i)^2/(4(1 + \tau)(1 - t_i))$, that is, country j's enforcement level is sufficiently high. In any symmetric equilibrium in tax rates $(t_i = t_j)$, the price to consumers in country i (resp. country j) will be positive as long as country j (country i) chooses a positive level of enforcement of the arm's-length principle.

8. This assumption is consistent with the actual behavior of most OECD countries. The source country typically has a first right to tax the profits of all firms operating within its borders. Then some residence countries exempt the foreign profits of their subsidiaries from domestic tax, in which case the source principle applies directly. Alternatively, residence countries can use the tax credit method of double taxation relief. Even in this case, the source principle often effectively remains in operation since foreign profits are taxed only upon repatriation, which can be deferred by MNEs. See Keen (1993), for example.

9. Following Kant (1988), the endogenous choice of the enforcement policy can be interpreted as a change in government's attitude toward MNEs, for example, due to a change in the government in either country or to a study and policy review by an existing government.

10. From a technical viewpoint, the convex specification of the enforcement cost function is needed for analytical tractability. This allows us to find a closed-form solution to the equilibrium enforcement policy, which depends on the ownership structure of MNEs and on trade costs. If we assume, for example, a linear cost of enforcement, $C_i(\delta_i) = d\delta_i$, $d > 0$, a symmetric equilibrium in enforcement policies still exists, but the government's first-order condition is satisfied for any level of enforcement of the arm's-length principle.

11. We can interpret the last assumption as a per unit penalty that tax authorities impose on the MNE when they detect transfer price manipulation.

12. If transfer price manipulation costs were tax deductible, fiscal authorities might not be able to distinguish them from production costs. The non-tax-deductibility assumption is in line with Peralta et al. (2003). Instead, Kind et al. (2002) treat such "concealment costs" as tax deductible.

13. The parameter α can also be seen as the weight that each government puts on profits when it maximizes national welfare. If, say, $\alpha < 1$ and MNEs are fully owned by domestic residents, the government values consumer surplus, tax revenue, and the cost of enforcement more than producer surplus.

14. Implicitly, I have in mind a situation where regulators commit themselves not to modify their enforcement policies after corporate tax rates have been set. I must also stress that the choice of an alternative timing where, before deciding on their enforcement policies, the two governments choose tax rates would make the model intractable, and we would not obtain clear-cut results for the equilibrium values of the two fiscal policy instruments.

15. As MNE_j's maximization problem is symmetric, we can restrict our attention to MNE_i's decisions.

16. Here and in what follows, I denote by an asterisk the value of all the variables corresponding to the case of symmetric tax rates $(t_i = t_j)$.

17. When $t_i > t_j$ $(t_i < t_j)$, we can reach the same conclusions by using the argument that a marginal increase in t_i will have a positive (negative) impact on MNE_j's profit-shifting and export incentives.

18. Alternatively, we can show that a marginal change in one of the tax rates starting from a symmetric equilibrium will not affect consumer surplus, the profit ownership effect (I), and the enforcement policy effect (IV).

19. Although the results of this section are qualitatively similar to those in sections 3.2 and 3.3 of Kind et al. (2002), it is instructive to derive and discuss them in some detail in order to convey the underlying economic intuition to readers.

20. This result is consistent with Huizinga and Nielsen (1997) whose model, however, does not consider transfer pricing by MNEs. They show that if economic integration means that a larger part of the corporate tax falls on foreigners, an incentive for tax exportation arises, leading to a higher corporate tax rate.

21. Ludema and Wooton (2000) obtain an analogous result in that lower trade costs may lead to higher equilibrium tax rates. Differently from us, they study the impact of tax competition on the location of manufacturing workers in an economic geography setup. Baldwin and Krugman (2004) instead show that by introducing agglomeration externalities into a standard tax competition model, greater economic integration may determine a race to the top in tax rates.

22. According to their estimates, an increase in foreign ownership by 1 percent would lead to an increase in the average corporate tax rate by between 0.5 and 1 percent.

23. See, for example, Wilson (1999) for a survey of the tax competition literature.

References

Baldwin, R. E., and P. Krugman. (2004). Agglomeration, Integration and Tax Harmonisation. *European Economic Review* 48, 1–23.

Bartelsman, E. J., and R.M.W.J. Beetsma. (2003). Why Pay More? Corporate Tax Avoidance through Transfer Pricing in OECD Countries. *Journal of Public Economics* 87 (9–10), 2225–2252.

Clausing, K. A. (2003). Tax-Motivated Transfer Pricing and US Intrafirm Trade Prices. *Journal of Public Economics* 87 (9–10), 2207–2223.

Elitzur, R., and J. Mintz. (1996). Transfer Pricing Rules and Corporate Tax Competition. *Journal of Public Economics* 60, 401–422.

Ernst & Young. (2000). *Transfer Pricing at-a-Glance Guide*. Rotterdam: Ernst & Young.

Gimme Shelter. (2000). *Economist*, January 27.

Gordon, R. H., and J. R. Hines. (2002). International Taxation. In A. J. Auerbach and M. Feldstein (eds.), *Handbook of Public Economics*, Vol. 4. Amsterdam: North-Holland.

Gresik, T. A. (2001). The Taxing Task of Taxing Transnationals. *Journal of Economic Literature* 39, 800–838.

Grubert, H., T. Goodspeed, and D. Swenson. (1993). Explaining the Low Taxable Income of Foreign-Controlled Companies in the United States. In A. Giovannini, G. Hubbard, and J. Slemrod (eds.), *Studies in International Taxation*. Chicago: University of Chicago Press.

Grubert, H., and J. Mutti. (1991). Taxes, Tariffs and Transfer Pricing in Multinational Corporate Decision Making. *Review of Economics and Statistics* 73 (2), 285–293.

Harris, D., R. Morck, J. Slemrod, and B. Yeung. (1993). Income Shifting in U.S. Multinational Corporations. In A. Giovannini, G. Hubbard, and J. Slemrod (eds.), *Studies in International Taxation*. Chicago: University of Chicago Press.

Haufler, A., and G. Schjelderup. (2000). Corporate Tax Systems and Cross Country Profit Shifting. *Oxford Economic Papers* 52, 306–325.

Hines, J. R. (1997). Tax Policy and the Activities of Multinational Corporations. In A. J. Auerbach (ed.), *Fiscal Policy: Lessons from Economic Research*. Cambridge, Mass.: MIT Press.

Hines, J. R. (1999). Lessons from Behavioral Responses to International Taxation. *National Tax Journal* 52 (2), 305–322.

Hines, J. R., and E. M. Rice. (1994). Fiscal Paradise: Foreign Tax Havens and American Business. *Quarterly Journal of Economics* 109 (1), 149–182.

Huizinga, H., and G. Nicodeme. (2006). Foreign Ownership and Corporate Income Taxation: An Empirical Evaluation. *European Economic Review* 50 (5), 1223–1244.

Huizinga, H., and S. B. Nielsen. (1997). Capital Income and Profit Taxation with Foreign Ownership of Firms. *Journal of International Economics* 42, 149–165.

Jenkins, G. P., and B. D. Wright. (1975). Taxation of Income of Multinational Corporations: The Case of the US Petroleum Industry. *Review of Economics and Statistics* 57 (1), 1–11.

Kant, C. (1988). Endogenous Transfer Pricing and the Effects of Uncertain Regulation. *Journal of International Economics* 24, 147–157.

Keen, M. (1993). The Welfare Economics of Tax Co-ordination in the European Community: A Survey. *Fiscal Studies* 14, 15–36.

Kind, H. J., K. H. Midelfart Knarvik, and G. Schjelderup. (2001). Corporate Taxation, Multinational Enterprises and Economic Integration. Discussion paper no. 2753, Centre for Economic Policy Research, London.

Kind, H. J., K. H. Midelfart Knarvik, and G. Schjelderup. (2002). Why Corporate Taxes May Rise: The Case of Trade Liberalization and Foreign Ownership. Discussion paper no. 3383, Centre for Economic Policy Research, London.

Kind, H. J., K. H. Midelfart Knarvik, and G. Schjelderup. (2004). Trade and Multinationals: The Effect of Economic Integration on Taxation and Tax Revenue. Discussion paper no. 4312, Centre for Economic Policy Research, London.

Kind, H. J., K. H. Midelfart Knarvik, and G. Schjelderup. (2005). Corporate Taxation, Multinational Enterprises, and Economic Integration. *Journal of International Economics* 65, 507–521.

Ludema, R. D., and I. Wooton. (2000). Economic Geography and the Fiscal Effects of Regional Integration. *Journal of International Economics* 52, 331–357.

Mansori, K. S., and A. J. Weichenrieder. (2001). Tax Competition and Transfer Pricing Disputes. *FinanzArchiv* 58 (1), 1–11.

Markusen, J. R. (2002). *Multinational Firms and the Theory of International Trade.* Cambridge, Mass.: MIT Press.

OECD. (1995). *Transfer Pricing Guidelines for Multinational Enterprises and Tax Administrations.* Paris: Organization for Economic Cooperation and Development.

OECD. (2003). *Model Tax Convention on Income and on Capital.* Paris: Organization for Economic Cooperation and Development.

Peralta, S., X. Wauthy, and T. van Ypersele. (2003). Should Countries Control International Profit Shifting? Discussion paper no. 2003/72, Center for Operations Research and Econometrics, Louvain-la-Neuve, Belgium.

Peralta, S., X. Wauthy, and T. van Ypersele. (2006). Should Countries Control International Profit Shifting? *Journal of International Economics* 68, 24–37.

Raimondos-Møller, P., and K. Scharf. (2002). Transfer Pricing Rules and Competing Governments. *Oxford Economic Papers* 54, 230–246.

U.S. Department of the Treasury. (1994). Intercompany Transfer Pricing Regulations under Section 482: Final Regulations. *Federal Register* 59 (130), 34971–35033.

Wilson, J. D. (1999). Theories of Tax Competition. *National Tax Journal* 52, 269–304.

7   Gains from Trade and Fragmentation

Alan V. Deardorff

7.1   Introduction

A hot topic these days in the trade field is international outsourcing, or what is coming to be called offshoring. This seems to mean the relocation of some aspect—but not all—of an industry's productive activity to another country. This has been happening for years in the form of trade in manufactured intermediate inputs, but recent advances in information technology have made it possible to do this with certain productive services as well, and the word *offshoring* seems to have accompanied that development. In the public mind, offshoring seems to mean the "exporting of jobs"; it suggests a pure loss to the country from which it occurs and especially for the workers who are replaced. This was no less true when the offshored jobs were primarily manufacturing jobs, but the recent inclusion of services has extended the threat from offshoring to an additional part of the population. The threatened workers do not so far include economists, however, and to many of us, offshoring just means the most recent manifestation of the international trade that we have been writing about for two centuries. It suggests to us gains to the participating countries and the world, though not necessarily to everyone within them.

There exist a variety of ways that offshoring could have adverse effects, at least to some, that I am not best qualified to deal with. These include macroeconomic effects if labor markets function poorly. They include intellectual property issues, if hosts of an offshored activity copy a technology that they did not previously possess. And they include the related effects that such a transfer of technology may have on the terms of trade, as was emphasized by Samuelson (2004) and has since been examined by Jones and Ruffin (2005). I will focus instead on a simpler and well-defined part of the issue: what happens, in static models of international production and trade, when it becomes possible to split a productive activity into parts that can now be done in different locations. If, as a result, production that was previously done in one country is now done in two, what effect does this have on the welfare of the world, of each country, and of groups within these countries? I will call this, as I and others have done before, the issue of trade and fragmentation.

In what follows, I recall some of the basic results of trade theory regarding the gains from trade and then ask how these results can inform us regarding the gains from fragmentation.

7.2   Lessons from the Gains from Trade

The gains from trade have been a major focus of economics almost since the discipline began. Our current understanding, though, seems to date from contributions of Samuelson (1939, 1962), as elaborated and extended by many authors such as Ohyama (1972) and Dixit and Norman (1980). Much of this literature has dealt carefully with delineating what is to be meant by a country's "gaining" from trade, an issue that I do not want to dwell on here. In the end, most treatments say, in essence, that if trade could potentially benefit all members of a country's population if their preferences and income were identical, then it is regarded as benefiting the country even though this assumption manifestly does not hold. The justifications for this inference are various, usually resting on the potential for some sort of income redistribution among the country's consumers.

The main lessons from the gains-from-trade literature for a country are the following:

Lesson 1: Free trade is better than autarky.

Lesson 2: Restricted trade (that is, trade that is less than free, restricted by trade barriers such as tariffs) is better than autarky.

Lesson 3: For a small country (that is, one too small to influence world prices), free trade is better than restricted trade.

Beyond these three results, which of course hold only under particular idealized assumptions, such as perfect competition or absence of externalities, the literature primarily tells us what we do not know. We do not know, even under idealized conditions, that any move in the apparent direction of free trade is necessarily beneficial, even for a small country.

For example, in the presence of multiple tariffs, reducing or eliminating just one of them may reduce welfare rather than raise it. Only if the tariff that is reduced is the highest of all tariffs in ad valorem terms can the case be made that this is welfare improving.[1] And certainly, reducing tariffs, even all of them, against one trading partner while keeping them unchanged against other countries may reduce the country's own welfare, as we have known since Viner (1950). About the only thing that we do know seems to be that an equiproportionate reduction in all tariffs, if they are specified and reduced in specific form rather than ad valorem form, will be welfare beneficial.[2]

What does this have to do with fragmentation? One way of interpreting what has happened with fragmentation is to imagine that international fragmentation has always been technologically possible, but that implicit barriers to trade have kept it from happening. The rise of international fragmentation can then be thought of as the manifestation of reductions in these barriers, from prohibitive to nonexistent. We can then apply the lessons of gains-from-trade theory to suggest what we do and do not know about the gains from fragmentation.

Most immediately, if a country were small and if trade were free aside from any trade that might arise from fragmentation, then the opportunity to engage in international fragmentation would be a move from restricted trade to free trade, and the country would have to gain, according to lesson 3. But that seems to be all that we can say, based on the above lessons, since the other two lessons start from autarky, and thus are not relevant to anything currently of interest. And on the contrary, the larger implication of this literature for fragmentation seems to be that if a country is either large enough to affect its terms of trade or if not all other aspects of its trade are free, then international fragmentation may cause its welfare to fall.

In the following sections, I look individually at several questions about the welfare effects of fragmentation. It is possible, of course, that the negative message just derived is not in fact correct if one takes into account more fully the nature of fragmentation. That is, to say that welfare may fall is not to say that it will fall, and there may be characteristics of fragmentation that make it different from other forms of trade liberalization. So I will look at some particular models that have appeared in the literature and provide examples of what may happen with fragmentation. In addition, I will look at more than just the effect on a country, first focusing more narrowly on groups of factor owners within a country and then more broadly at effects on the world as a whole.

7.3   Can Fragmentation Hurt a Country?

The answer, as I have already suggested, is yes. The most obvious way that fragmentation can hurt a country as a whole is by causing a worsening of its terms of trade. Of course, if a country is too small to affect world prices and if fragmentation becomes a new possibility only for itself and not for other countries (perhaps because others already have it), then this cannot alter world prices and cannot hurt the country on that account. But the introduction of fragmentation, because it tends to be based in part on new technologies, is unlikely to be confined to a single country unless that country is simply a laggard behind its adoption in the rest of the world. And if fragmentation becomes a new possibility for all countries, then of course that can easily alter world prices to the benefit of some and the detriment of others.

An example can be found in Deardorff (2001b), where a Ricardian model has two countries producing and trading two goods, initially without fragmentation. For one of the goods, it then becomes possible to fragment the production technology into two parts, with each country having its own labor requirements for performing each part. The model illustrates the possibility that this new ability to fragment may cause a change in world equilibrium relative prices, and it is possible that one country's terms of trade could worsen sufficiently that it is made worse off, even accounting for the new technological ability that fragmentation represents.

That model is abstract, so it may be helpful to sketch a more concrete example that is loosely based on the model. Suppose that the world produces two products: a numeraire good in the production of which all countries are equally productive, and a traded service, which I will call banking, in which their productivities differ. The technology of banking requires two activities: data entry and accountancy. Our country of interest is more productive than the world in accountancy but less productive in data entry. Initially, however, these two activities must be done in the same place, and it happens that we have a large enough advantage in accountancy to more than offset our disadvantage in data entry, with the result that we have a comparative advantage in banking. Thus, at the start, we export banking even though we are not so good at one of the activities that it requires. Suppose further that even though we produce only banking services, the world demands somewhat more than we can produce, and therefore the world price of banking is determined in the rest of the world, where the world's comparative disadvantage in banking makes the relative price higher, in terms of the numeraire, than the cost to us if we were to produce the numeraire ourselves. Indeed, it is this higher world price that yields our country a substantial gain from trade.

Now suppose that a new communication technology makes it possible to produce banking services with data entry and accountancy being done in different locations. Our banks will naturally begin to outsource the data entry, which can now be done more cheaply abroad. The problem for us as a country can be seen quite simply: by outsourcing data entry, we push down the world price of banking, which is our export, and we hurt our terms of trade.

Now if it were possible for us to outsource all data entry, then our gain from trade would only increase, since we would be specializing even more completely than we had before in what we do best, accountancy. But suppose that the world does not demand enough banking services for us to occupy our entire labor force doing only accountancy now that we are no longer doing data entry. If that is the case, then we will have to produce the numeraire good as well, and this does indeed require a fall in the relative price of banking.

Notice, incidentally, that this example—in both the abstract model of Deardorff (2001b) and the banking example described here—does not involve any transfer of technology to the rest of the world such as occurs in Samuelson (2004). In the example here, productivities differ across countries in both data entry and accountancy, but these productivities do not change when fragmentation becomes possible. However, fragmentation does in general permit activities within industries to be allocated more efficiently across the globe, and this tends to reduce those industries' costs. It is not surprising, then, that such a fall in costs can lower prices as well, and thus worsen a country's terms of trade.

A second way that fragmentation can hurt a country is if its markets are already distorted and fragmentation makes a distortion worse. The adverse effect of that worsening may more than offset the cost reduction permitted by fragmentation.

In tariff theory, we know, for example, that a reduction of a single tariff, if it is not the country's highest tariff, can be welfare worsening. This might occur, for example, if the liberalized good is a strong substitute for another good with a higher tariff. Then the fall in price of the first good reduces demand for the second, reducing still further its imports, which were already made too low by its own tariff. By thus worsening the distortionary effect of the higher tariff, the tariff reduction may lower welfare. By a similar mechanism, fragmentation might permit the outsourcing of an activity that is strongly substitutable for an input that is imported subject to a high tariff. In such a case, it might make the distortion caused by the tariff worse, and thus reduce the country's welfare.

I do not doubt that there may be other mechanisms by which fragmentation might reduce a country's welfare, both if fragmentation becomes newly possible for only a country's own industry and especially if it alters the structure of production throughout the world. Countries differ greatly in their positions in world markets, as well as in their own trade and other policies, and it would be surprising if examples of loss from what is in effect a new technology could not be constructed. But this is not at all to suggest that loss from fragmentation will be, in some sense, more common than gain. I will say more about this below, but for now, it bears mentioning that it is just as easy, if not more so, to construct examples in which countries gain from fragmentation.

7.4   Can Fragmentation Hurt Groups within a Country?

Again the answer is yes, even more easily. We know from Heckscher-Ohlin (HO) trade theory that a change in relative prices is very likely to reduce the real wage of at least one factor of production. So if groups within a country derive their incomes from different factors, some group will lose from any change in relative prices. Furthermore, fragmentation is sure to cause prices to change. The only chance for owners of a losing factor not to lose would be if fragmentation creates some other source of gain in which these factor owners share sufficiently to offset their lower factor price. That may happen, but it certainly is not assured.

The effect of changing relative prices on real factor returns is familiar as the Stolper-Samuelson theorem, which takes its strongest form in the textbook two-good, two-factor model with incomplete specialization.[3] But a fall in the real wage of some factor is equally assured in a more general HO model if there is incomplete specialization and if there are many goods and factors, as well as in the specific-factors model. To offset this, we would need additional benefits from complete specialization, or perhaps benefits from some non-HO properties such as increasing returns to scale, imperfect competition, or variety.[4]

Exactly which groups of factor owners may lose from fragmentation is very much an open question. The presumption in much public discussion has always been that outsourcing would be of unskilled-labor-intensive inputs and that it would therefore drive down the wage of unskilled labor. More recent concern with offshoring has focused on services, sometimes provided by more skilled workers such as computer programmers, medical technicians, and engineers, and the expectation has been that it would lower the wages of these occupations. That may well be the case, although theory has suggested that this outcome is not assured.

Jones and Kierzkowski (2001), for example, showed that international fragmentation could as easily have one effect on relative factor prices as another, depending on the detailed factor intensities of the fragments and the industries prior to fragmentation. Deardorff (2001a) explored further such options, showing in particular that fragmentation may actually drive relative factor prices in different countries further apart. All of this was reinforced in the simulations of Markusen (2005).

7.5   Can Fragmentation Hurt the World?

Here I argue that the answer is no, or at least that this is so in the absence of distortions with which fragmentation might adversely interact.

The argument is simple if we keep in mind the definition of fragmentation as a new technology that becomes available to a country or to the world. Such a technology, since it does not reduce the availability of any previous technology, can only expand the world's production possibilities. Then, in the absence of distortions, a perfectly competitive free-trade world economy is known to maximize the value of world output on the world production possibility set, and this maximum cannot fall. On the contrary, it must rise if the new technology is used at all by those who find it strictly preferable to previous practice.

From this one concludes that while fragmentation may hurt particular countries or groups within countries, as the previous sections suggested, it must always benefit other countries or groups by at least as much, and probably more. This means, in turn, that if it were possible to redistribute income across countries or groups without creating distortions, then such redistribution could accompany the introduction of fragmentation so as to leave everybody in the world at least as well off.

As usual with our gains-from-trade propositions, the gain to others may be of little comfort to those who lose, since no one seriously expects sufficient compensation to be provided. But from the safety of the academic ivory tower, we trade economists are accustomed to inferring benefit from just this possibility of redistribution, and therefore in this case, we infer that fragmentation is good. I ask in the next section whether there might be some other interpretation to buttress this conclusion.

But first I want to address the rather serious qualification to the result just mentioned: that it holds only in a perfect world with no distortions. Like the role of distortions in section 7.3, the presence of distortions here can render harmful an otherwise desirable change if it makes the impact of the distortion worse. This is of course the message of the theory of the second best, which we owe to Lipsey and Lancaster (1956). Although this theory is customarily applied to the effects of reducing one distortion, such as a tariff, in the presence of another, it applies just as well to any change that would otherwise be welfare improving, such as an improvement in technology. And fragmentation is exactly such a new technology.

How might fragmentation therefore hurt a distorted world? It is not hard to construct an example, although it is purely hypothetical. Suppose that there existed a good the production or consumption of which imposed a large negative externality[5] on the world, and the production of which required two activities or inputs that, as it happened, did not both exist in any single country of the world. Suppose, for example, that production of cigarettes required both tobacco, which could be grown in only a few places on earth where the soil or climate were appropriate, and also the delicate hands of a genetically distinct population of cigarette rollers to roll the tobacco into cigarettes, with this population living only in parts of the world that lacked the potential to grow tobacco. To avoid letting simple trade solve this problem, suppose that tobacco before it is rolled into cigarettes is extremely perishable, so that once cut from the plant, it becomes useless in minutes if not rolled immediately. The result of these tortuous assumptions clearly is that the world would have no cigarettes and—here the strain on reality is less severe—people would be healthier.

Now suppose that fragmentation of this technology becomes possible, so that growing tobacco and rolling it into cigarettes can be done in different locations after all. How? Perhaps a preservative allows the tobacco to survive shipment. Or perhaps there is some extraordinary extension on the arms of the cigarette rollers so that they can reach from where they live to where the tobacco is grown and do their job. (I did say that this was hypothetical.) Now suddenly, the world gets a thriving cigarette industry, and people start to die of lung cancer, though before they die, some of them live more happily because of the joys of smoking. Whether the world is better off or worse off depends on weighting the internalized benefits against the externalized costs, but it is certainly possible, at least if the costs do include truly external ones from second-hand smoke, that the introduction of fragmentation here has lowered world welfare.

As usual with second-best arguments, however, the cause of the loss is not really fragmentation, but rather the absence of a first-best policy to deal with the externality. If countries had been willing and able to tax cigarette smoking by an amount that equaled the external cost to society, then whatever smoking took place after fragmentation would provide private benefits exceeding this cost, and the world would have gained. If such benefits could not exceed the costs, then the industry would not appear at all in the presence of the tax, even when fragmentation made it technically possible, and the possibility of fragmentation would have had no effect at all.

This example rests on the existence of an externality, the presence of which is well known to undermine the welfare theorems of economics. What if the only distortion were a tariff? Again I think one can construct an example of welfare loss due to fragmentation, although it is not as stark.

Suppose that the manufacture of cars requires an input of steel, as well as the combined activities of design, which does not use the steel, and assembly, which does. Consider a country that has comparative advantage in both design and assembly due to its endowments of various types of workers, perhaps, but a comparative disadvantage in producing steel. Also, suppose that initially design and assembly have to be done in the same place. If there were free trade, the country would import steel and produce (both design and assemble) cars and export them. But now suppose that for some extraneous political reason, the country has a tariff on imports of steel, pushing its domestic price above the world price. Depending on the sizes of its advantages in design and assembly, it may still have a comparative advantage in producing cars, in spite of the higher-priced steel.

Now suppose that it becomes possible to fragment production into separate design and assembly stages that can be done in different locations. By moving assembly abroad, car companies can continue to exploit their comparative advantage in design while giving up their comparative advantage in assembly in return for lower-priced steel. Steel imports go down, as do car exports which are presumably shipped directly from the now-foreign assembly plants to their final markets.

I believe that this change could be harmful for the world. The tariff on steel was reducing steel imports below their free-market levels, and it was presumably also reducing the extent to which the world took advantage of the home country's comparative advantages in design and assembly. Fragmentation here reduces steel imports still further, although it may increase the use of steel in producing cars. More important, it reduces the extent to which the world benefits from the country's comparative advantage in assembly, which has moved offshore to a place where, if it were not for the lower-priced steel, costs would be higher. But it has also made it possible for the world to benefit more from the country's services in car design. So the outcome may be good or bad. But it seems clear that this is an example in which, in the presence of a tariff, the introduction of a form of fragmentation could be harmful to the world.

7.6   Should We Care about the World?

Of course, we should, in the sense of caring about everybody in the world. But what I mean here is, Should we care about the effect of fragmentation on the aggregate welfare of the world, as defined both here and routinely in international trade theory? That is, if we believed that the world were close enough to an undistorted state for the results there to be meaningful, would we then find useful the result that fragmentation benefits the world? Or alternatively, if we believed not only that distortions exist but also that they correlate with the effects of fragmentation in a way that it will lower world welfare, should we then oppose fragmentation on that account alone?

Perhaps not, in both cases. Some might argue that since compensating income redistribution will never in fact occur, what matters is how we weight the effects on winners and losers, not whether the winners could compensate the losers if we made them do it. Most likely, I think, many would regard a change that benefits the rich and hurts the poor as undesirable, even if the money value of the gain in the sense of, say, equivalent variation is somewhat larger than that of the loss. And a change that does the opposite might be welcomed, again even if it fails the compensation test. If so, then the questions about trade and fragmentation should focus not on their aggregate welfare effects but on their effects on income distribution. That would take us back to section 7.4, where we would ask, for example, how fragmentation affects the wages of skilled versus unskilled workers. And it would take us into the literature on trade and wages where such questions have been addressed theoretically and empirically.[6]

But while I certainly think that questions about income distribution are important, I also think that results concerning aggregate world welfare are worth pursuing for fragmentation just as they are for more traditional questions of international trade. The truth is that we are incredibly ignorant about what distributional affects will be, especially when we think about fragmentation in general rather than in very specific circumstances. If the theoretical literature teaches us anything, it is that anything can happen. For any given country or even any given group within a country, the general possibility of fragmentation may be helpful or harmful. And while it might be possible, with sufficient information about the details of a particular example of fragmentation, to remove this ambiguity empirically, this could surely not be done for all the instances of fragmentation that are arising over time in the world.

In our ignorance, therefore, the best that we may be able to do is to take a bet on whether fragmentation overall is likely to be good or bad. And for that, in the case of an undistorted world economy, the aggregate welfare result is clear. Because it says that fragmentation must raise world welfare, it is also saying that it raises individual welfare on average across the world's countries and groups. Unless, therefore, you have good reason to think that a person, group, or country that you care about (the poor, for example) will be affected systematically differently from the average, for all forms of fragmentation, then you should bet in favor of fragmentation rather than against it.

Now in the case of traditional trade—in contrast to fragmentation—we actually do have reason to expect systematic departures from the average. That reason is the Stolper-Samuelson theorem. If we view the world as comprising relatively high-paid skilled workers and relatively low-paid unskilled workers, the former more abundant in the rich world and the latter more abundant in the poor world, then Stolper-Samuelson tells us systematically that more liberal trade will make the income distribution more uneven in the rich world and more even in the poor, or more important, that it will raise real wages of unskilled workers in the South and lower them in the North. One could easily have an opinion on which of these effects to take most seriously. And even without that, one could hardly comfort the losers from trade with the argument that they might just as well have been born into a different group or country, so the average is all that matters.

But although the message of Stolper-Samuelson is clear, it is not at all clear that it tells the whole story of the effects of trade, for all sorts of reasons that trade theorists have explored. And these reasons tend—as I see it, at least—to add all sorts of reasons that particular groups may be affected differently by trade than Stolper-Samuelson suggests, both within the framework of the Heckscher-Ohlin model (adding more factors, for example, or allowing for complete specialization) and outside it (the New Trade Theory).

These same extensions and modifications of simple trade theory also tend to add more reasons that the effects of trade on aggregate world welfare are likely to be positive, with the gain presumably therefore larger than might have been expected from the simple model. Therefore, they reinforce the conclusion both that, in our ignorance, we should look at the average effects of trade and that these average effects are probably positive.

Returning to the question of fragmentation, I would say that this conclusion is even stronger. In the case of fragmentation, we do not even have a simple result like Stolper-Samuelson. That is, even in the simplest model where Stolper-Samuelson tells the whole story for trade, the introduction of fragmentation in a particular industry may help or hurt, say, unskilled labor in either country. This is the message we saw above from Jones and Kierzkowski (2001) and Deardorff (2001a). And of course more complicated models will yield even greater confusion, if that is possible (see Markusen 2005). That being the case, the result that fragmentation raises total, and therefore average, world welfare may be the best that we can do.

Of course, this result is true only in an undistorted world, which most people would regard as pretty remote from the one in which we live. What do distortions do to this conclusion? I argued in section 7.5 that in the presence of distortions, fragmentation can lower aggregate world welfare. But to say that it can does not by any means say that it will. For every example where fragmentation hurts a distorted economy, I am sure one could construct another example where it helps.

The issue, in all cases, will be whether fragmentation makes the harm done by the distortion worse, usually by shifting activity further away from what would have been optimal, or whether it reduces that harm by shifting activity toward the optimum. On average one might suppose—again if we are completely ignorant about the details of what will happen, as I believe in essence that we are—that fragmentation is as likely to do one as to do the other. And in that case, the fact that fragmentation must systematically expand what the world is able potentially to do with its given resources should mean that, again, on average fragmentation will be beneficial.

7.7   Conclusion?

My conclusions about the gains from fragmentation, then, are similar to the conclusions of trade theory more generally about the gains from trade. It is certainly true that examples of fragmentation can be found that lower the welfare of particular individuals, groups, and countries. Even the world as a whole may lose from fragmentation if it interacts adversely with existing distortions such as externalities and tariffs. But in an important average sense, fragmentation is very likely to expand world welfare.

So what? I have treated fragmentation here as a technological change that makes it possible to do something that was not possible before, on the grounds that much of the visible fragmentation today seems to have been made possible by improvements in the technologies of communication and transportation. Does anyone seriously propose reversing those technological changes even if it were possible? Of course not. So perhaps it does not matter from a policy perspective whether fragmentation is good or bad. It is simply an unavoidable fact of modern life.

But people do propose using policies to prevent or limit the use of those technologies, especially through fragmentation. In my own state of Michigan, our governor (whom I otherwise largely respect) has tried to limit the state government's purchases from firms that outsource abroad. John Kerry (whom I also otherwise respect), in his run for U.S. president, railed against "Benedict Arnold companies" that betray our nation by sourcing abroad, and he proposed a change in the tax code that was supposed to discourage this. And while at the moment U.S. concerns about trade seem to be more traditional—textiles from China, sugar from the Caribbean—I will be surprised if we do not hear more demands for policies to interfere somehow with firms that shift activities abroad.

These policies will seldom be as simple as an import tariff because fragmentation today often does not involve a physical product crossing a border. Therefore our standard arguments against tariffs, and the associated labeling of those who favor them as "protectionists," will seem not to apply. We will need to be creative in arguing against them. This will be especially hard given our tendency, illustrated in this chapter, to find particular cases in which fragmentation has adverse effects.

Notes

This chapter was motivated by serving as discussant of Markusen (2005). I have benefited particularly from talking with Juan Carlos Hallak about this topic. I also have had useful comments from an anonymous referee.

1. See Kowalczyk (1992).

2. Again, see Kowalczyk (1992), who shows the negative result that equiproportionate reductions in ad valorem tariffs may lower welfare.

3. See Stolper and Samuelson (1941) and, for a review of more recent developments, Deardorff (1994).

4. See Brown, Deardorff, and Stern (1993) for a discussion of how these "new trade theory" effects may interact with the Stolper-Samuelson mechanism.

5. The referee has suggested that this example is less than ideal since it involves trade in a "bad" rather than a "good" and that other propositions about gains from trade are invalidated if countries trade "bads." I disagree and cite the example of trade in garbage (of which Michigan happens to be an importer from Canada), for which importers simply pay a negative price. The key to the example here, as I note below, is simply the presence of an externality that is not internalized through an optimal tax or subsidy. The referee may well be right, however, that some other distortion, such as a subsidy to trade, would have provided a more compelling example.

6. See Freeman (1995).

References

Brown, Drusilla K., Alan V. Deardorff, and Robert M. Stern. (1993). Protection and Real Wages: Old and New Trade Theory and Their Empirical Counterparts. Research seminar in International Economics, University of Michigan, post-print paper no. 6, May 18.

Deardorff, Alan V. (1994). Overview of the Stolper-Samuelson Theorem. In Alan V. Deardorff and Robert M. Stern (eds.), *The Stolper-Samuelson Theorem: A Golden Jubilee*. Ann Arbor: University of Michigan Press, 7–34.

Deardorff, Alan V. (2001a). Fragmentation across Cones. In Sven W. Arndt and Henryk Kierzkowski (eds.), *Fragmentation: New Production Patterns in the World Economy*. Oxford: Oxford University Press, 35–51.

Deardorff, Alan V. (2001b). Fragmentation in Simple Trade Models. *North American Journal of Economics and Finance* 12, 121–137.

Dixit, Avinash K., and Victor Norman. (1980). *Theory of International Trade*. Cambridge: Cambridge University Press.

Freeman, Richard B. (1995). Are Your Wages Set in Beijing? *Journal of Economic Perspectives* 9, 15–32.

Jones, Ronald W., and Henryk Kierzkowski. (2001). Globalization and the Consequences of International Fragmentation. In R. Dornbusch, G. Calvo, and M. Obstfeld (eds.), *Money, Capital Mobility and Trade: Essays in Honor of Robert A. Mundell*. Cambridge, Mass.: MIT Press.

Jones, Ronald W., and Roy Ruffin. (2005). International Technology Transfer: Who Gains and Who Loses? *Review of International Economics* 15, 209–222.

Kowalczyk, Carsten. (1992). Paradoxes in Integration Theory. *Open Economies Review* 3, 51–59.

Lipsey, Richard G., and Kelvin Lancaster. (1956). The General Theory of Second Best. *Review of Economic Studies* 24, 11–32.

Markusen, James. (2005). Modeling the Offshoring of White-Collar Services: From Comparative Advantage to the New Theories of Trade and FDI. Centre for Economic Policy Research, Discussion Paper No. 5408, London.

Ohyama, M. (1972). Trade and Welfare in General Equilibrium. *Keio Economic Studies* 9, 3773.

Samuelson, Paul A. (1939). The Gains from International Trade. *Canadian Journal of Economics and Political Science* 5, 195–205.

Samuelson, Paul A. (1962). The Gains from International Trade Once Again. *Economic Journal* 72, 820–829.

Samuelson, Paul A. (2004). Where Ricardo and Mill Rebut and Confirm Arguments of Mainstream Economists Supporting Globalization. *Journal of Economic Perspectives* 18(3), 135–146.

Stolper, Wolfgang, and Paul A. Samuelson. (1941). Protection and Real Wages. *Review of Economic Studies* 9, 58–73.

Viner, Jacob. (1950). *The Customs Union Issue*. New York: Carnegie Endowment for International Peace.

II   Empirics

8 Spacey Parents: Spatial Autoregressive Patterns in Inbound FDI

Bruce A. Blonigen, Ronald B.
Davies, Helen T. Naughton,
and Glen R. Waddell

8.1 Introduction

Of the many directions in the current work on foreign direct investment (FDI), the effort to expand our understanding of multinational enterprises (MNEs) to include the influence of third countries is one of the most promising. Working from a strong base of theory and evidence describing the influence of parent and host country factors on FDI, much of which is summarized in Caves (1996) and Markusen (2002), recent work examines the influence of additional potential host countries on the outbound FDI decision. Papers in this vein include those of Ekholm, Forslid, and Markusen (2007), Yeaple (2003), and Bergstrand and Egger (2004), who analyze what has been termed "export platform FDI." In contrast to Markusen's (1984) horizontal model in which the MNE serves each of its markets through a local plant, in the export platform model, the MNE establishes a single overseas plant in one of the many potential hosts. Output from this centrally located plant is then sold in both the host and other nearby markets. Recent evidence by Blonigen, Davies, Waddell, and Naughton (2007), Baltagi, Egger, and Pfaffermayr (2007), and Ekholm, Forslid, and Markusen (2007), finds compelling evidence for this export platform motivation in outbound FDI data.

Although this work has focused on outward investment and the choice among host locations, it is just as important to recognize that third-country effects may be important for inbound FDI as well. In this chapter, we identify two potential channels for such effects using a simple model of the MNE. First, we show that the parent (or home) country's proximity to additional markets alters the margin of whether to service the host market through exports from the parent or through FDI. When the parent country has low-cost access to large markets, this increases the opportunity cost of exporting to the host. Therefore, subsidiary production in the host will rise even though the host itself is not an export platform. We call this the *parent market proximity effect*, which contrasts with host country market proximity effects (often called market potential effects) in previous literature such as Head and Mayer (2004) and Blonigen et al. (2007). Second, when there are MNEs from many countries active in the host, they may influence each other. If the various MNEs compete for scarce resources, then FDI from any single parent country may be crowded out by FDI from other parent countries. Alternatively, if FDI from other parent countries provides positive production externalities in the host country through technological transfer or market linkages, then greater third-country FDI could encourage FDI from the parent country in question.

This then suggests two testable hypotheses. First, we expect that more FDI will come from countries near large third-country markets. Second, more FDI from third countries in the host can mean more or less FDI from the parent depending on whether spillover or crowding-out effects dominate. To analyze these issues, we turn to a data set on U.S. inbound FDI from twenty Organization for Economic Cooperation and Development (OECD) countries over 1983 to 1998. We find strong evidence for parent market proximity effects—evidence that is robust to a variety of specifications. The effect of FDI from third countries, however, depends on the sample. When using our full OECD data set, we find no robust result for this variable. When restricting the analysis to a European subsample, which excludes the geographically distant countries of Australia, Canada, and Japan, we find a fairly robust negative impact of third-country FDI. Thus, at least for the European sample, it seems that FDI from one country may crowd out investment from another.

This chapter proceeds as follows. In section 8.2, we sketch out a simple, partial equilibrium model of the multinational firm in order to frame our predictions. In section 8.3, we discuss our empirical strategy and data. Section 8.4 presents our results and section 8.5 concludes.

8.2   A Simple Model of the Multinational Firm

In this section our goal is to frame our empirical methodology with a simple, partial equilibrium model of a multinational firm. Although this model clearly lacks many of the general equilibrium properties that typify fully specified models such as Markusen (2002) or Helpman, Melitz, and Yeaple (2004), our goal here is simply to elucidate some of the ways in which third-country effects may be important for a country's inbound FDI from a particular parent country.

Consider a firm that produces in two countries, the parent and the host.[1] Countries are numbered such that the host country is country 1 and the parent country is country 2. In addition, there is a third country 3. The output from the parent country 2 is produced at a total variable production cost $C(Q)$ where Q is the total amount produced in the parent country.[2] This output can be sold in any of the three countries, where Q_i is the amount of parent-produced output sold in country i. To do so, the firm must incur a per unit shipping cost $t \geq 0$, where $t_2 = 0$: parent country production can be sold in that country without additional cost. In addition to parent production, the multinational produces in the host, incurring the total variable production cost $C^*(Q^*; \Omega)$ where Q^* is the total host production and Ω is a function of the other (nonmodeled) MNEs active in the host (more on this below). Both production cost functions are increasing, convex functions. Note that this assumption differs from many models in which production is constant returns to scale (CRS). If we assume CRS production in our partial equilibrium model, then host production will not depend on third-country variables, although it would still depend on Ω. We assume that all output from the host plant is sold in the host, that is, that this is a purely horizontal MNE, in order to eliminate any effects that would arise from an export platform motivation for host production. We also assume that in equilibrium, all quantities will be positive, implying that the firm does not import from the host.[3]

Defining q_i as the total amount sold in each country, each country's local price is $P_i(q_i; \beta_i)$. Note that for the host country, $q_1 = Q_1 + Q^*$, whereas the total amount sold in the other two countries is equal to their respective Q_i. We assume that these inverse demand functions are decreasing in their respective quantities and that the associated marginal revenue functions are declining in quantity.[4] The β_i term in the inverse demand is a shift parameter. We assume that, all else equal, an increase in a country's β increases both the price and the slope of the price function, that is, where superscripts denote derivatives, that both P_i^{β} and $P_i^{q_i\beta}$ are positive. These β terms capture effects from an increase in the size of a given market; the bigger the market for a given quantity, the higher and the less sensitive the price will be. Finally, in addition to its variable costs, each plant costs the firm a fixed cost γ_i, and the firm incurs a firm-level fixed cost α.

The MNE's profits are given by

$$\Pi^{MNE} = \sum_{i=1}^{3} P_i(q_i; \beta_i)q_i - C(Q) - C^*(Q^*; \Omega)$$

$$- \sum_{i=1}^{3} t_i Q_i - \gamma_1 - \gamma_2 - \alpha. \tag{8.1}$$

Profit maximization implies that

$$P_i^{q_i}(q_i; \beta_i)q_i + P_i(q_i; \beta_i) = C^Q\left(\sum_{i=1}^{3} Q_i\right) + t_i \quad \text{for } i = 1, 2, 3 \tag{8.2}$$

and

$$C^{*Q^*}(Q^*; \Omega) = C^Q\left(\sum_{i=1}^{3} Q_i\right) + t_1. \tag{8.3}$$

Equation 8.2 shows the standard markup conditions for a monopolist in each of the three markets. Note that unlike many other models of FDI, we ignore competition in output markets with other firms (either domestic, foreign, or multinational). We take this partial equilibrium approach for simplicity, since demonstrating these interactions is not the primary goal of our theory, which is instead to highlight the role of third countries. Equation 8.3 highlights the trade-off of this horizontal firm between parent production (and exports) and host production. From the four first-order conditions, we can calculate how host production moves in response to changes in our exogenous parameters. This is given in the following proposition:

Proposition 1   Host production is:

a. Increasing in country 1's transport cost

b. Decreasing in country 3's transport cost

c. Increasing in any country's market size

Proof   It will prove convenient to define some notation. Denote the change in a country's marginal revenue with respect to the quantity sold there by

$$\tilde{P}_i \equiv P_i^{q_i q_i}(q_i; \beta_i)q_i + 2P_i^{q_i}(q_i; \beta_i) < 0. \tag{8.4}$$

Also, define

$$\Phi \equiv C^{QQ}(Q)C^{*Q^*Q^*}(Q^*;\Omega)[\tilde{P}_1\tilde{P}_2 + \tilde{P}_1\tilde{P}_3 + \tilde{P}_2\tilde{P}_3]$$

$$- \tilde{P}_1\tilde{P}_2\tilde{P}_3[C^{QQ}(Q) + C^{*Q^*Q^*}(Q^*;\Omega)] > 0. \tag{8.5}$$

Using equations 8.2 and 8.3, we can calculate the following comparative statics (dropping the arguments of functions):

$$\frac{dQ^*}{dt_1} = \Phi^{-1}\tilde{P}_1[C^{QQ}(\tilde{P}_2 + \tilde{P}_3) - \tilde{P}_2\tilde{P}_3] > 0, \tag{8.6}$$

$$\frac{dQ^*}{dt_3} = \Phi^{-1}[-C^{QQ}\tilde{P}_1\tilde{P}_2] < 0, \tag{8.7}$$

$$\frac{dQ^*}{d\beta_1} = \Phi^{-1}\tilde{P}_2\tilde{P}_3 C^{QQ}[P_1^{q_i\beta}q_1 + P_1^{\beta}] > 0 \tag{8.8}$$

$$\frac{dQ^*}{d\beta_2} = \Phi^{-1}\tilde{P}_1\tilde{P}_3 C^{QQ}[P_2^{q_i\beta}q_2 + P_2^{\beta}] > 0 \tag{8.9}$$

$$\frac{dQ^*}{d\beta_3} = \Phi^{-1}\tilde{P}_1\tilde{P}_2 C^{QQ}[P_3^{q_i\beta}q_3 + P_3^{\beta}] > 0 \tag{8.10}$$

The intuition behind these results is straightforward. When the transport cost to the host rises, this lowers the relative marginal cost of host production compared to producing in the parent country and exporting. Thus, the MNE shifts production to the host. When the transport cost to country 3 rises, it reduces exports from the parent to country 3. This frees up parent-produced output for exporting to the host, leading to a reduction in host output. When the host market size rises, this increases the return to selling there, thereby increasing host production (as well as exports from the parent to the host). When the market size of either of the nonhost countries rises, the MNE will divert parental-produced output toward the expanding market and away from the host. This then leads to higher host-country production to replace a portion of the fall in imports from the parent.[5]

It is worth reiterating the importance of our convex cost assumption for this result. If marginal costs are constant, there is no need to divert parental output from the host to country 3 when its trade costs fall or its market size rises. Thus, with constant returns to scale production, host output is independent of country 3. If marginal costs are decreasing, and production is increasing returns to scale, then when country 3's trade costs fall or its market size rises, this will lead to an increase in parental production, lowering marginal costs in the parent. Thus, under increasing returns to scale, host production will fall as the size of country 3 increases or as its trade costs fall. These competing alternatives imply the need for empirical analysis to choose among these assumptions.

This illustrates one way in which third countries can affect FDI in the host. When the parent country has easy access to large third markets, the firm's parent country activities will be geared more heavily toward those markets. As a result, firms from such countries will expand host production to serve that particular market. The second way in which third countries can affect the MNE's decision is through the effect of their multinationals on the firm's host production costs, that is, through Ω. Again using the first-order conditions, we find that

$$\frac{dQ^*}{d\Omega} = \Phi^{-1} C^{*Q^*\Omega} [\tilde{P}_1 \tilde{P}_2 \tilde{P}_3 - C^{QQ}[\tilde{P}_1 \tilde{P}_2 + \tilde{P}_1 \tilde{P}_3 + \tilde{P}_2 \tilde{P}_3]], \tag{8.11}$$

which has the opposite sign of $C^{*Q^*\Omega}$. If $C^{*Q^*\Omega}$ is positive (greater MNE activity by other firms increases this firm's marginal cost of host production), then more FDI from other countries will reduce the output of MNEs from the parent country. This would be consistent with a situation in which MNEs compete for scarce host resources.

Alternatively, if we were to embed this Ω in the host price function, such an impact could arise due to greater output competition in the host. But more FDI from other countries could lower the marginal cost of host production due to spillovers. As discussed by Blomström and Kokko (1998), a sizable body of evidence suggests that multinationals provide positive production externalities to other firms, benefits that may well extend to other MNEs in the host. Given these conflicting possibilities, we have no a priori expectations on the net effect of third countries' FDI and therefore turn to the data for additional insights.

8.3   Empirical Methodology and Data

8.3.1   Empirical Specification
Our empirical approach will use U.S. inbound FDI data and apply a modification of the commonly used gravity model of FDI. Ignoring time subscripts for notational purposes and where all nondiscrete vari-

ables are measured in natural logs, our primary regression specification is given by

$$FDI = \lambda_0 + \lambda_1 \ ParentVariables + \lambda_2 \ Trends$$

$$+ \ \lambda_3 \ ParentMarketProximity + \rho \cdot W \cdot FDI + \varepsilon. \tag{8.12}$$

As in other gravity specifications for FDI, including those of Eaton and Tamura (1994) and Brainard (1997), we include several controls for the parent country. Thus, *ParentVariables* in equation 8.12 includes parent-country GDP and parent country population.[6] In addition, following the insights of Carr, Markusen, and Maskus (2001), we include a measure of parent country skill. Typically gravity models include a comparable set of host country variables. In our case, since the United States is always the host country, these variables were insignificant once trends were included.[7] Therefore, we omit these in favor of *Trends*, which is a quadratic time trend.[8]

In addition to the standard set of controls guided by prior literature, the theory also suggests the inclusion of two additional variables. The first of these is a measure of the parent country's proximity to nonhost markets. In their study of Japanese outbound FDI into Europe, Head and Mayer (2004) use several different measures of host country market proximity and find that a distance-weighted sum of proximate countries' GDPs provides the best fit for the data.[9] Taking their lead, we construct a comparable variable, parent market proximity, which for parent country i is equal to $\sum_{j \neq i}(173/d_{ij})GDP_j$ where d_{ij} is the distance between the parent country in question (i) and other non-US countries (j).[10] Note that although the construction of this variable is analogous to the host market potential measure of Head and Mayer (2004) and Blonigen et al. (2007), its interpretation is quite different because of the parent versus host country distinction. In this previous work, we analyzed outbound FDI data, and the variable measures the proximity of the host country to additional surrounding markets that can be served by exports from this host. In this chapter we are constructing a variable that measures proximity of the parent country to other surrounding markets and thus is a measure of the ease with which firms can export from their parent country location. Also note that this variable differs from the distance between the parent country i and the United States, a standard gravity model control variable that we include separately. This parent market proximity variable captures two aspects of the theory. First, third-country GDP (GDP_j) corresponds to the demand shift parameter, β_3, in our theory section. Second, t_3, the trade costs between the parent country and country 3, are captured by the distance between the parent country and this third country. A rise in β_3 or a fall in t_3 would imply an increase in parent market proximity. Since the theory predicts that either change would increase FDI in the host, we expect that $\lambda_3 > 0$.

In addition to parent market proximity, we include information about concurrent FDI from other parent countries. This is done to investigate whether there is indeed any evidence supporting the Ω effect in the theory. The primary difficulty in doing so is that, due to the fact that FDI from i affects FDI from j and vice versa, there is an endogeneity problem that must be addressed. One possible approach is to construct instruments for the other countries' investment. An alternative, and the one we choose here, is the use of autoregressive spatial estimation. As detailed in Anselin (1988), this maximum-likelihood procedure deals with the endogeneity problem present in ordinary least squares. The spatial autocorrelation problem here is similar to the problem of time-series autocorrelation where a structure is specified through which the dependent variable in one time period predicts what occurs in the next time period.[11] Here, though, we specify a richer, two-directional structure through which a country's investment both influences and is influenced by the investment behavior of other countries. This is done using a spatial weighting matrix that assigns a larger weight to country pairs believed to influence each others' decisions more and a smaller weight to country pairs that are less likely to respond to each other.

In equation 8.12, the effect of Ω is represented by $\rho \cdot W \cdot FDI$, where FDI is a vector of investment into the United States and W is the spatial lag weighting matrix, which is an $n \times n$, block-diagonal matrix, with each block capturing a single year's observations (where n is the number of observations). In our baseline case, we weight FDI using a simple inverse distance function where the shortest distance within the sample (the 173 kilometers separating Brussels and Amsterdam) gets a weight of one and all other distances get a weight that declines with distance. This inverse distance weighting scheme results in a control variable for FDI from country i in year t of $\sum_{j \neq i}(173/d_{ij})FDI_{j,t}$ that is, a distance-weighted average of FDI from the other parent countries in year t. As is standard in spatial econometrics, we then row-standardize so that the sum of these weights equals one for each parent country. The coefficient on this term, ρ, is referred to as the spatial lag. If the spatial lag is negative, this would be consistent with the crowding-out story discussed above in which more FDI from other locations implies less FDI from the parent country in question. A positive spatial lag would be consistent with the spillover story. Note that in either case, the spatial lag only captures the net effect of FDI from other countries and does not rule out coexistence of these mechanisms. Also note that this spatial lag indicates the impact of other countries' inbound FDI and does not consider the interaction of firms from country i or capture spillovers or crowding out by U.S. firms (the effect of which is captured by the trend terms). Because the particular choice of weighting scheme is ad hoc, we use several alternative functional forms below. Furthermore, it is not clear that we should weight FDI by distance if what matters for Ω is total FDI from other sources regardless of where it comes from. Therefore, one of our alternative weighting schemes will consider this possibility.

Although spatial studies of outbound FDI have been undertaken by Coughlin and Segev (2000), Baltagi et al. (2007), and Blonigen et al. (2007), to our knowledge this technique has yet to be applied to inbound FDI data. Therefore, we are the first to consider the interaction between FDI from various parent countries. In particular, our use of inbound data implies an important difference in the interpretation of their spatial lag variable and ours. In their estimates, the spatial lag estimates the impact of FDI from a single parent country i into third country k on its FDI into j. In our estimates, the spatial lag captures the impact of FDI from third country k into j on FDI from parent country i into j. Note that this also differs from the interpretation of the results of Head, Ries, and Swenson (1995), who find evidence of agglomeration of Japanese subsidiaries in the United States, since there too the estimated effect is how FDI from a single source in one location depends on FDI from the same source in other locations.

8.3.2   Data

For our data set, we use a panel of annual data on U.S. inbound FDI from the major developed countries between 1983 and 1998, as listed in table 8.1. We chose these data for several reasons. First, the FDI from these countries is more likely homogeneous and may be more comparable across parent countries. As noted by Blonigen and Davies (2004), combining rich and poor countries in FDI data can often lead to implausible coefficient estimates. Furthermore, since the motivations behind investment from developed and developing countries may be

Table 8.1
Sample of countries and number of years in the sample

Country	Years in sample	Number of years in the sample
Australia	1984–1998	15
Austria	1984–1998	15
Belgium	1984–1998	15
Canada	1984–1998	15
Denmark	1984–1996, 1998[a]	14
Finland	1986–1996, 1998[a]	12
France	1984–1998	15
Germany	1984–1998	15
Greece	1984–1996[a]	13
Ireland	1984–1996, 1998[a]	14
Italy	1984–1998	15
Japan	1984–1998	15
Netherlands	1984–1998	15
Norway	1984–1996, 1998[a]	14
Portugal	1984–1997[a]	14
Spain	1984–1998	15
Sweden	1984–1998	15
Switzerland	1984–1998	15
Turkey	1991–1998[a]	8
United Kingdom	1984–1998	15

[a] Missing years are due to one of two reasons: either FDI data were censored by the Bureau of Economic Analysis due to confidentiality, or FDI sales reported were zero.

quite different, combining FDI from the two groups may introduce undesirable noise into the data. In addition, as demonstrated by Markusen and Maskus (2001) and Blonigen, Davies, and Head (2003), estimates relying on pooled outbound and inbound data can give very different results for variables such as skill when compared to separate regressions on each subsample. Our second reason for choosing these data is that restricting ourselves to a relatively small sample of countries greatly eases the computation time that spatial autoregressive techniques require. This is a particular issue when the weighting matrix gives positive weight to all countries in the sample, an issue we must grapple with in many of our specifications. Third, utilizing this set of countries allows a better comparison to the results of Blonigen et al. (2007), who consider U.S. outbound FDI to this same set of countries. Despite the limitations utilizing this group of countries causes, it

is worth noting that in 1996, the countries in our full sample consti-
tuted 91 percent of affiliate sales by foreign MNEs in the United States.
Finally, one added benefit of using U.S. inbound data is that compared
to European countries, the United States is far less likely to be an export platform since most output by MNEs in the United States is sold
in the United States.

Our dependent variable is the real sales by foreign affiliates in the
United States as reported by the Bureau of Economic Analysis. In unreported results, FDI stocks were used instead of affiliate sales. These
yielded qualitatively identical results to the sales results: significantly
positive parent market potential and significantly negative spatial lags
for the European subsample. (These alternative estimates are available
upon request.) We convert affiliate sales into real millions of dollars
using the chain-type price index for gross domestic investment from the
Economic Report of the President.[12] Availability of these data limits
our time period to 1983–1998. Parent country real GDP per capita and
population data come from Penn World Tables (PWT). These data run
up to 2000.[13] As is standard in gravity regressions, we included the
distance between the United States and the parent country. One interpretation of this variable is as a proxy for trade costs between the
United States and the parent, which in our model would yield a positive coefficient. It should be noted, however, that this distance can also
capture the difficulty in managing a distant subsidiary and may therefore capture the impact of such a barrier to FDI. Distance is measured
using great circle distances between capital cities, denominated in kilometers.[14] Parent country skill is measured by the average years of
schooling for those over age twenty-five, reported every five years for
1960–2000.[15] We used linear interpolation to construct values for other
years. Summary statistics for our data are found in table 8.2.

One admitted shortcoming of this data set is that it utilizes country-
level data, a potential issue since the theory of section 8.2 does not
provide clear guidelines in the mapping between an individual firm's
decisions and a country's aggregate amount of FDI. This shortcoming
plagues many studies of FDI, particularly those that seek to identify
effects generated in firm-level models. Although firm-level studies do
exist (e.g., Head and Mayer 2004), the use of country-level data is still
popular in the literature. To the extent that more aggregate country-
level data mask heterogeneous patterns at the firm or industry level,
it will bias our analysis toward not finding any statistically significant effects. For example, crowding out effects may outweigh positive

Table 8.2
Descriptive statistics

Variable	Mean	Standard deviation	Minimum	Maximum
FDI ($millions)	59,658	90,461	1	500,400
Parent GDP ($billions)	510	617	27	3,121
Parent population (thousands)	30,411	32,159	3,506	126,486
Parent skill	8.5	1.8	3.5	11.8
Parent distance from United States (km)	6,967	2,791	734	15,958
Parent market proximity ($billions)	1,107	711	78	3,332

production externalities in some industries, with the opposite true in other industries. Such patterns in the data would make an estimate of the spatial lag likely insignificant when using country-level data. As we next show, despite this aggregation bias, we find generally statistically significant results using country-level data.

8.4   Results

In our estimation, we begin with the full OECD sample. Following this, we restrict ourselves to a European subsample in order to test the sensitivity of our results. In Blonigen et al. (2007), which used U.S. outbound FDI, the results on the spatial lag term depend somewhat on whether geographic outliers such as Japan and Australia are included. Therefore it is important to look for comparable sensitivity in U.S. inbound FDI.

8.4.1   OECD Results

Table 8.3 presents our initial results from the OECD sample. Column 1 provides the standard OLS gravity estimates so that we can determine to what extent they are sensitive to the inclusion of third-country effects. As is common in gravity models of FDI, we find that most U.S. inbound FDI comes from large, skilled economies. We also find that more FDI tends to come from countries with small populations. Under the log specification, this would be consistent with more FDI from wealthy countries (i.e., holding GDP equal, those with smaller populations). In column 1 we also find that more FDI comes from countries near the United States.

Table 8.3
Spatial analysis of U.S. inbound FDI

Independent variable	OLS		ML	
	(1)	(2)	(3)	(4)
Ln(Parent GDP)	2.660	2.045	2.403	1.996
	(0.392)***	(0.347)***	(0.360)***	(0.337)***
Ln(Parent Population)	−1.279	−0.485	−0.985	−0.441
	(0.406)***	(0.363)	(0.374)***	(0.353)
Ln(Parent Skill)	6.627	7.539	6.586	7.391
	(0.444)***	(0.398)***	(0.406)***	(0.390)***
Ln(Distance from US in km)	−0.133	−0.098	−0.188	−0.132
	(0.117)	(0.102)	(0.108)*	(0.100)
Trend	−0.190	−0.216	−0.167	−0.201
	(0.068)***	(0.060)***	(0.063)***	(0.058)***
Trend^2	0.006	0.007	0.002	0.004
	(0.004)	(0.003)*	(0.004)	(0.003)
Spatially weighted FDI (i.e., $W*FDI$)			0.594	0.311
			(0.085)***	(0.117)***
Parent market proximity		0.683		0.588
		(0.072)***		(0.079)***
Constant	−41.826	−53.722	−44.555	−53.495
	(3.199)***	(3.052)***	(2.954)***	(2.965)***
Observations	284	284	284	284
Adjusted R^2/log likelihood	0.84	0.88	−410.21	−382.99

Note: Standard errors in parentheses. *Significant at 10 percent. **Significant at 5 percent. ***Significant at 1 percent.

In column 2, we add parent market proximity to the baseline gravity specification. We find that it is both positive and significant, consistent with our hypothesis that a larger market surrounding the parent country increases the opportunity cost of exporting to the host, thus increasing FDI and affiliate production in the host country. It is important to note that this is only one reason that parent market proximity may be positively correlated with FDI. An alternative explanation is that, as in many general equilibrium models of FDI with fixed costs, scale matters. Here, with a larger notion of parent market size, this positive coefficient could instead be evidence that greater parent market size, which includes nearby markets as well as the actual source country, makes it possible for a parent country to sustain more firms, increasing the number of MNEs and therefore the amount of FDI. Our other coefficients change little in terms of either significance or magnitude. In column 3, we omit the parent market proximity but include the spatial lag in the baseline gravity specification. We find that the spatial lag is positive and significant. Nevertheless, it is important to note that its inclusion does not greatly change our estimates relative to column 1. Finally, column 4 includes both the spatial lag and parent market proximity. Again, parent market proximity is significantly positive. This result is useful because it is consistent with our modeling assumption of increasing marginal production costs. Furthermore, the spatial lag is again significantly positive, although this is sensitive to the weighting scheme used.

8.4.2   Robustness to Alternative Weighting Schemes

One potential issue with the spatial lag estimates in table 8.3 is that the weighting matrix construction is ad hoc. In the theory, the term Ω represents the influence that FDI from third countries exerts on FDI from another country. There is no a priori reason to expect that this influence is an inverse function of geographic distance. Furthermore, the inverse distance weights used in table 8.3 assign positive weight to all countries, regardless of their distance from the parent country in question. Finally, it seems just as possible that distance between parent countries should not factor into Ω at all and that what matters is simply the total FDI from third countries. To examine whether these alternatives provide a different picture of the effect of third country FDI, in table 8.4 we use several alternative specifications for the weighting matrix used to construct the spatial lag term.[16]

The first alternative (the results are in column 1), uses a negative exponential weight, that is, for an observation from country i, the weight on FDI into the United States from country j is

$$w_y(d_{i,j}) = e^{-d_{i,j}/1000} \quad \forall \quad i \neq j. \tag{8.13}$$

As with the inverse distance, this too assigns positive weight to all other parent countries. Therefore, the next alternative assigns zero weight to other parent countries j beyond a certain distance from parent country i. In column 2, we use the weights

$$w_y(d_{i,j}) = \left(1 - \left(\frac{d_{i,j}}{11,155}\right)^2\right)^2 \quad \forall i \neq j \text{ if } d_{i,j} \leq 11,155; \ 0 \text{ otherwise.} \tag{8.14}$$

Table 8.4
Spatial analysis of U.S. inbound FDI: Sensitivity Tests

Independent variable	Table 8.3 (4)	Alternative weighting matrices			
		(1)	(2)	(3)	(4)
Ln(Parent GDP)	1.996	1.957	2.033	2.058	1.952
	(0.337)***	(0.343)***	(0.342)***	(0.341)***	(0.338)***
Ln(Parent Population)	−0.441	−0.375	−0.465	−0.521	−0.433
	(0.353)	(0.360)	(0.360)	(0.358)	(0.353)
Ln(Parent Skill)	7.391	7.456	7.541	7.491	7.432
	(0.390)***	(0.392)***	(0.392)***	(0.393)***	(0.388)***
Ln(Distance from US)	−0.132	−0.194	−0.126	−0.048	−0.094
	(0.100)	(0.112)*	(0.114)	(0.110)	(0.099)
Trend	−0.201	−0.213	−0.217	−0.218	−0.057
	(0.058)***	(0.058)***	(0.059)***	(0.059)***	(0.079)
Trend^2	0.004	0.006	0.006	0.008	−0.001
	(0.003)	(0.003)	(0.003)*	(0.004)**	(0.004)
Spatially weighted FDI (i.e., W^*FDI)	0.311	0.147	0.046	−0.185	−0.022
	(0.117)***	(0.079)*	(0.091)	(0.164)	(0.007)***
Parent market proximity	0.588	0.725	0.714	0.624	0.671
	(0.079)***	(0.074)***	(0.094)***	(0.088)***	(0.070)***
Constant	−53.495	−54.313	−54.479	−51.157	−49.055
	(2.965)***	(3.005)***	(3.361)***	(3.761)***	(3.365)***
Observations	284	284	284	284	284
Adjusted R^2/log likelihood	−382.99	−384.41	−386.00	−385.47	−381.89

Note: The nondiagonal weights used for the spatially weighted FDI are as follows: Table 8.3(4), $w_{i,j} = 173/d_{i,j}$; Table 8.4(1), $w_{i,j} = e^{-d_{i,j}/1000}$; Table 8.4(2), $w_{i,j} = (1 - (d_{i,j}/11,155)^2)^2$ if $d_{i,j} \le 11,155$; Table 8.4(3), $w_{i,j} = (1 - (d_{i,j}/18,074)^2)^2$ if $d_{i,j} \le 18,074$; Table 8.4(4), $w_{i,j} = 1/19$ (when all 20 countries are in the sample). All w_{ii} are set equal to zero.

Standard errors in parentheses. *Significant at 10 percent. **Significant at 5 percent. ***Significant at 1 percent.

In our sample, the smallest maximum separation of any country pair (the distance between Lisbon and Tokyo) is 11,155 kilometers, whereas the largest maximum separation is 18,074 kilometers (the distance between Lisbon and Sydney). As such, this scheme gives positive weight only to pairings closer than 11,155. Because this weighting scheme uses the minimum maximum distance as a cutoff, with apologies to game theorists everywhere, we refer to this as the minmax weight. The third weighting scheme, found in column 3, is similar to the minmax weight in form but assigns positive weights to all countries except the pair with the greatest distance. This scheme is is given by

$$w_y(d_{i,j}) = \left(1 - \left(\frac{d_{i,j}}{18,074}\right)^2\right)^2 \quad \forall i \neq j \text{ if } d_{i,j} \leq 18,074; \text{ 0 otherwise.} \quad (8.15)$$

Since this weighting scheme uses the maximum maximum distance between countries as the cutoff point, we refer to it as the "maxmax" weight. Finally, column 4 does not weight by distance at all. Here, the weight is

$$w_y(d_{i,j}) = 1 \quad \forall i \neq j; \text{ 0 otherwise} \quad (8.16)$$

implying that the spatial lag is the total FDI from all other countries j.[17] We refer to this as equal weights.

As table 8.4 shows, similar to table 8.3's column 4, which is repeated in table 8.4, the magnitude and significance of the standard gravity model variables change little across the various weighting matrix specifications. Parent market proximity also does not change greatly across the various specifications and is significantly positive across specifications. Thus, it appears that this too is reasonably robust to the way in which third-country FDI is included in the regression. The spatial lag term, however, is rather dependent on the choice of weighting matrix. Across the five weighting matrices, the spatial lag is negative once, insignificant twice, and positive twice. It is worth noting that the one negative coefficient is the one that assigns the greatest relative weight to distant countries, suggesting lines of possible future exploration. Thus, no clear-cut conclusions can be drawn regarding the potential impact or importance of third-country FDI in the OECD data. Although the specification with the highest log likelihood is the negative exponential weight where the spatial lag is positive and significant, the difference in log likelihoods is small. Unfortunately, as discussed by Anselin (1988), there is no good mechanism for choosing a preferred

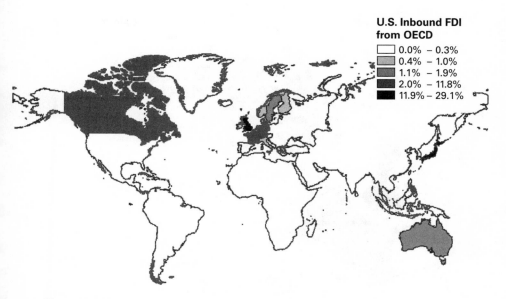

Figure 8.1
Sample of OECD in 1996
Note: Sample countries were Australia, Austria, Belgium, Canada, Denmark, Finland, France, Germany, Greece, Ireland, Italy, Japan, Netherlands, Norway, Portugal, Spain, Sweden, Switzerland, Turkey, and the United Kingdom.

weighting matrix.[18] We must therefore conclude that although the parent market proximity effect is reasonably robust in the OECD data, the same is not true for the spatial lag.

8.4.3   European Results

As illustrated in figure 8.1, nearly 40 percent of U.S. inbound FDI in our sample comes from three countries: Australia, Canada, and Japan in 1996. One factor that sets these three countries apart from the others is their geographic isolation; the others are relatively tightly packed into Europe. To examine the extent to which these geographic outliers influence our results, we next restrict our data set to the European countries as illustrated in figure 8.2.[19] In table 8.5, we repeat our regressions from table 8.3 using this subsample. In column 1, we include only the standard set of gravity model variables. As in the full sample, we find that most FDI comes from large, skilled parent countries. Also like the OECD results, we find that as in most other studies of FDI, distance from the United States is a detriment to FDI. Unlike the OECD results, parent population is insignificant.

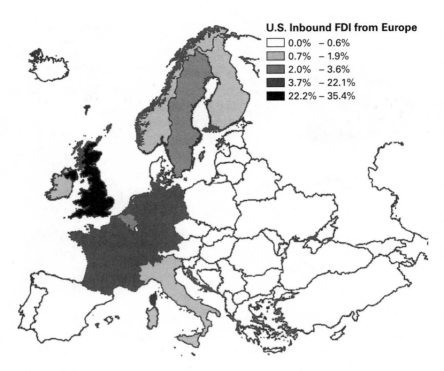

Figure 8.2
Sample of European OECD in 1996
Note: Sample countries were Austria, Belgium, Denmark, Finland, France, Germany, Greece, Ireland, Italy, Netherlands, Norway, Portugal, Spain, Sweden, Switzerland, Turkey, and the United Kingdom.

Turning to the parent market proximity variable, as in OECD regressions, it is positive and significant. A key difference between the European and OECD results, however, is that including parent market proximity does affect the coefficients of two gravity model variables: parent country GDP and parent country population. In both columns 2 and 4, including parent market proximity reduces the point estimate of parent country GDP by about half. This suggests that at least in this sample, excluding this variable tends to overstate the importance of the parent country's size. In addition, including parent market proximity switches the sign of parent country population from negative to positive (although it remains insignificant).

Like the OECD results, the European data yield a significantly positive spatial lag in column 3. However, as the results of column 4 demonstrate, this is sensitive to the inclusion of parent market proximity.

Table 8.5
Spatial analysis of U.S. inbound FDI from European OECD

Independent variable	OLS		Spatial ML	
	(1)	(2)	(3)	(4)
Ln(Parent GDP)	1.778	0.993	1.707	0.954
	(0.413)***	(0.365)***	(0.392)***	(0.360)***
Ln(Parent Population)	−0.220	0.369	−0.168	0.400
	(0.431)	(0.375)	(0.408)	(0.369)
Ln(Parent Skill)	7.953	7.132	7.680	7.165
	(0.470)***	(0.414)***	(0.451)***	(0.406)***
Ln(Distance from U.S. in km)	−3.665	−0.833	−3.070	−0.817
	(0.696)***	(0.673)	(0.675)***	(0.659)
Trend	−0.172	−0.244	−0.160	−0.254
	(0.073)**	(0.063)***	(0.069)**	(0.063)***
Trend^2	0.007	0.009	0.004	0.010
	(0.004)	(0.004)**	(0.004)	(0.004)***
Spatially weighted FDI (i.e., $W*FDI$)			0.435	−0.162
			(0.106)***	(0.157)
Parent market proximity		1.713		1.857
		(0.187)***		(0.230)***
Constant	−6.859	−55.772	−14.590	−57.009
	(7.755)	(8.534)***	(7.589)*	(8.447)***
Observations	239	239	239	239
Adjusted R^2/log likelihood	0.85	0.89	−345.44	−314.56

Note: Standard errors in parentheses. *Significant at 10 percent. **Significant at 5 percent. ***Significant at 1 percent.

This omitted variable bias suggests that parent market proximity and the FDI from third countries are positively correlated, a finding reinforced by the rise in the coefficient on parent market proximity when the spatial lag is included. Since, as our estimates indicate, large countries tend to undertake more FDI, it is not surprising that proximity to large countries also tends to mean proximity to large sources of FDI. In any case, the results of the preferred specification in column 4 suggest at most a crowding-out story in which the presence of multinationals from other countries decreases the net benefit of FDI from the country in question. Note that this is quite different from the results in columns 3 and 4. Thus, as in Blonigen et al. (2007), the exclusion of the geographic outliers tends to increase the estimated coefficient of the spatial lag.[20]

In table 8.6, we again use four alternative weighting matrices for the spatial lag.[21] Note that both the minmax and the maxmax weights were adjusted to reflect changes in the maximum distances the sample change created. Here, our results change little across the various weighting matrices. In each, parent market proximity is significantly positive. The spatial lag is negative in each specification, although again it is significant only when using weighting schemes that give relatively greater importance to distant countries. Using the results of column 4, we find that a 1 percent rise in FDI by all other parent countries decreases FDI by the remaining parent country by 0.02 percent.[22] This suggests that to the extent that crowding out occurs, it happens on a less than one-to-one basis. Thus, regardless of how we combine third countries' FDI, we find that more FDI comes from countries nearer to other large markets. Furthermore, our estimates suggest that more FDI from one European country appears to crowd out FDI from another and that this effect is less than one-to-one.

Finally, in unreported results, we in turn dropped Belgium, the Netherlands, and the Scandinavian countries.[23] In each of these, we found a positive parent market proximity coefficient and a negative spatial lag. This indicates that the European results are robust to subsamples within Europe and that the exclusion of the three geographic outliers is the driving force of the difference between the OECD and European samples.

8.5   Conclusion

The goal of this chapter has been to provide some initial insights into how the presence of other parent countries might affect how much FDI a particular parent country undertakes into a given host country. This line of thought is intended to complement the existing work on how the presence of additional host countries affects how much FDI a given host receives. Using a simple model, we suggest two avenues for such effects: parent market proximity and interaction between FDI from different parents. Using data of OECD and European FDI flows into the United States, we find strong evidence for a positive effect of parent market proximity. However, only in the European subsample do we find a consistent effect of FDI from other countries. There, we find that the more FDI that other countries have in the United States, the less FDI a given parent country will have. This would be consistent with increased competition in input or output markets by these other coun-

Table 8.6
Spatial analysis of U.S. inbound FDI: Sensitivity tests from European OECD

Independent variable	Table 5 (4)	Alternative weighting matrices			
		(1)	(2)	(3)	(4)
Ln(Parent GDP)	0.954	1.020	1.224	1.156	0.930
	$(0.360)^{***}$	$(0.357)^{***}$	$(0.403)^{***}$	$(0.345)^{***}$	$(0.354)^{***}$
Ln(Parent Population)	0.400	0.319	0.121	0.080	0.396
	(0.369)	(0.369)	(0.418)	(0.360)	(0.364)
Ln(Parent Skill)	7.165	7.160	7.125	6.960	7.036
	$(0.406)^{***}$	$(0.405)^{***}$	$(0.405)^{***}$	$(0.390)^{***}$	$(0.402)^{***}$
Ln(Distance from US)	−0.817	−0.971	−1.231	−1.662	−0.814
	(0.659)	(0.665)	$(0.732)^{*}$	$(0.668)^{**}$	(0.651)
Trend	−0.254	−0.254	−0.262	−0.228	−0.105
	$(0.063)^{***}$	$(0.062)^{***}$	$(0.063)^{***}$	$(0.059)^{***}$	(0.080)
Trend^2	0.010	0.010	0.010	0.013	0.002
	$(0.004)^{***}$	$(0.004)^{***}$	$(0.004)^{***}$	$(0.004)^{***}$	(0.004)
Spatially weighted FDI (i.e., W^*FDI)	−0.162	−0.227	−0.153	−0.849	−0.021
	(0.157)	(0.167)	(0.123)	$(0.229)^{***}$	$(0.008)^{***}$
Parent market proximity	1.857	1.805	1.727	1.456	1.676
	$(0.230)^{***}$	$(0.195)^{***}$	$(0.183)^{***}$	$(0.188)^{***}$	$(0.182)^{***}$
Constant	−57.009	−54.496	−53.127	−35.836	−51.839
	$(8.447)^{***}$	$(8.394)^{***}$	$(8.620)^{***}$	$(9.629)^{***}$	$(8.395)^{***}$
Observations	239	239	239	239	239
Adjusted R^2/log likelihood	−314.56	−314.16	−314.33	−307.85	−311.56

Note: The nondiagonal weights used for the spatially weighted FDI are as follows: Table 8.5(4), $w_{i,j} = 173/d_{i,j}$; Table 8.6(1), $w_{i,j} = e^{-d_{i,j}/1000}$; Table 8.6(2), $w_{i,j} = (1 - (d_{i,j}/11{,}155)^2)^2$ if $d_{i,j} \leq 11{,}155$; Table 8.6(3), $w_{i,j} = (1 - (d_{i,j}/18{,}074)^2)^2$ if $d_{i,j} \leq 18{,}074$; Table 8.6(4), $w_{i,j} = 1/19$ (when all twenty countries are in the sample). All w_{ii} are set equal to zero.

Standard errors in parentheses. *Significant at 10 percent. **Significant at 5 percent. ***Significant at 1 percent.

tries' multinationals. An alternative explanation is that this represents the fact that the bulk of FDI occurs through mergers and acquisitions. If the supply of acquisition targets is limited, acquisition of a target by one country naturally reduces opportunities for acquisition FDI by other countries. We leave further investigation of this intriguing possibility for future research.

This latter effect suggests that such crowding out appears to be the dominant force at play in the European sample. However, two critical caveats must be noted. First, this is only the net effect from third-country FDI. As such it should not be interpreted as implying that no positive production externalities exist. Second, we are dealing with highly aggregated data for the purpose of comparing our results to the bulk of the literature. This level of aggregation may mask important interactions at the industry or firm level that we do not capture. In addition to the obvious possibility that spillovers dominate crowding out in some industries but not others, there is the possibility for reincorporation issues. For example, suppose that due to a favorable tax environment in a country j proximate to a given parent country i, firms initially located in i will find it beneficial to reincorporate in country j. Thus, as FDI from j rises, FDI from i would fall. Nevertheless, our hope is that our results here highlight the potential usefulness of considering the impact of other parent countries on FDI and that they spur both more detailed theory and empirical work in this area.

Notes

We thank participants at the CES-Ifo's Venice Summer Institute's Workshop, "Recent Developments in International Trade: Globalization and the Multinational Enterprise." In particular, we thank Maarten Bosker, Joseph François, James Markusen, and three anonymous referees for useful comments. Any errors or omissions are our responsibilities.

1. In the interest of brevity, we assume that the firm is a multinational. Such decisions lie at the heart of many models of FDI as discussed by Markusen (2002). Our model could easily be broadened to include the choice of whether to go multinational. There, because of the need to cover additional fixed costs when setting up the host plant, this choice would depend on host market size and the relative cost savings (avoiding transport costs and the increasing parent country marginal cost). Since formal presentation of this possibility does not significantly contribute to our goals for this section, we omit it.

2. In the rest of this section we refer to parent country 2 as simply the "parent country."

3. Our theory can certainly encompass this possibility, however. The primary change is that an increase in trade costs between 1 and 2 would decrease the need for overseas production.

4. This latter assumption is guaranteed if the inverse demand functions are concave.

5. In an alternative model, suppose that the MNE has a fixed supply of a factor that it must allocate between production facilities in each of the three countries. In this case, an increase in the size of country 3 would lead the firm to reallocate this limited resource away from country 1 toward country 3. This would yield an opposite effect from the one here. In any case, our results reject such an effect in the data.

6. In unreported results, we also included the inverse of parent openness, measured as Parent GDP/(Parent imports + Parent exports) to proxy for parent trade costs. However, since the theory treats parent country trade as an endogenous variable, using this as a control variable created some problematic interpretative issues. In any case, when this was included, we found qualitatively identical results for our variables of interest. The only notable change is that when including this additional variable (which was typically significantly negative in the regressions), the distance between the parent and the United States was typically insignificant in the OECD results. These alternative estimates are available on request.

7. These alternative results are available on request. The omitted variables include U.S. GDP, population, openness, skill, and an index of investment barriers.

8. In unreported specifications, we replace *Trends* with a set of year dummies. This did not alter the qualitative results of our estimation.

9. Since our host country is the United States in all observations, as with the other U.S. variables, we exclude host market potential in favor of quadratic trends.

10. In line with the FDI weighting matrix discussed below, the 173 is the shortest distance between country pairs, implying that Belgium's GDP gets a weight of one for the Netherlands and vice versa. Since this is a constant, this simply scales the estimated coefficient on parent market proximity.

11. This similarity is the root of the term *spatial lag*.

12. The Bureau of Economic Analysis FDI data can be found at http://www.bea.gov/bea/di/home/directinv.htm. The price deflator can be found at http://www.gpoaccess.gov/usbudget/fy05/sheets/b7.xls.

13. The PWT Version 6.1 data are available online at http://pwt.econ.upenn.edu/php_site/pwt_index.php.

14. With the exception of Belgium, these data were provided by Raymond Robertson at his Web site. Belgian distances were acquired from http://www.indo.com. Alternatives to measuring distance between capital cities may result in different estimates for our spatial lag, particularly for geographically large countries such as Canada. This is an additional benefit to investigating the European subsample as this is presumably less of a problem in these geographically smaller countries.

15. Acquired from Barro and Lee (2001), International Data on Educational Attainment.

16. Throughout table 8.4 we use the same inverse-distance weighting scheme for parent market proximity. We do this to isolate the impact the weighting matrix has on the spatial lag's estimated coefficient.

17. Note that with this scheme, unlike the others, we do not row-standardize. This is because doing so converts this term into average FDI from countries other than i. By construction, this average is going to be bigger for countries with small amounts of FDI and

smaller for countries with large amounts of FDI. This then will tend to lead to a negative coefficient on the spatial lag simply as a result of the variable's construction.

18. As Anselin (1988) discusses in chapter 14, depending on the criterion used, the relative ranking of weighting matrices can change dramatically. Furthermore, since choosing a different weighting matrix is tantamount to choosing a different control variable, such comparisons do not have analogies to comparisons between restricted and unrestricted estimations.

19. In 1996, this subsample was 55 percent of total U.S. inbound FDI; therefore, we are still discussing a large share of overall U.S. inbound FDI.

20. It is worth noting that in the OECD results with equal weights, the results look similar to the European results. Thus, in the one regression using the OECD data in which space does not affect the spatial lag (the one in which spatial outliers do not appear as such), we find similar results in the two samples.

21. As in table 8.2, throughout table 8.6 we use the same inverse-distance weighting scheme for parent market proximity.

22. Note that this is a partial equilibrium effect since this decrease in FDI from the parent in question would feed back into the FDI from the other parent countries creating a multiplier effect. In this case, the comparative static would depend on the parent country in question because the particular weighting matrix to calculate this "spatial externality" varies by country. For details on this, see Anselin (2003).

23. The Scandinavian countries excluded were Denmark, Norway, Sweden, and Finland. When we drop those countries that in 1996 composed less than 1 percent of U.S. inbound FDI, from Europe the results using sales data do not converge.

References

Anselin, Luc. (1988). *Spatial Econometrics: Methods and Models*. Norwood, Mass.: Kluwer.

Anselin, Luc. (2003). Spatial Externalities, Spatial Muliapliers, and Spatial Econometrics. *International Regional Science Review* 26, 153–166.

Baltagi, Badi H., Peter Egger, and Michael Pfaffermayr. (2007). Estimating Models of Complex FDI: Are There Third-Country Effects? *Journal of Econometrics* 127, 260–281.

Barro, R., and J. W. Lee. (2001). International Data on Educational Attainment: Updates and Implications. *Oxford Economic Papers* 53(3), 541–563.

Bergstrand, Jeffrey H., and Peter Egger. (2004). A Theoretical and Empirical Model of International Trade and Foreign Direct Investment with Outsourcing: Part I, Developed Countries. Mimeo.

Blomström, Magnus, and Ari Kokko. (1998). Multinational Corporations and Spillovers. *Journal of Economic Surveys* 12, 247–277.

Blonigen, Bruce A., and Ronald B. Davies. (2004). The Effects of Bilateral Tax Treaties on US FDI Activity. *International Tax and Public Finance* 11(5), 601–622.

Blonigen, Bruce A., Ronald B. Davies, and Keith Head. (2003). Estimating the Knowledge-Capital Model of the Multinational Enterprise: Comment. *American Economic Review* 93, 980–994.

Blonigen, Bruce A., Ronald B. Davies, Glen R. Waddell, and Helen T. Naughton. (2007). FDI in Space: Spatial Autoregressive Relationships in Foreign Direct Investment. *European Economic Review* 51, 1303–1325.

Brainard, S. Lael. (1997). An Empirical Assessment of the Proximity-Concentration Trade-off Between Multinational Sales and Trade. *American Economic Review* 87(4), 520–544.

Carr, David L., James R. Markusen, and Keith E. Maskus. (2001). Estimating the Knowledge-Capital Model of the Multinational Enterprise. *American Economic Review* 91(3), 693–708.

Caves, Richard E. (1996). *Multinational Enterprise and Economic Analysis*. Cambridge: Cambridge University Press.

Coughlin, Cletus, and Eran Segev. (2000). Foreign Direct Investment in China: A Spatial Econometric Study. *World Economy* 23(1), 1–23.

Eaton, Jonathan, and Akiko Tamura. (1994). Bilateralism and Regionalism in Japanese and US Trade and Direct Foreign Investment Patterns. *Journal of the Japanese and International Economies* 8(4), 478–510.

Ekholm, Karolina, Rikard Forslid, and James R. Markusen. (2007). Export-Platform Foreign Direct Investment. *Journal of the European Economics Association* 5, 776–795.

Head, Keith, and Thierry Mayer. (2004). Market Potential and the Location of Japanese Investment in the European Union. *Review of Economics and Statistics* 86, 959–972.

Head, Keith, John Ries, and Deborah Swenson. (1995). Agglomeration Benefits and Location Choice: Evidence from Japanese Manufacturing Investments in the United States. *Journal of International Economics* 38(3–4), 223–247.

Helpman, Elhanan, Marc J. Melitz, and Stephen R. Yeaple. (2004). Export Versus FDI with Heterogeneous Firms. *American Economic Review* 94(1), 300–316.

Markusen, James R. (1984). Multinationals, Multi-Plant Economies, and the Gains from Trade. *Journal of International Economics* 16(3–4), 205–226.

Markusen, James R. (2002). *Multinational Firms and the Theory of International Trade*. Cambridge, Mass.: MIT Press.

Markusen, James R., and Keith E. Maskus. (2001). Multinational Firms: Reconciling Theory and Evidence. In Magnus Blomström and Linda S. Goldberg (eds.), *Topics in Empirical International Economics: A Festschrift in Honor of Robert E. Lipsey*. Chicago: University of Chicago Press.

Yeaple, Stephen R. (2003). The Complex Integration Strategies of Multinationals and Cross Country Dependencies in the Structure of Foreign Direct Investment. *Journal of International Economics* 60(2), 293–314.

9   Do Italian Firms Improve Their Performance at Home by Investing Abroad?

Giorgio Barba Navaretti and
Davide Castellani

9.1   Introduction

The effects at home of the transfer of economic activities abroad, either through foreign investment or through arm-length contracts, is a widely debated issue. This chapter contributes to this debate by assessing how the home activities of manufacturing firms in Italy change following the setting up of foreign subsidiaries abroad.

The debate on outsourcing in the United States and in the United Kingdom has mostly focused on services. In contrast, continental European countries are concerned with the loss of manufacturing jobs, particularly in traditional industries. Accordingly, policymakers in several European countries and in the European Union (EU) have responded to public concerns by introducing measures hindering this process.

However, public opinion and policy responses are often formed on a superficial understanding of outsourcing. Indeed, the issue is not simple. Theoretically, the transfer of national resources from home to foreign countries, either developed or developing, taking place through outward investment or arm's-length contracts may be predicted to have both positive and negative consequences on home activities. Empirically this process is hard to gauge, as it needs to be observed at the firm level, and sufficiently detailed firm-level data are rarely available.

This chapter contributes to the assessment of the effects of outsourcing by focusing on foreign direct investment, one of the channels through which firms transfer their activities abroad. It is based on a firm-level data set of Italian firms with foreign investment between 1993 and 1998. It has two key features.

First, it focuses on firms that change status from national to multinational by investing abroad for the first time. By restricting this analysis to firms changing status, we believe we are in a better position to isolate the effect of investing abroad. In fact, while we agree that the effects of the investment by nonswitchers are also important and should be taken into account, our aim here is capturing the effects of discrete changes in investment behavior (new investments rather than ongoing ones) on performance. We believe that focusing on first-time investors is an original way to isolate this factor. Including non-switchers would make it difficult to isolate the impacts of new investments from those of ongoing ones.

Second, it uses propensity score matching to construct an appropriate counterfactual of national firms that do not invest abroad and a difference-in-difference (DID) estimator to compare the performance of the two types of firms. Constructing an appropriate counterfactual is essential. The effects of outward investments on home activities are relevant not only for themselves but also with respect to what would have happened if firms had not invested abroad. For example, although home employment is observed to decline, perhaps it would have declined even more if these firms had not invested. Albeit this cannot be observed, their hypothetical behavior can be proxied by the behavior of a sample of other firms that have not invested. Furthermore, the use of DID reinforces a causal interpretation of our results by comparing performance trajectories before and after the investment.

We find that the home performance of Italian firms that invested abroad for the first time during the period analyzed improved after the investment. The postinvestment rate of growth of output and productivity is higher than the one observed over the same period for the counterfactual of noninvesting firms. Also, there is no significant evidence of a slowdown of the rate of employment growth. Thus, the evidence supports the view that foreign investments strengthen rather than deplete economic activities at home.

This result is in line with those of Egger and Pfaffermayr (2003), who used a methodology similar to ours on a sample of Austrian firms and found that firms investing abroad also raised their investments in R&D and in intangible assets at home. Other studies on foreign direct investment (FDI) based on other methodologies also generally find evidence that outward investments do not deplete home activities. These earlier empirical works have examined the effects of outward FDI on output (Head and Ries 2001, Blonigen 2001), home employment (Brainard and Riker 1997a, 1997b; Braconier and Ekholm 2001; Konigs and Murphy 2001; Bruno and Falzoni 2003; Blomstrom, Fors, and Lipsey 1997; Lipsey 1999; Mariotti, Mutinelli, and Piscitello 2003; Marin 2004), and productivity (Braconier, Eckholm, and Midelfart Knarvik 2001; Van Pottelsberghe de la Potterie and Lichtenberg 2001). However, they focus at either the sectoral/regional level or, when addressing the question at the firm level, on the activities of multinational enterprises (MNEs) and thus fail to take into account the appropriate counterfactual to this problem.

Our result is also in line with other studies that analyzed this issue but by looking at other measures of outsourcing. For example, Gorg, Hanley, and Strobl (2004), measuring outsourcing by the share of imported inputs at the firm level, find that in a sample of Irish firms, the effect of outsourcing tends to be positive, particularly for large firms and those based in broader international exports (they are foreign owned or are exporters). Finally, work on outsourcing based on industry data does not find negative effect, for the outsourcing of services and material inputs (Amiti and Wei 2004).

The next section outlines the main analytical issues and our empirical strategies. Section 9.3 discusses the methodology used to construct DID estimators. Section 9.4 describes the sample and section 9.5 the construction of the counterfactual. Section 9.6 estimates the effects of investing abroad, and section 9.7 concludes.

9.2   Analyzing the Performance of Investing Firms: The Issue

9.2.1   Analytical Issues
The key concern for policymakers is the effect of foreign investment on the size of economic activity at home. Theories of horizontal and vertical investment do not provide a clear answer to this concern. In particular, both rationales for an increase and for a decrease of employment and output at home can be found in this literature (see Barba Navaretti et al. 2004 for a thorough discussion of this issue). The direction of the effect mainly depends on whether firms substitute domestic labor and output with foreign activities or whether expanding foreign activities complement domestic ones.

Typically horizontal investment is carried out to serve a foreign market and tends to be an alternative to exporting. In this perspective, it could cause a reduction in domestic output. Yet a number of arguments may counter this prediction. First, export may not always be a convenient option in certain sectors and markets (e.g., if tariffs of transport cost are too high), so horizontal investment need not substitute for exporting. Second, in multiproduct firms, FDI, by allowing access to foreign markets, may induce a sort of bandwagon effect for other varieties produced by the same firm, which could eventually be produced in home plants and exported. Third, horizontal investments may well determine an increase in the need for coordination activities and other headquarter services (such as finance, advertising, and R&D), which would largely be carried at home.

Vertical investment involves breaking up activities and the transfering part of them abroad. This is likely changing the division of labor within a firm and shedding relatively more unskilled labor at home but increasing the need for skilled workers. Yet by transferring part of their production abroad, the firm may reduce unit costs and become more competitive; it could gain market shares finally increase output in the other home plants.

The other key effect is the contribution of FDI to productivity growth. Even in this case, theoretical predictions are not clear-cut, for both horizontal and vertical investment. There are three main reasons why opening and running foreign subsidiaries affect domestic productivity: the exploitation of firm-level and plant-level scale economies, the change in the composition of inputs used in production, and the opening of new channels of international sourcing of technological and managerial knowledge. These sources of productivity change may work in both directions, depending on the features of the investment.

The effect of changes in output induced by horizontal investment depends on the interplay between plant- and firm-level scale economies; if firm-level scale economies are predominant, then productivity is likely to be enhanced by the expansion of the worldwide activities of the firm; if plant-level scale economies dominate instead, duplicating activities may increase unit costs.

As for vertical investment, home activities could be strengthened or impoverished by changes in their factor use. If, for example, labor-intensive activities are transferred abroad, human-capital-intensive activities at home might become more efficient. In contrast, if there are strong economies of integration between both types of activities, splitting them apart could be costly.

Finally, whatever the type of investment, technologies could be acquired in foreign markets or get dispersed to foreign competitors;

In other words, the fact that we find both positive and negative outcomes of outward investment on the scale and the efficiency of home activities is not inconsistent with theory. For this reason, the issue essentially boils down to an empirical one.

9.2.2   The Empirical Setting

An empirical test of the effects of foreign investments on performance at home poses several methodological problems. First, if we observe only MNEs, we cannot single out the hypothetical benchmark: performance if the firm had not invested abroad. Moreover, if we observe only MNEs, we do not know if changes in performance are due to unobservable shocks equally affecting all firms, national and multinational alike. It is therefore important to benchmark MNEs to a sample of national firms. However, when comparing the performance of MNEs and national firms, we face a second problem: we do not know if differences are due to other observable or unobservable characteristics of the two types of firms (e.g., size, ability of management) rather than to their being multinational or strictly national. In particular, foreign investments and performance are jointly determined. Given that investing abroad has large costs, with imperfect financial markets only the (ex ante), most productive firms will invest abroad. The recent theoretical literature on the decision to export and invest abroad with heterogeneous firms establishes a very clear link between ex ante performance and international activities (Helpman, Melitz, and Yeaple 2004). Thus, if we observe that ex post MNEs perform better than national firms, we do not know if this is so because of foreign investments or because these firms performed better anyway, even before the investment.

To address these problems empirically, it is possible to draw on the well-established literature investigating the effects of exporting on firms' performance (Bernard and Jensen 1999; Clerides, Lach, and Tybout 1998; Aw, Chung, and Roberts 2000; Castellani 2002; Delgado, Farinas, and Ruano 2002; Girma, Kneller, and Pisu 2005; Kraay 1999). The exporter faces the same problem as a firm investing abroad. Consequently, the analysis of the effects of these two decisions raises similar methodological problems.

To illustrate the kind of exercise we carry out in this chapter, it is useful to discuss figure 9.1 which we adapt to the case of foreign investments. We draw average hypothetical trajectories in home performance for three types of firms: those that are always MNEs, with at least one foreign subsidiary during the period observed; those that never have a foreign subsidiary in the period observed (NATIONAL); and those that open their first foreign subsidiary in the period observed and therefore switch from being national to being MNEs (SWs, or switching firms) at time t.

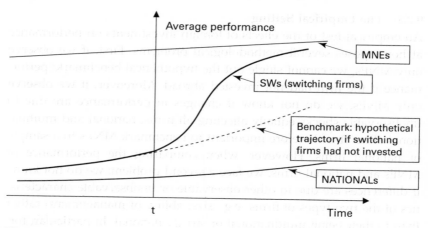

Figure 9.1
Performance trajectories in home plants
Source: Clerides, Lach, and Tybout (1998).

Compare the trajectory of MNEs and NATIONALs. We assume that MNEs perform better than NATIONALs. This assumption reflects what emerges from all available studies: on average, MNEs at home always perform better than NATIONALs (Barba Navaretti et al. 2004; Castellani and Zanfei 2006; Criscuolo and Martin 2002; Girma et al. 2003; Doms and Jensen 1998; Pfaffermayr and Bellak 2002; Bellman and Jungnickel 2002). However, the trajectory of MNEs could lie above the one of NATIONALs because they were the best-performing firms even before becoming multinational or because performance improved as a result of international production

More can be learned if we now focus on SWs—those that invest for the first time at t_0. If the investment has a positive effect on productivity, their trajectory becomes steeper at t_0 and performance converges to the one of MNEs. Thus, our empirical question can be answered by comparing their trajectory after the investment to the one that they would have followed had they not invested. If the investment does indeed improve performance, this hypothetical trajectory lies below the one of the SWs after t, as represented by the dotted line in figure 9.1. This comparison is important; if we focus on just effective performance, even if we observe that it improves, this could be the outcome of other unobserved random factors that have nothing to do with the investment. Unfortunately, the dotted line cannot be observed, and we need to proxy it. Good candidates for the counterfactual are NATIONAL firms, so we could compare the performance trajectory of SWs with the one of NATIONALs. However, we still have a problem. The trajectory of the appropriate counterfactual should differ from the one of SWs because of the different investment decision. But firms are heterogeneous, even within the same industry, and SWs could be different from NATIONALs even before the investment. The assumption of most of the literature is that operating in a foreign environment involves additional costs and risks, so only firms possessing some intangible capital, giving them a competitive edge over national firms, are able to overcome such disadvantages and invest abroad (Dunning 1993, Markusen 1995). Because of this self-selection, the average NATIONAL is not a good benchmark: it is ex ante different from the SW, and this difference may affect ex post performance. Accordingly, we draw the performance trajectory of SWs before the investment above the one of NATIONALs. If we want to isolate the effect of investing, we need to build a counterfactual made of NATIONALs that are as similar as possible to firms that have invested.

To do so, we derive a control group from a propensity score matching procedure. The performance trajectory of this control group is the closest approximation to the dotted line. We will then be able to compare postinvestment performances in the two groups. We will use standard matching estimators that essentially compare the post-t slope of the thick line to the one of the dotted line and DID estimators, which compare the change in the slope of the thick line and of the dotted line before and after t.

9.3   The Evaluation Problem: Propensity Score Matching and Difference-in-Difference Estimators

Our aim is to evaluate the effect of becoming a multinational firm on economic performance at home, Δy (where Δy denotes the rate of growth of employment, output, or total factor productivity, TFP).[1] To gather this effect, we need to understand what would have happened to the firm's economic performance had it not invested abroad. Let SW_{it} be an indicator taking a value equal to one if firm i switches to becoming a multinational by investing abroad for the first time at time t (i.e., between $t-1$ and t). Let also $\Delta y^1_{i,t+1}$ be firm i's postinvestment performance and $\Delta y^0_{i,t+1}$ the hypothetical performance achieved at $t + 1$ had i not invested abroad. The effect of investing abroad on economic performances for firm i would then be measured by $\Delta y^1_{i,t+1} - \Delta y^0_{i,t+1}$. More formally, this average effect can be expressed as follows:[2]

$$\hat{\alpha} = E(\Delta y^1_{t+1} - \Delta y^0_{t+1} | SW_{it} = 1)$$

$$= E(\Delta y^1_{t+1} | SW_{it} = 1) - E(\Delta y^0_{t+1} | SW_{it} = 1). \qquad (9.1)$$

The key problem is that the last term is unobservable, that is, we do not know what would have been the average performance of SWs if they had not invested. We need to find an appropriate measure for the last term in our sample; in other words, we need to construct an appropriate counterfactual based on the right control group. If we were to run a natural experiment, we could randomly draw a sample of firms from a population and let half invest and the other half not invest. The latter group would be the appropriate control group. Unfortunately, as argued in section 9.2, firms choose endogenously whether to invest.

To overcome the problem of self-selection, we use the method of matching, which aims at reestablishing the conditions of a natural experiment with nonexperimental data (Heckman, Ichimura, and Todd 1997; Blundell and Costa Dias 2002). This methodology has also been used to evaluate the effects of exporting and of acquisitions on firms' performances and returns to scale by Girma, Greenaway, and Kneller (2004), Girma et al. (2005), Wagner (2002), and Girma and Gorg (2007). Egger and Pfaffermayr (2003) use matching estimators to analyze the effects of outward investments on the decision to invest at home in tangible assets and in R&D.

The idea is to construct an appropriate counterfactual by matching each investing firm with one with similar characteristics drawn from a sample of noninvesting ones. Here we use the nearest-neighbour matching, based on the propensity score method, which computes the probability of investing (the propensity score) conditional on a number of observables. To obtain a measure of the effect of investing abroad on performance at home as free as possible from any self-selection bias, we first estimate a probit model of the decision to become an MNE, which can be represented as

$$P(SW_{it} = 1 | X_{i,t-1}),$$

where $X_{i,t-1}$ is a vector of observable firm i's characteristics at $t - 1$.

It is then possible to compute the probability of switching (propensity score) for each firm and pair each investor with its nearest neighbor, that is, the noninvesting firm with the closest propensity score. In other words, we build a sample where for each investing firm, there is a firm that had a very similar ex ante probability of switching but remained national. This latter group is our counterfactual. Subsequently, the average treatment effect on the treated can be obtained by comparing average performances in the group of investing firms and in the counterfactual, as illustrated by the following equation,

$$\hat{\alpha}_{SM} = \Delta \bar{y}_{t+1}^1 - \Delta \bar{y}_{t+1}^0 \qquad (9.2)$$

where $\Delta \bar{y}_{t+1}^1$ is the mean performance growth of investing firms after switching and $\Delta \bar{y}_{t+1}^0$ is a weighted mean of performance growth of the control group over the same period.[3] In other words, the average treatment effect on the treated (ATT) can be thought of as a test for the equality of means in performance growth over the switching and the matched control groups.

For the ATT, we also compute a DID estimator. Whereas the ATT compares postinvestment performance growth for the two groups of firms, the DID estimator compares the difference between pre- and postinvestment performance growth in both groups. Formally DID, is given by

$$\hat{\alpha}_{DID} = (\Delta \bar{y}_{t+1}^1 - \Delta \bar{y}_{t-1}^1) - (\Delta \bar{y}_{t+1}^0 - \Delta \bar{y}_{t-1}^0), \qquad (9.3)$$

where the over bars denote averages in each group performance before $t-1$ and after $t+1$, the investment year. In substance, the DID measures the differential performance in the group of investing firms relative to the noninvesting ones once ex ante differences in performance are accounted for. It eliminates time-invariant unobserved heterogeneity that might not be captured by matching.

Both ATT and DID can be obtained from ordinary least squares (OLS) estimation. In particular, DID can be estimated from the following regression (Meyer 1995),

$$\Delta y_{it}^j = c + \gamma_1 d_t + \gamma_2 d^j + \alpha_{DID} d_t^j + x_{it}^{j'} \delta + \varepsilon_{it}^j, \qquad (9.4)$$

where $j = 0, 1$ denote the control and the switching firm's groups, respectively; $t = 0, 1$ denote the pre- and postinvestment periods; and the d's are dummies taking the following values:

$d_t = 1$ if $t = 1$ and zero otherwise (the postswitching dummy)

$d^j = 1$ if $j = 1$ and zero otherwise (the switching firm dummy)

$d_t^j = 1$ if $t = 1$ and $j = 1$ and zero otherwise (the DID dummy)

The OLS estimate of $\hat{\alpha}_{DID}$ is the DID estimator of the effect of investing on performance growth. One of the advantages of this specification of DID is that it allows conditioning on a vector of covariates x, which might capture other sources of heterogeneity in the dependent variable. Setting $t = 1$, we can estimate

$$\Delta y_i^j = a + \alpha_{ATT} d^j + x_i^{j'} \delta + v_i^j, \tag{9.5}$$

where the OLS estimate of α_{ATT} is now the ATT.

9.4   Data and Description of the Sample

The data set we use combines the Reprint database of the Politecnico of Milan (which contains information on Italian multinationals and foreign firms operating in Italy) with the Aida database of Bureau Van Dijck (which has information on balance sheet and other economic data of Italian firms). The two databases have been merged by the Centro Studi Luca d'Agliano. The panel used in this chapter includes Italian firms with more that twenty employees with observations between 1993 and 1998. The Reprint database is the main source of information on multinational firms in Italy and provides a good approximation to the universe of activities of both foreign multinationals in Italy and Italian multinationals abroad. For the purpose of this work, we use the issues from 1993 to 1997 of the outward section of Reprint. For each firm in the Reprint database, we were able to count the number of foreign affiliates carrying out manufacturing activity. We thus excluded all sales offices and plants carrying out other nonmanufacturing activities abroad. This allows us to focus on investments involving the transfer of production by Italian firms to a foreign country. By comparing various issues of this directory, we have built an indicator flagging when each firm created its first establishment abroad. This allowed us to select a sample of 193 firms that became multinationals between 1993 and 1997.[4] In order to compute propensity score and DID estimates, we dropped firms switching in the first years of the period analyzed, since for these cases, we were not able to gather any preinvestment information. We ended up with a sample of 119 firms switching between 1995 and 1997. This was complemented with a sample of 1,000 firms with more than twenty employees randomly drawn from the Aida data set,[5] which will be the control group. For each firm from those two sources, we gathered balance sheet information from Aida on the period 1993–1997. In particular, we used information on the year of establishment, the sector of activity, turnover, number of employees, value added, cash flow, operating profits, return on investments (ROI), cost of intermediate materials, tangible fixed capital, capitalized R&D, total assets, and total liabilities. A measure of total factor productivity was derived from these data by estimating a Cobb-Douglas production function with fixed capital, materials, and labor as inputs. We controlled for endogeneity in input use by estimating a fixed-effect model and allowing autocorrelated disturbances (which should account for persistence in productivity). Furthermore, we allowed each sector to have different production functions by having input coefficients interact with sector dummies. Due to missing values in some of the variables, we were forced to drop a few observations. Table 9.1 summarizes the distribution of firms used in the analysis. In particular, we ended up with 114 switching firms and 2,918

Table 9.1
Number and distribution of firms in the sample, by year, sector, size class, and investing status

	National firms	Switching firms	Total
Year			
1995	962	28	990
1996	962	44	1,006
1997	968	42	1,020
Total	2,918	114	3,016
Pavitt sectors			
Scale intensive	28.7	24.6	28.5
Science based	4.9	7.0	5.0
Specialized suppliers	25.7	25.4	25.7
Supplier dominated	40.7	43.0	40.8
Employment classes			
21–49 employees	48.1	20.2	47.1
51–249 employees	45.1	51.8	45.4
250–499 employees	3.8	17.5	4.4
More than 500 employees	2.8	10.5	3.1
Total	100	100	100

observations in the control group. The sectoral distribution of the sample reflects the actual distribution of firms in the Italian economy, where a large proportion of firms is in traditional (supplier-dominated) or specialized supplier industries. Switching firms appear to be relatively more frequent in science-based industries than those in the control group. As far as size is concerned, the sample reflects the large weight of small and medium-sized enterprises in the Italian economy (approximately 50 percent of cases have fewer than fifty employees), but remarkable differences emerge between switching and controls, with the former being significantly more frequent in larger-sized classes. This suggests that switching firms may be very different from the average firm in the control group, so that a simple comparison of these two groups of firms may lead to biased conclusions, as the latter may not provide the more accurate approximation to the counterfactual. In table 9.2 we provide further support for this view by looking at means over a number of characteristics of both switching and control groups and show that the former are significantly larger, more productive, and more profitable (in terms of both ROI and operating profits per employee), while differences are not significant in terms of age, share of capitalized R&D in total assets, share of liabilities on total assets, and cash flow on fixed capital.

9.5 Construction of the Counterfactual

The previous section highlighted that the switching firms are significantly different from the average firm in the control group. Therefore, we need to build an appropriate counterfactual group from a subsample of nationals that did not invest over the 1995–1997 period. To do so, we use the propensity score matching technique. We start by running a probit regression to derive the probability of investing as a function of observable firm-specific characteristics,

$$P(SW_{it} = 1 | Z_{i,t-1}, E_{i,t-1}, F_{i,t-1}, S_i, P_i, yr95, yr96), \qquad (9.6)$$

where $Z_{i,t-1}$ is a vector of firms' attributes such as size, age, and share of intangible assets on total assets; $E_{i,t-1}$ is a vector of efficiency and profitability measures such as TFP, lagged TFP growth, operating margin per employee, and ROI; $F_{i,t-1}$ is a vector of financial variables such as the ratio of debt to total assets and the share of cash flow in total capital; S_i and P_i are sector and province dummies; and $yr95$ and $yr96$

Table 9.2
Switching firms and unmatched control group, various characteristics (means)

Unmatched sample	Control	Switching	Differential	SE	Number of observations
$(Log)TFP_{i,t-1}$	−0.128	0.321	0.449**	(0.060)	3,016
Growth of $TFP_{i,t-2}$	0.010	0.003	−0.007	(0.010)	3,016
$(Log)N.$ employees$_{i,t-1}$	4.113	4.957	0.844**	(0.106)	3,016
Profits per employee$_{i,t-1}$	0.219	0.385	0.166**	(0.048)	3,016
$ROI_{i,t-1}$	0.069	0.086	0.017**	(0.008)	3,016
$(Log)Age_{i,t-1}$	2.940	3.031	0.091	(0.062)	3,016
Capitalized R&D / total assets$_{i,t-1}$	0.001	0.002	0.001	(0.001)	3,016
Debt / total assets$_{i,t-1}$	0.671	0.678	0.008	(0.015)	3,016
Cash flow / fixed capital$_{i,t-1}$	0.756	0.521	−0.234	(0.154)	3,016

$**p < .05$

Table 9.3
Determinants of the probability of switching

Variable	(1) Whole sample	(2) Matched sample	(3) Matched sample
$(\text{Log})\text{TFP}_{i,t-1}$	0.346**	−0.213	−0.144
	(0.157)	(0.156)	(0.365)
Growth of $\text{TFP}_{i,t-2}$	−0.678	−1.130	−1.303
	(479)	(0.938)	(1.204)
$(\text{Log})\text{N. employees}_{i,t-1}$	0.422**	0.040	−0.010
	(0.067)	(0.093)	(0.155)
Profits per employee$_{i,t-1}$	0.004**	0.003	0.002
	(0.001)	(0.003)	(0.004)
$\text{ROI}_{i,t-1}$	0.015*	0.245	0.193
	(0.008)	(1.444)	(1.950)
$(\text{Log})\text{Age}_{i,t-1}$	0.138*	0.114	0.165
	(0.081)	(0.137)	(0.181)
Capitalized R&D/total assets$_{i,t-1}$	0.047	−1.175	−2.625
	(0.031)	(4.559)	(5.459)
Debt/total assets$_{i,t-1}$	0.532*	0.460	0.006
	(0.309)	(0.625)	(0.788)
Cash flow/fixed capital$_{i,t-1}$	−0.108**	−0.119	−0.170
	(0.033)	(0.086)	(0.139)
Sector dummies	Yes	No	Yes
Province dummies	Yes	No	Yes
Year dummies	Yes	Yes	Yes
Number of observations	3,016	224	207
Pseudo R-squared	0.212	0.019	0.096
LR test[a]	206.48**	6.12	27.56

[a] Test for the hypothesis that all coefficients are jointly equal to zero.
**$p < .05$. *$p < .10$.

are two time dummies. The results of the estimation of equation 9.6 are reported in table 9.3 in column 1 and support the hypothesis that size, productivity, and profitability are important determinants for becoming a multinational firm. In other words, we confirm that multinationals have some ex ante advantage over national firms that likely compensate for the higher costs and risks of running a business abroad.

With the propensity score obtained from the estimation of equation 9.6, we are now able to build an appropriate counterfactual to our sample of switching firms by matching each of them to the control firms

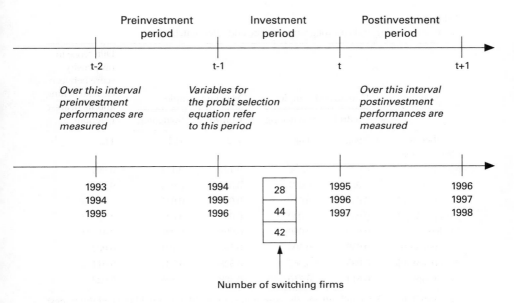

Figure 9.2
Time structure of investment patterns

with the closest propensity score (this is called nearest-neighbor matching). We run the nearest-neighbor algorithm[6] year by year, so that we match each switching firm to an observation from the control group in the same year the switching occurs. By doing this, we ensure that, for example, a firm switching in 1995 will be matched to a firm that prior to investment (in 1994) was similar to it. Then, as illustrated in figure 9.2, performance one year after the investment (1995–1996) will be compared in switching and control firms.

As we have already suggested, propensity score matching should account for ex ante differences in the sample of switching firms and in the counterfactual, therefore, generating a counterfactual with characteristics as close as possible to those of the investing firms. In formal terms, the matched sample should satisfy the balancing property, that is, the distribution of the vector of observables should be balanced across switching and control firms. We therefore need to assume conditional independence when we derive propensity scores, that is, we need to rule out that the choice of investing abroad is significantly affected by unobservable variables that also determine postinvestment performance. Because of data limitations, we cannot fully exclude that unobservables do indeed play a role, so we proceeded with caution. In

Table 9.4
Score of switching and control groups, before and after matching

	Unmatched sample		Matched sample		Difference in propensity score between each switching and its nearest neighbor
	Control	Switching	Control	Switching	
Number of observations	2,902	114	112	112[a]	112
Mean	0.033	0.150	0.141	0.141	0.004
Minimum	0.000	0.001	0.001	0.001	9.7E-08
10th percentile	0.002	0.019	0.019	0.019	6.6E-06
25th percentile	0.005	0.042	0.041	0.041	4.3E-05
Median	0.013	0.099	0.096	0.096	2.4E-04
75th percentile	0.039	0.208	0.192	0.191	0.002
90th percentile	0.085	0.362	0.328	0.339	0.011
Maximum	0.614	0.710	0.589	0.566	0.023

[a] Two switching firms fell outside the common support (the interval between the largest propensity score of a control firm and the lower propensity score of a switching firm) and were dropped by the matching algorithm.

what follows, we discuss all the steps taken to ensure that the balancing property is satisfied.

First, in estimating equation 9.6, we control for as many observable firms' characteristics as possible (including a large set of sector and province dummies) and reach a satisfactory result in terms of explained variance, as indicated by a pseudo-R^2 of 21.2 percent, which is in line with most existing works using matching techniques.

Second, in table 9.4 we provide some statistics on the propensity score of the switching and control groups before and after matching. The probability of switching is much higher in the group of firms that actually switched than in the unmatched control group. In the final column of table 9.4, we compare switching firms to the matched counterfactual. The two groups of firms have very similar propensity scores in terms of both mean and various percentiles. Furthermore, from the last column of table 9.4 we see that the difference in propensity scores between switching firms and their matched neighbor is very small (for more than 50 percent of the cases, it is lower than 0.02 percent, and on average it is only 0.4 percent). This result is confirmed by the graphical representation of these distributions provided in figure 9.3, where it is

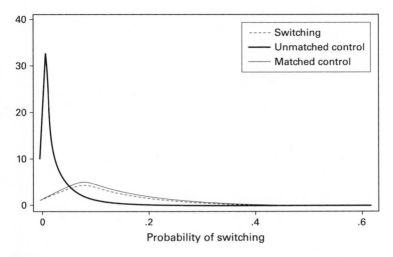

Figure 9.3
Distribution of the propensity score in switching and (matched and unmatched) control firms

clear that the distribution of the propensity score of the unmatched control group is very skewed leftward (thick line), whereas the one for the matched subsample (thin solid line) is very close to the one for the switching firms (dotted line).

Third, in table 9.5 we compare the characteristics of the matched control group with the switching firms and find that differences between the two groups of firms are nonsignificantly different from zero in all the characteristics used to estimate the propensity score. This result should be compared to the one reported in table 9.2, where the unmatched counterfactual is significantly different from the switching sample for several of the variables considered.

Fourth, we follow Sianesi (2004) and run the selection probit on the matched sample with and without sector and location controls (third and second column of table 9.3, respectively). As expected, we find that pseudo-R^2 drops significantly (from .212 in the whole sample to .096 in the matched sample), and no regressor is significant either individually or jointly.[7] These results support the presumption that the characteristics included in the probit are not statistically significant either individually or jointly when we use the matched sample.

Fifth, and finally, we test that the whole distribution, not only the means, of the characteristics of firms in the switching and control

Table 9.5
Switching firms and matched control group, various characteristics (means)

Matched sample	Control	Switching	Differential	SE	Number of observations
$(\text{Log})\text{TFP}_{i,t-1}$	0.422	0.308	−0.114	(0.094)	224
Growth of $\text{TFP}_{i,t-2}$	0.018	0.004	−0.015	(0.014)	224
$(\text{Log})\text{N. employees}_{i,t-1}$	4.994	4.934	−0.059	(0.149)	224
Profits per employee$_{i,t-1}$	0.432	0.377	−0.055	(0.098)	224
$\text{ROI}_{i,t-1}$	0.091	0.087	−0.004	(0.011)	224
$(\text{Log})\text{Age}_{i,t-1}$	2.986	3.021	0.035	(0.088)	224
Capitalized R&D / total assets$_{i,t-1}$	0.003	0.003	−0.001	(0.003)	224
Debt / total assets$_{i,t-1}$	0.666	0.676	0.010	(0.021)	224
Cash flow / fixed capital$_{i,t-1}$	0.870	0.526	−0.344	(0.302)	224

Table 9.6
Kolmogorov-Smirnov test for equality of distribution functions: Switching versus control firms (various characteristics)

	Unmatched sample		Matched sample	
	K-S	p-value	K-S	p-value
(Log)TFP$_{i,t-1}$	0.337	[0.000]	0.085	[0.795]
Growth of TFP$_{i,t-2}$	0.056	[0.854]	0.090	[0.732]
(Log)N. employees$_{i,t-1}$	0.422	[0.000]	0.160	[0.103]
Profits per employee$_{i,t-1}$	0.162	[0.004]	0.079	[0.859]
ROI$_{i,t-1}$	0.079	[0.444]	0.119	[0.377]
(Log)Age$_{i,t-1}$	0.109	[0.116]	0.133	[0.253]
Capitalized R&D / total assets$_{i,t-1}$	0.041	[0.990]	0.045	[1.000]
Debt / total assets$_{i,t-1}$	0.048	[0.943]	0.084	[0.803]
Cash flow / fixed capital$_{i,t-1}$	0.115	[0.085]	0.111	[0.471]

group, does not differ after matching. This is done by testing for the difference in the distribution function using the Kolmogorov-Smironov statistics (in table 9.6). This analysis suggests that the distribution of all variables becomes very similar in the matched controls and in the switching group, regardless of how different they are in the whole sample. Furthermore, the Kolmogorov-Smirnov does not reject equality of distribution in any of the variables in the matched sample.

9.6 Effects of Investing Abroad: Results

We now use the matched sample to estimate the impact of the creation of foreign subsidiaries on firms' performances. We estimate both the average treatment effect (ATT) and the difference-in-difference (DID) estimator.[8] Our outcome variables are three indicators of firms' economic performances: TFP growth, employment growth, and output (measured by total sales) growth. Here we mainly concentrate on a robust estimation of the partial effect of investing abroad on the three indicators, but since we are aware of possible relations among these three indicators, we partially allow the possibility that the effect of investment on the expansion of output might also explain the growth in employment and productive efficiency (through economies of scale). However, a full account of the interlinkages (such as the impact of an increase in TFP on output growth, through an increase of international competitiveness or through factor mix reallocation) and the channels through which these effects occur is left for further investigation.

Table 9.7
Effect of investing abroad on firms' performances, 1993–1998

Dependent variable	Turnover growth			
Estimator	SM	DID		
Effect of investing (α)	0.079**	.110**		
	(0.027)	(.043)		
Switching firm dummy (γ_2)		−0.030		
		(0.029)		
Postswitching dummy (γ_1)		−0.146**		
		(0.032)		
Constant	−0.044**	0.101**		
	(0.023)	(0.021)		
Observations	224	448		
R^2	0.03	0.05		
Dependent variable	TFP growth			
Estimator	ATT	DID	ATT	DID
Effect of investing (α)	0.041**	0.059**	0.004	0.014
	(0.021)	(0.025)	(0.010)	(0.016)
Switching firm dummy (γ_2)		−0.016		−0.004
		(0.014)		(0.010)
Postswitching dummy (γ_1)		−0.043**		0.016
		(0.020)		(0.010)
Turnover growth			0.457**	0.407**
			(0.121)	(0.065)
Constant	−0.021	0.020	−0.001	−0.021**
	(0.017)	(0.011)	(0.008)	(0.009)
Observations	224	448	224	448
R^2	0.01	0.02	0.39	0.44

In table 9.7 we report estimates of the effect of investing abroad, using both DID and ATT (from equations 9.4 and 9.5). We compute bootstrapped standard errors to adjust for additional sources of variability introduced by the estimation of the propensity score as well as the matching process. As illustrated in figure 9.2, switching may occur at three different points in time (1995, 1996, or 1997). In the estimation of the effect of investing abroad on performance at home, we pooled all firms investing in the three years. However, we made sure that each switching firm is compared with observations from the same period of time, as we have matched them year by year. For example, per-

Table 9.7
(continued)

Dependent variable	Employment growth			
Estimator	ATT	DID	ATT	DID
Effect of investing (α)	0.042**	0.036	0.013	−0.005
	(0.021)	(0.031)	(0.019)	(0.030)
Switching firm dummy (γ_2)		0.004		0.014
		(0.023)		(0.020)
Postswitching dummy (γ_1)		−0.090**		−0.036**
		(0.020)		(0.019)
Turnover growth			0.368**	0.385**
			(0.080)	(0.062)
Constant	−0.010	0.083**	0.006	0.046
	(0.017)	(0.013)	(0.013)	(0.014)
Observations	224	448	224	448
R^2	0.01	0.05	0.23	0.28

Note: DID estimates are gathered from the following equation: $\Delta y_{it}^j = c + \gamma_1 d_t + \gamma_2 d_t^j + \alpha_{DID} d_t^j + x_{it}^{j\prime}\delta + \varepsilon_{it}^j$, where d^j takes value 1 for switching firms (both before and after investing) and zero for controls, d_t takes value 1 in the year after investment (for both groups of firms), and d_t^j takes value 1 for switching only after investment. The coefficient associated with the last term (α) is the DID estimate of the effect of investing abroad. ATT have been obtained from estimating the same equation, after setting $d_t = 1$. Asterisks denote significance level at 5 percent (**) and 10 percent (*), based on bootstrapped standard errors (500 repetitions).

formance of a firm switching in 1995 will be observed one year after investment (in the period 1995–1996), and the control firm will be observed over the same time interval.

Results support a significant effect of investing abroad for the first time on output growth: switching firms have a 7.9 percent higher growth rate in output than their counterfactual in the year following the investment. This effect is even larger (11 percent) if we account for preswitching output dynamics (DID estimators). The ATT and DID are positive (although slightly lower than in the case of output) and significant also in terms of TFP, though we find no significant effect on the rate of employment growth after accounting for preinvestment performance (DID). In columns 3 and 4 of table 6, we investigate to what extent the effect of investment on TFP and employment may be due to scale economies and an indirect effect of output growth. For this purpose, we estimate ATT and DID in terms of TFP and employment growth controlling for the contemporaneous growth in output. Results suggest that the effect of investing on TFP and employment is much lower once we account for output growth and both ATT and DID turn nonsignificantly different from zero.

9.7 Conclusions

This chapter examines the effects of foreign investment on the home activities of MNEs in Italian manufacturing. Contrary to widespread concerns about international outsourcing, we find that investing abroad significantly boosts performance at home. The rate of growth of total factor productivity and output is significantly higher for investing firms, and it accelerates after the investment takes place. This result is robust to the inclusion of different controls. We also find that investing has no significant effect on employment growth. In this perspective, actions aimed at discouraging foreign investments and the creation of foreign employments seem shortsighted and risk weakening the domestic economy rather than strengthening it.

As a note of caution, we should stress that our analysis provides a limited picture of the outsourcing process. First, our sample includes all types of investments. We cannot distinguish between vertical investments aimed at fragmenting production internationally (which is what is normally meant by outsourcing) and horizontal investments aimed at entering foreign markets that do not necessarily involve the transfer abroad of activities previously carried out at home. Second, we cannot control whether firms in our sample internationally outsource their activities through channels other than FDI, for example, by undertaking arm's-length agreements with firms based in foreign countries.

Notes

1. This is usually defined the outcome in the evaluation literature. See Blundell and Costa Dias (2000, 2002) and Wooldridge (2002, chap. 18) for reviews.

2. In the literature, this is referred to as the average treatment effect on the treated (ATT). The original idea is derived from natural sciences, where some outcome from individuals who receive a treatment (such as a medical treatment) is compared to identical individuals (randomly drawn from a population) who did not receive treatment. In economics, things are complicated by the fact that nontreated individuals are nonrandomly selected.

3. In the nearest-neighbor matching used in this chapter, weighting is simply used to account for the fact that one control can be matched to more than one switching firm.

4. One referee noted that the analysis should also include subsequent investments made by firms that are already multinationals. Although we agree that the effects of investment

by nonswitchers are also important and should be taken into account, we prefer to focus this chapter on the effects of discrete changes in investment behavior (new investments rather than ongoing ones) on performance at home. We believe that focusing on first-time investors is a good and original way to isolate this factor. Including all investors would make it difficult to isolate the impacts of new investments from those of ongoing ones.

5. The draw was carried out on firms that appeared not to be multinational firms in the 1993–1997 period and were not foreign owned.

6. We used the -psmatch2- command in Stata.

7. The second column drops sector and province dummies, and the third column also includes those dummies. The number of observation drops in the latter case as some observations are perfectly predicted by those dummies (there may be only one firm in each sector-province).

8. Bertrand, Duflo, and Mullainathan (2004) raise some concerns on the use of DID estimators. They warn that standard errors in DID estimators may be inconsistent due to serial correlation, and this may yield a false rejection of the null hypothesis of no treatment effect. However, their problem is not likely to affect our results, for both theoretical and empirical reasons. From the theoretical point of view, at least two of the three sources of serial correlation in DID mentioned in Bertrand et al. (p. 251) do not seem to apply in our context. In fact, (1) we do not have a long time series, since our data span only five years, and (2) our dependent variables are growth rates, which usually do not display strong serial correlation patterns. From an empirical point of view, we implement two of the solutions proposed by Bertrand et al. In particular, we consider only the information on pre- and postinvestment, thus collapsing the time series into two points, and we rely on bootstrapped standard errors.

References

Amiti, M., and S. Wei. (2004). Fear of Outsourcing: Is it Justified? Discussion Paper 4719, Centre for Economic Policy Research, London.

Aw, B., S. Chung, and M. Roberts. (2000). Productivity and the Decision to Export: Micro Evidence from Taiwan and South Korea. *World Bank Economic Review* 14(1), 65–90.

Barba Navaretti, G., and A. J. Venables. (2004). *Multinational Firms in the World Economy.* Princeton, N.J.: Princeton University Press.

Bellman, L., and R. Jungnickel. (2002). (Why) Do Foreign-Owned Firms in Germany Achieve Above-Average Productivity? In R. Jungnickel (ed.), *Foreign-Owned Firms: Are They Different?* Houndmills: Palgrave-Macmillan.

Bernard, A., and B. Jensen. (1999). Exceptional Exporter Performance: Cause, Effect or Both? *Journal of International Economics* 47, 1–25.

Bertrand, M., E. Duflo, and S. Mullainathan. (2004). How Much Should We Trust Differences-in-Differences Estimates? *Quarterly Journal of Economics* 19(1), 249–275.

Blomstrom, M., G. Fors, and R. Lipsey. (1997). Foreign Direct Investment and Employment: Home Country Experience in the United States and Sweden. *Economic Journal* 107, 1787–1797.

Blonigen, B. (2001). In Search of Substitution between Foreign Production and Exports. *Journal of International Economics* 53, 81–104.

Blundell, R., and M. Costa Dias. (2000). Evaluation Methods for Non-Experimental Data. *Fiscal Studies* 21(4), 427–468.

Blundell, R., and M. Costa Dias. (2002). Alternative Approaches to Evaluation in Empirical Microeconomics. Working paper CWP 10/02, Cemmap.

Braconier, H., and K. Ekholm. (2000). Swedish Multinationals and Competition from High- and Low-Wage Locations. *Review of International Economics* 8, 448–461.

Braconier, H., K. Ekholm, and K. Midelfart Knarvik. (2001). In Search of FDI-Transmitted R&D Spillovers: A Study Based on Swedish Data. *Weltwirtshaftliches Archiv* 137(4), 644–665.

Brainard, L., and D. Riker. (1997a). Are US Multinationals Exporting US Jobs? Working paper no. 5958, National Bureau of Economic Research, Cambridge, Mass.

Brainard, L., and D. Riker. (1997b). US Multinationals and Competition from Low-Wage Countries. Working paper no. 5959, National Bureau of Economic Research, Cambridge, Mass.

Bruno, G., and A. Falzoni. (2003). Multinational Corporations, Wages and Employment: Do Adjustment Costs Matter? *Applied Economics* 35, 11, 1277–1290.

Castellani, D. (2002). Export Behavior and Productivity Growth: Evidence from Italian Manufacturing Firms. *Welwirtshaftliches Archiv* 138(4), 605–628.

Castellani, D., and A. Zanfei. (2006). *Multinational firms, innovation and productivity*. Cheltenham UK: Edward Elgar.

Clerides, S. K., S. Lach, and J. R. Tybout. (1998). Is Learning by Exporting Important? Micro-Dynamic Evidence from Colombia, Mexico, and Morocco. *Quarterly Journal of Economics* August, 903–948.

Criscuolo, C., and R. Martin. (2002). Multinationals, Foreign Ownership and US Productivity Leadership: Evidence from the U.K. Paper presented at the Royal Economic Society Conference.

Delgado, M., J. Farinas, and S. Ruano. (2002). Firm Productivity and Export Markets: A Non-Parametric Approach. *Journal of International Economics* 57, 397–422.

Doms, M., and B. Jensen. (1998). Comparing Wages, Skills, and Productivity between Domestically and Foreign-Owned Manufacturing Establishments in the Unites States. In R. Baldwin, R. Lipsey, and J. Richardson (eds.), *Geography and Ownership as Bases for Economic Accounting*. Chicago: University of Chicago Press.

Dunning, J. (1993). *Multinational Enterprises and the Global Economy*. Wokingham, England: Addison-Wesley.

Egger, P., and M. Pfaffermayr. (2003). The Counterfactual to Investing Abroad: An Endogenous Treatment Approach of Foreign Affiliate Activity. Working paper in economics, 2003/02, University of Innsbruck.

Girma, S., and H. Gorg. (2007). Multinationals Productivity Advantage: Scale or Technology? *Economic Inquiry* 45, 350–362.

Girma, S., and H. Gorg. (2007). Evaluating the Foreign Ownership Wage Premium Using Difference-in-Differences Matching Approach. *Journal of International Economics* 72, 97–112.

Girma, S., D. Greenaway, and R. Kneller. (2004). Does Exporting Lead to Better Performance? A Microeconometric Analysis of Matched Firms? *Review of International Economics* 12(5), 855–866.

Girma, S., R. Kneller, and M. Pisu. (2005). Exports versus FDI: An Empirical Test. *Review of World Economics* 141, 193–218.

Girma, S., R. Kneller, and M. Pisu. (in press). Do Exporters Have Anything to Learn from Foreign Multinationals. *European Economic Review* 51, 993–1010.

Gorg, H., A. Hanley, and E. Strobl. (2004). Outsourcing, Foreign Ownership, Exporting and Productivity: An Empirical Investigation with Plant Level Data. Globalization and Economic Policy Research Paper Series, University of Nottingham, 2004/08.

Head, K., and J. Ries. (2001). Overseas Investment and Firm Exports. *Review of International Economics* 91(1), 108–122.

Heckman, J., H. Ichimura, and P. Todd. (1997). Matching as an Econometric Evaluation Estimator: Evidence from Evaluating a Job Training Program. *Review of Economic Studies* 64, 605–654.

Helpman, E., M. Melitz, and S. Yeaple. (2004). Exports vs. FDI with Heterogeneous Firms. *American Economic Review* 94, 300–316.

Konings, J., and A. Murphy. (2001). Do Multinational Enterprises Substitute Parent Jobs for Foreign Ones? Evidence from European Firm-Level Panel Data. Discussion paper no. 2972, Centre for Economic Policy Research, London.

Kraay A. (1999). Exports and Economic Performance: Evidence from a Panel of Chinese Enterprises. *Revue d'Economie du Developpement* 1–2/1999, 183–207.

Lipsey, R. E. (1999). Foreign Production by US Firms and Parent Firm Employment. Working paper no. 7357, National Bureau of Economic Research, Cambridge, Mass.

Marin, D. (2004). A Nation of Poets and Thinkers: Less So with Eastern Enlargement? Austria and Germany. Discussion paper no. 4358, Centre for Economic Policy Research, London.

Mariotti, S., M. Mutinelli, and L. Piscitello. (2003). Home Country Employment and Foreign Direct Investment: Evidence from the Italian Case. *Cambridge Journal of Economics* 57, 419–431.

Markusen, J. (1995). The Boundaries of Multinational Firms and the Theory of International Trade. *Journal of Economic Perspectives* 92, 169–189.

Meyer, B. (1995). Natural and Quasi-Natural Experiments in Economics. *Journal of Business and Economic Statistics* 13, 151–162.

Pfaffermayer, M., and C. Bellak. (2002). Why Foreign-Owned Are Different: A Conceptual Framework and Empirical Evidence for Austria. In R. Jungnickel (ed.), *Foreign-Owned Firms: Are They Different?* Houndmills: Palgrave-Macmillan.

Sianesi, B. (2004). An Evaluation of the Swedish System of Active Labour Market Programmes in the 1990s. *Review of Economics and Statistics* 86, 133–155.

van Pottelsberghe de la Potterie, B., and F. Lichtenberg. (2001). Does Foreign Direct Investment Transfer Technology across Borders? *Review of Economics and Statistics* 83, 490–497.

Wagner, J. (2002). The Causal Effect of Exports on Firm Size and Labor Productivity: First Evidence from a Matching Approach. *Economics Letters* 77, 287–292.

Wooldridge, J. (2002). *Econometric Analysis of Cross Section and Panel Data*. Cambridge, MA: MIT Press.

10

Is Human Capital Losing from Outsourcing? Evidence for Austria and Poland

Andzelika Lorentowicz, Dalia Marin, and Alexander Raubold

10.1 Introduction

The debate about globalization has shifted recently to a new frontier. Firms in rich countries are outsourcing white-collar work to India, China, and Eastern Europe, raising fears that this will adversely affect the long-run growth potential of industrialized economies and will result in an increase in unemployment for high-skilled workers in Europe and a decline in the skill premium in the United States.[1] Marin (2004) has shown that German and Austrian firms offshore skill-intensive stages of production to eastern Europe, relocating high-skilled jobs to this region. She also finds that German affiliates in eastern Europe are on average almost three times as skill intensive compared to their parent companies in Germany. The skill intensity of the offshoring activity of Austrian firms is slightly above that of the activity of parent firms in Austria.

In this chapter, we examine empirically whether outsourcing to new Europe can explain changes in relative wages of skilled workers in old and new Europe.[2] Figure 10.1 gives the ratio of skilled to unskilled wages in the past decade in Germany and Austria, on the one hand, and in Poland, Hungary, and the Czech Republic on the other. We use as a proxy for the skill-wage ratio relative wages of nonproduction to production workers. The data show a strong increase in the relative wage for skills in Poland, Hungary, and the Czech Republic, while this ratio appears to have remained almost constant in Germany and Austria.[3]

These wage data do not show a pattern of factor prices that trade economists usually expect from trade and investment integration. Typically, when a skill-rich country like Germany (relative to Poland) integrates with a skill-poor country like Poland, we expect relative wages

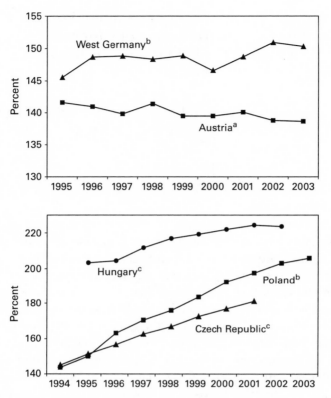

Figure 10.1
Relative wages of nonproduction workers to production workers
Note: [a]Manufacturing and mining; [b]manufacturing; [c]industry.
Source: Own calculations based on data gathered from Statistic Austria, Central Statistical Office of Poland, and PAIilZ.

for skills to go up in Germany and decline in Poland. The reason is that trade integration leads a country to specialize in those sectors that use the country's abundant factor intensively. Thus, skill-rich Germany specializes in the skill-intensive sectors, and labor-rich Poland specializes in labor-intensive sectors. As a result, the relative demand for skills goes up in Germany and declines in Poland, leading to an increase in the relative wage for skills in Germany and a decline of those in Poland.

Why have relative wages for skilled workers increased in new Europe and remained somewhat constant in old Europe? Why do we observe a perverse Stolper-Samuelson effect in these countries? We explore these questions on the example of two countries from old and

Table 10.1
Foreign direct investment pattern in Austria and Poland

	Austria's outgoing FDI		Poland's incoming FDI		
	1992–1994	2002–2004	1994–1996	2001–2003	
CEE	33.83	58.00	7.86	19.07	France
Hungary	18.03	10.93	21.07	10.74	United States
Czech Republic	9.87	7.19	14.27	13.94	Germany
Poland	0.59	10.40	7.81	18.08	Netherlands
Croatia	1.00	6.36	4.79	9.22	United Kingdom
Slovak Republic	1.53	3.10	10.37	2.15	Italy
Slovenia	2.00	3.86	3.16	5.21	Sweden
Romania	0.18	10.35	0.51	7.96	Belgium
Russia	0.15	1.15	2.33	4.11	Denmark
Bulgaria	0.23	1.35	0.00	0.00	Russia
EU-15	35.24	28.30	1.07	0.45	Ireland
Germany	9.66	10.30	3.33	1.83	Switzerland
United Kingdom	6.67	3.52	1.31	−1.01	Austria
Other	30.93	13.69	22.12	8.25	Other
Total	100.00	100.00	100.00	100.00	Total

Note: The numbers show the percentage distribution of foreign direct investment flows. Countries are ranked according their average (1992–2004 for Austria and 1994–2003 for Poland) importance as source and as host country, respectively.
Source: Own calculations based on data of the Austrian National Bank, OeNB, and the Polish Information and Foreign Investment Agency, PAIiIZ.

new Europe: Austria and Poland. Austria and Poland are not a natural pair to consider. Although Austria's foreign direct investment (FDI) to Poland accounts for 10.4 percent of total outgoing Austrian FDI to Eastern Europe in 2002–2004 and has shown a tremendous increase since the fall of communism (see table 10.1), Austria's share in total incoming FDI in Poland is negligible (see table 10.1). Still, we chose these two countries because Poland is the largest country in new Europe and Austria is the country in old Europe most integrated with new Europe. The Central and Eastern European Countries (CEE) account for 58 percent of total outgoing FDI in Austria in 2002–2004 (see table 10.1).[4]

Table 10.2 takes a closer look at outsourcing in selected countries and the development in their labor markets. With an annual growth rate of the skill-wage ratio of 4.4 percent, Poland shows the strongest increase in the skill premium since the announcement of eastern

Table 10.2
Outsourcing and labor market outcomes in selected countries

	Poland, 1994–2002	Austria, 1995–2002	Germany, 1990–2000	United States, 1979–1990	Mexico, 1975–1988
Outsourcing	6.91[c]	6.01[d]	3.86	3.82[e]	17.60[f]
Relative wages[a]	4.42	−0.29	0.23	0.72	1.39[g]
Relative employment[a]	1.22	2.25	1.98	—	—
High-skilled workers' wage bill share[b]	3.74	1.14	1.16	1.67	1.50[h]

Note: The numbers show annual average growth rates.
[a] Nonproduction to production workers in manufacturing for Poland, Germany, the United States, and Mexico and in mining and manufacturing for Austria.
[b] (Nonproduction workers' wage ∗ number of nonproduction workers)/((nonproduction workers' wage ∗ number of nonproduction workers) + (production workers' wage ∗ number of production workers)) in manufacturing for Poland, Germany, the United States, and Mexico, in mining and manufacturing for Austria.
[c] 1 + (foreign fixed assets/domestic fixed assets), manufacturing.
[d] Narrow definition of outsourcing: (imported inputs from the same sector/value added of sector) ∗ 100, mining and manufacturing.
[e] (Imported inputs from the same sector/total nonenergy material purchases) ∗ 100, manufacturing.
[f] Incoming FDI/total fixed investment.
[g] For U.S.-border region only, manufacturing.
Source: Poland, Austria and Germany: own calculations; United States: data from Feenstra and Hanson (1996b); Mexico: data from Feenstra and Hanson (1997).

enlargement. Compared to Poland, Mexico's increase in the relative wage for skills appears to be small in the face of the North American Free Trade Agreement (NAFTA). The annual increases in the skill premium in Germany and the United States are of the same order of magnitude, while Austria's skill premium declined modestly.

At the same time, Austria and Poland experienced a sharp increase in outsourcing between 1995 and 2002. In both countries, outsourcing has grown annually by 6 and 7 percent, respectively. This can also be seen in figure 10.2, which shows that the measure for outsourcing in Austria (the share of imported inputs in percent of output) increased from 20 percent in 1990 to 30 percent in 2000, while remaining constant over the previous decade. In Poland, foreign assets in percentage of domestic assets increased from 4 to 80 percent between 1994 and 2002. Thus, outsourcing is a candidate for explaining the evolution of the skill premia in both countries.[5]

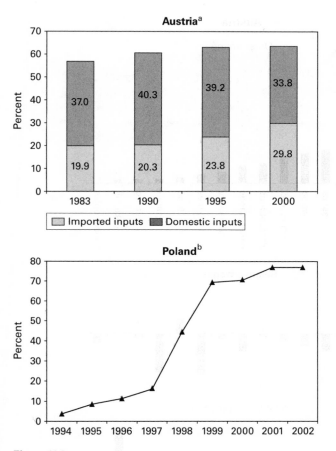

Figure 10.2
Outsourcing in Austria and Poland
Note: [a]Domestic and imported inputs in percentage of output, manufacturing and mining; [b]foreign fixed assets relative to domestic fixed assets, manufacturing.
Source: Own calculations based on data gathered from Statistic Austria, Central Statistical Office of Poland, and PAIilZ.

The described wage pattern can also be seen at the sectoral level in both countries. In Austria relative wages of skilled workers declined during 1995–2002 in all sectors except food with very little outsourcing (see figure 10.3), while relative wages for skilled workers in Poland increased substantially in all sectors except coke over 1994–2002.

This chapter explores the role of outsourcing for the decline in the skill premium in Austria and the increase of the skill premium in Poland. In sections 10.2 and 10.3, we develop the theoretical framework

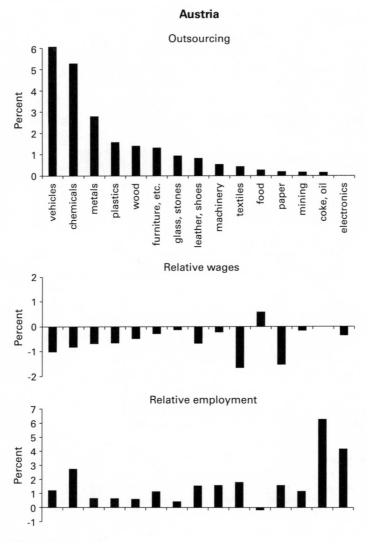

Figure 10.3
Outsourcing, relative wages and relative employment
Note: Average annual changes in percentage points (1995–2002 for Austria and 1994–
2002 for Poland). Sectors ranked by outsourcing (defined in the narrow way) for Austria
and the share of foreign fixed assets in domestic fixed assets.
Source: Own calculations based on data gathered from Statistics Austria, the Central Statistical Office of Poland, and PAIiIZ.

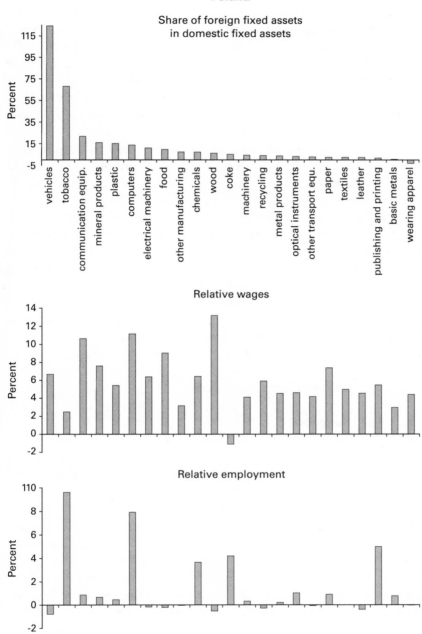

Figure 10.3
(continued)

and its empirical implementation along the lines of Feenstra and Hanson (1996b, 1997), who have argued that the increase in the skill premium in the United States as well as in Mexico in the face of NAFTA can be explained by capital movements in the form of FDI from the United States to Mexico. U.S. multinationals started to outsource the labor-intensive stages of production to Mexico. Then so-called *maquiladoras* emerged in Mexico. *Maquiladoras* are affiliates of U.S. multinationals in Mexico that specialize in the low-skill-intensive part of the value chain. U.S. multinationals' outsourcing activities to Mexico lead relative wages for skills to increase in the United States as well as in Mexico. The increase in the skill premium in Poland and its decline in Austria suggests that an inverse *maquiladoras* effect is emerging in Austria and Poland. Austrian firms are outsourcing the more skill-intensive stages of production to eastern Europe and specializing in the more labor-intensive stages of production in Austria, leading to a decline in the skill premium in Austria.[6] Poland, on the other hand, is receiving outsourcing of multinational activities from more skill-rich countries like the United States, the Netherlands, and France, resulting in an increase in the skill premium in Poland. Section 10.4 examines whether such an inverse *maquiladoras* effect can be identified for Austria and whether the decline in the skill premium in Austria can be attributed to outsourcing. Section 10.5 then examines whether multinational outsourcing has been contributing to the increase in the skill premium in Poland. Section 10.6 concludes.[7]

10.2 The Framework

In Feenstra and Hanson's (1996a) model, the world economy consists of two countries: North and South. Each country is endowed with three factors of production: capital, high-skilled labor, and low-skilled labor. These endowments are assumed to be sufficiently different that factor prices are not equalized. Returns to capital and the relative wages of high-skilled labor are assumed to be higher in the South, reflecting a relative scarcity of capital and high-skilled labor in the South. Initially there is no international factor mobility, but there is labor mobility between skill categories within each country. In other words, the supply of skilled and unskilled workers can react to changes in the relative wages. On the production side, there is a single final good assembled from a continuous range of intermediate inputs

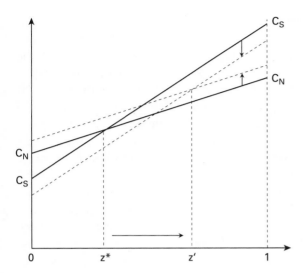

Figure 10.4
Outsourcing from the North to the South

at no additional cost. These inputs are produced using all factors and differ only with regard to the relative amounts of high-skilled and low-skilled labor engaged in their production since capital enters the production function with the same cost share for all inputs. They are indexed by $z \in [0, 1]$ and ranked in a way that high-skilled-labor intensity is increasing with z. Assuming that for constant wages, the minimum cost of producing one unit of input is a continuous function of z and that all inputs are produced in both countries, figure 10.4 depicts the minimum cost locus for intermediate goods produced in the North $(C^N C^N)$ and the South $(C^S C^S)$.

z^* is defined as the cutoff intermediate input where the minimum production cost in the South and the North is equal. $C^S C^S$ lies below $C^N C^N$ to the left of z^* since the relative wage of low-skilled labor, which is relatively intensively used in the production of these inputs, is lower in the South. The opposite holds for intermediates lying to the right of z^*. Thus, the South has a cost advantage in producing inputs, which are relatively low-skilled labor intensive, and the North has a cost advantage producing inputs that are relatively high-skilled intensive. The following trade pattern emerges: the South exports intermediate goods in the range $z \in [0, z^*)$, while the North exports those in the range $z \in (z^*, 1]$.

What will happen in the model if northern firms are allowed to invest in the South? They will have an incentive to do so in order to earn the higher returns to capital in the South. The flow of capital from the North to the South will cause a reduction in the southern return to capital and an increase in return to capital in the North. Consequently, at constant wages, this change will alter the minimum cost loci shown in figure 10.4. $C^S C^S$ will move down and $C^N C^N$ up, increasing the critical value of z^* to z'. That is, the production of inputs in the range $[z^*, z')$ now will take place in the South rather than in the North. In other words, in the South, the range of intermediate production will spread toward inputs that engage a higher ratio of high-skilled to low-skilled labor. The inputs, which still will be produced in the North, will use a higher ratio of high-skilled to low-skilled labor relative to those that will leave. Therefore, both countries will experience an increase in the average skill intensity of production and an increase in the relative demand for high-skilled labor. As a result, the relative wage of skilled labor will rise in both countries. Summing up, z^* is increasing with the southern-to-northern capital ratio. Thus, the relative wage of skilled workers will be positively affected by the accumulation of capital in the South relative to the North. Feenstra and Hanson (1996a) show that this result also holds for exogenous relative capital accumulation in the South not necessarily caused by northern firms' investment.

Following Feenstra and Hanson's (1996a) interpretation of the model, the activities outsourced by industrialized countries to developing countries are relatively low skilled from the perspective of the home country and relatively high skilled for the host country. Thus, outsourcing increases the relative demand for high-skilled workers in both countries, resulting in a higher relative wage for high-skilled labor.

10.3   The Empirical Model

The model of Feenstra and Hanson (1996a) provides a formalization of the idea that outsourcing induces a shift in the factor intensities in domestic and foreign production. As described in the previous section, the countries are, by assumption, endowed with three factors of production: low-skilled labor, high-skilled labor, and capital. In the production process, these three factors are combined, which leads to the following unit variable cost function for each sector i and for each point in time t:

$$cv_{it} = cv(w_{it}^{LS}, w_{it}^{HS}, r_{it}, OUTS_{it}, TECH_{it}). \tag{10.1}$$

We include in addition to the factor prices w^{LS}, w^{HS}, and r_{it} two variables: outsourcing ($OUTS$) and technical change ($TECH$). Following the existing literature, the inclusion of outsourcing as well as technical progress in the unit cost function is justified by arguing that merely including the factors of production will not capture other factors that might influence production costs. In this context, outsourcing can be thought of as a form of technical change since it acts as an "endogenous technical change."[8]

Berman, Bound, and Griliches (1994) suggested that a translog cost function can be derived from the unit cost function. Assuming capital as a fixed factor of production, the differentiation of the translog cost function with respect to the prices of the variable factors, w^{LS} and w^{HS}, gives the factor demand equation in the form of the factor's share in total variable cost. In our analysis, the factor's share in total variable cost is defined as the high-skilled workers' wage bill in the total wage bill. This wage bill share of the high-skilled workers (WBS^{HS}) measures the relative demand for high-skilled labor.

We undertake our estimations with fixed effects, since any variation between units not accounted for by the independent variables creates unobserved heterogeneity in the model. Given that industries differ from each other in the characteristics not included in our empirical model, estimating with ordinary least squares (OLS) would relegate the omitted heterogeneity to the error term, and the coefficients would be biased.[9] Furthermore, we also incorporate time-fixed effects. This is important, since we have neglected the fact that international outsourcing might be determined by some foreign factors. Due to obvious reasons, we cannot include these variables in the regression. By including time dummies, we assume that the foreign variables' impact is the same across industries and varies only over time. Moreover, there might exist some aggregate exogenous factors that are correlated with the industry-level relative labor demand.

We have performed Breusch-Pagan and White tests to identify heteroscedasticity in the data. Both tests cannot reject the null hypothesis of homoscedasticity, after including the time and industry fixed effects. In any case we report standard errors, which are robust to heteroscedastictiy.

10.4   Outsourcing in Austria

In this section we analyze the consequences of increased competition due to imported intermediate goods for the Austrian labor market. Particularly, we want to address the question of how international outsourcing affects the demand for high-skilled labor in Austria. What is an appropriate measure of this competition in imported inputs? In the existing literature, there are two definitions known that use the data of input-output tables: wide and narrow definitions of outsourcing. The wide definition refers to the intermediate goods that a particular sector imports from all sectors all over the world. In contrast, the narrow definition of outsourcing is related to just the imported inputs from the firm's own sector. The reasoning for favoring the latter definition is that the workers of a particular sector might be solely affected by decisions of firms at the sectoral level over make-or-buy inputs.[10] Firms of a particular sector are not able to produce inputs that they buy from other sectors. Therefore, the factor intensities and the demand for high-skilled labor should not be affected by the decision if inputs from other sectors are sourced domestically or from abroad. In this chapter, we will therefore use the narrow definition of international outsourcing.

10.4.1   Data and Variables

The sample contains annual data of fifteen industrial sectors that are pooled over the years 1995–2002. The sectors are classified according to the European NACE (Nomenclature generale des Activités Economiques) system at the two-letter level.[11] The sample period starts in 1995, because consistent data with respect to sector classification are available only for the years after Austria's accession to the European Union (EU).

The labor demand data are taken from the Association of Austrian Social Insurance. The skill levels are proxied by the commonly used broad definition of production (*Arbeiter*) and nonproduction workers (*Angestellte*) for low-skilled and high-skilled workers. The statistics show the wages and the employment separately for production and nonproduction workers.

We define the variable international outsourcing $OUTS$ as the share of imported inputs in value added. The narrow definition of outsourcing takes the imported inputs of the NACE two-letter sector into account. Some other studies use the imported intermediate inputs as a share of the sum of domestic and imported inputs.[12] The advantage of our measure $OUTS$ is that it controls for changes in the degree of value added and, consequently, for overall changes in the use of intermediate goods. Since we want to analyze the importance of outsourcing for the labor market, it might not be appropriate to look just at the relative importance of imported inputs compared to total inputs.

As control variables, we use data on output Y, value-added VA, and gross fixed capital formation K from the Organization for Economic Cooperation and Development (OCED) STAN database. Since no industry-level measure of capital stocks is available,[13] we use gross fixed capital formation data to construct a measure for the capital stocks. For this calculation, we employ the perpetual inventory method.

Technical change is proxied by the variable $R\&D\ L$ measuring the R&D personnel as a proportion of the sector's employment. (See appendix 10A for further description of the data and their sources.)

For the empirical implementation of equation 10.1, we estimate

$$WBS_{it}^{HS} = \beta_0 + \beta_1\ ln\ Y_{it} + \beta_2\ ln\ K_{it}/Y_{it} + \beta_3 OUTS_{it}$$

$$+ \beta_4 TECH_{it} + u_{it}. \tag{10.2}$$

The dependent variable (WBS^{HS}) in this equation is a composite measure, incorporating relative wages of nonproduction workers and their relative employment.

10.4.2 Empirical Results

We first estimate our basic equation, 10.2, with the wage bill share as the dependent variable in table 10.3.

In column 1 of table 10.3, the wage bill share of the high-skilled workers WBS is regressed on $OUTS$ and the control variables, Y and the capital output ratio K/Y. The results suggest that outsourcing has a significant negative effect on the demand for high-skilled labor. Thus, rather than saving on low-skilled labor as is commonly assumed, outsourcing saves on high-skilled labor relative to low-skilled labor. Furthermore, the sector's output and capital output ratio have a positive impact on the nonproduction workers' share of the wage bill.[14]

Table 10.3
Outsourcing and demand for high-skilled labor in Austria

Dependent variable	Wage bill share of high-skilled workers			
	(1)	(2)	(3)	(4)
OUTS	−0.018*	−0.030**	−0.034***	−0.036***
	(0.011)	(0.012)	(0.010)	(0.010)
ln Y	3.999*	4.256**	3.721*	2.704
	(2.100)	(1.962)	(1.964)	(2.031)
ln K/Y	3.440*	4.740**	4.098*	2.826
	(2.059)	(2.064)	(2.067)	(2.098)
R&D L		0.414**	0.362*	0.365**
		(0.198)	(0.183)	(0.179)
R&D SUB			0.829***	0.974***
			(0.303)	(0.311)
FDI L				−0.039**
				(0.019)
Adjusted R^2	0.997	0.997	0.997	0.997
N	120	120	120	120

Note: Parameters are estimated by OLS regressions; *** (**) [*] indicates significance at the 1 (5) [10] percent level; robust standard errors are reported in parentheses; constant, industry dummies, and time dummies are included but for expositional ease are not shown.

Variables are defined as follows: wage bill share = (wage bill of nonproduction workers/industry wage bill) $*$ 100; OUTS = (imported inputs from the same sector/ value added) $*$ 100; ln Y = log real output; ln K/Y = log[(capital/output) $*$ 100]; R&D L = (R&D employment/employment) $*$ 100; R&D SUB = (R&D subsidies/value added) $*$ 100; FDI L = (employment in foreign affiliates in Austria/employment) $*$ 100.

This suggests that the output elasticity is higher for high-skilled labor than for low-skilled labor.

Additionally, specification 2 includes the *R&D L* as a proxy for technical change,[15] which is positively signed and statistically significant at the 5 percent level. This indicates that labor-saving technical change shifts the demand toward nonproduction workers. It is interesting to note that the inclusion of *R&D L* in column 2 magnifies the negative impact of OUTS on high-skilled labor and raises the significance to the 5 percent level.

We include two additional variables, *R&D SUB* and *FDI L*, in the regression to control for further factors that may have put pressure on the relative demand for skilled labor in Austria. *R&D SUB* measures public subsidies to the private sector in percentage of value added. The reason we include this variable in the regression is that the govern-

Table 10.4
Who contributes to R&D

	Financing R&D in 2001				
	Austria	United States	France	Japan	Finland
State aid	38.2%	27.8%	36.9%	18.5%	25.5%
Domestic firms	41.8	67.3	54.2	73.0	70.8
Foreign firms	19.7	—	7.2	0.4	2.5

Note: Due to other (not specified) contributors, the numbers do not sum to 100 for each country.
Source: Statistische Nachrichten 6/2004, Statistics Austria.

ment in Austria pursued an active technology policy, driving up relative wages of skilled labor in Austria. *R&D SUB* is supposed to control for this policy-induced effect on relative wages of skilled workers.[16] Compared to other OECD countries, governmental R&D policy plays an important role in Austria. In 2001, 38.2 percent of R&D expenditures was financed by the government, whereas only 29.1 percent of R&D expenditures was state financed on average in the OECD. Since these state-financed R&D expenditures are used as a policy instrument, they might be unequally distributed among sectors. As a proxy for R&D subsidies, we use in our analysis the R&D subsidies of the state-owned research foundation for enterprises (*Österreichische Forschungsförderungsgesellschaft*). The subsidies vary from 2.3 percent of the sector's R&D expenditures in the coke and oil sector to 21.6 percent in the wood sector.

The positive and highly significant coefficient on *R&D SUB* indicates that an increase of state-aided R&D expenditures in percentage of value added by 1 percentage point is pushing up the relative wage bill of high-skilled workers by 0.83 percentage points. Furthermore, the inclusion of *R&D SUB* increases the statistical significance of *OUTS* to the 1 percent level.

In the last specification of table 10.3, we include *FDI L*, measuring the percentage of employment of foreign affiliates in Austria by sector. The reason we include this variable is that foreign firms play an important role in the R&D and trade activity taking place in Austria. In 2001, 20 percent of R&D expenditures was financed by foreign firms (see table 10.4). This share is the largest one among OECD countries.[17] In addition, foreign affiliates in Austria generate a large share of Austrian imports. Table 10.5 shows that around one-third of all imports are by

Table 10.5
Role of foreign firms for Austria's trade and labor market

	1995	1998	2002
Share of FDI employment in total employment	16.26	17.00	16.65
Share of FDI imports in total imports	—	21.75	32.08

Source: Own calculations based on data from the Austrian National Bank, OeNB, the OECD STAN database, and Eurostat Comext database.

foreign multinationals in Austria. The presence of foreign firms in Austria varies strongly according to sector. The share of employment of foreign affiliates in percentage of the sector's employment ranges from 3.8 percent in the furniture sector to 70 percent in the coke and oil sector.[18]

Foreign multinationals tend to increase the relative demand for unskilled labor in Austria, suggesting that they invest in unskilled-labor-intensive sectors. This is consistent with the fact that Austria is a relatively human-capital-poor country.[19] The estimated coefficient on *FDI L* is negative and significant at the 5 percent level. A 1 percentage point increase in the share of imported inputs (*OUTS*) and the share of employment in foreign multinationals in Austria lowers the relative demand for high-skilled labor by about 0.04 percentage points.

The economic impact of international outsourcing implied by these estimates is substantial over the period considered. The observed increase in the nonproduction wage bill share in the period 1995–2002 is 3.36. Multiplying the coefficient on outsourcing from column 4 in table 10.3 by the change in outsourcing (12.67 percentage points) and dividing this by the change in the wage bill share $[(-0.036 * 12.67)/3.36]$ results in a negative contribution of 0.136. This implies that the wage bill share of human capital would have increased by 13.6 percent more in the absence of outsourcing in the previous decade.

How robust are these results? A decomposition of the wage bill share into relative wages and relative employment may deliver interesting insights. In table 10.6, we replace the dependent variable *wage bill share* with the new dependent variables, *relative wages*[20] and *relative employment* of high-skilled labor, respectively. We then run similar regressions as in table 10.3. The coefficient on *OUTS* is negative and statistically significant at the 1 percent level in all three relative wage regressions and somewhat less significant in the relative employment regressions.[21]

Table 10.6
Outsourcing and decomposed demand for high-skilled labor in Austria

	Relative wages			Relative employment		
	(1)	(2)	(3)	(4)	(5)	(6)
OUTS	−0.155***	−0.148***	−0.179***	−0.109*	−0.149**	−0.142***
	(0.056)	(0.055)	(0.061)	(0.063)	(0.067)	(0.051)
ln VA	−20.131**	−27.179***	−22.592***	67.617***	52.529***	66.058***
	(8.557)	(9.386)	(8.270)	(14.162)	(9.758)	(15.608)
ln K/VA	−17.521*	−22.064**	−19.831**	57.372***	51.123***	54.806***
	(9.145)	(9.115)	(8.724)	(10.280)	(7.831)	(11.164)
R&D L		2.637*			3.074***	
		(1.516)			(1.073)	
R&D SUB			2.349			4.923**
			(1.664)			(2.025)
Adjusted R^2	0.975	0.976	0.975	0.994	0.995	0.994
N	96	96	96	120	120	120

Note: Parameters are estimated by OLS regressions; *** (**) [*] indicates significance at the 1 (5) [10] percent level; robust standard errors are reported in parentheses; constant, industry dummies, and time dummies are included but for expositional ease are not shown.

Variables are defined as follows: relative wages = (70 percentile wage of nonproduction workers/30 percentile of production workers) * 100; relative employment = (number of nonproduction workers/number of production workers) * 100; OUTS = (imported inputs from the same sector/value added) * 100; ln VA = log real value added; ln K/VA = log[(capital/value added) * 100]; R&D L = (R&D employment/employment) * 100; R&D SUB = (R&D subsidies/value added) * 100.

The R&D measures have a strong and significant impact on the relative employment. The *R&D L* ratio and the *R&D SUB* influence the relative employment of high-skilled workers positively, whereas the *FDI L* ratio has a strong negative impact, which is not reported in the table. These variables, however, have only a minor effect on relative wages.[22]

International outsourcing can explain 38 percent of the decrease in the wage gap between the 70 percentile of the nonproduction workers and the 30 percentile wage of the production workers. Relative employment would have grown by 24 percent more in the absence of outsourcing activities that occurred in the eight-year period considered. As shown in table 10.6, outsourcing has a negative impact on relative wages, as well as on relative employment. However, while the wage gap is decreasing, outsourcing contributes significantly to this development, and it acts against the rise in relative employment.

10.5   Multinational Outsourcing to Poland

In this section we investigate how outsourcing by foreign firms has affected the evolution of the skill premium in Poland. We capture outsourcing of foreign firms to Poland by the share of foreign-owned fixed assets in domestic fixed assets $(1 + K_{it}^{FDI}/K_{it}^{D})$. This measure arises from disaggregating of the capital stock (K) into domestic capital (K^{D}) and foreign capital (K^{FDI}) as in Feenstra and Hanson (1997).[23]

10.5.1   Data and Variables

We study the relative labor demand for skilled workers in Poland on the manufacturing industry. Our data set consists of an unbalanced panel[24] of twenty-three ISIC (International Standard Industry Classification) industries over a nine-year period (1994–2002).[25] We measure the employment of high-skilled (low-skilled) workers as an annual average employment of nonproduction (production) workers and the wage of skilled (unskilled) workers as an annual average gross wage of nonproduction (production) workers. Unfortunately, especially at the level of disaggregation we use in our empirical work, no better proxies for high-skilled and low-skilled labor are available. Hence, the high-skilled labor wage share is measured as the nonproduction workers' wage share in the total wage bill.

Our data allow us to separate foreign- and domestic-owned fixed assets.[26] To control for the restructuring processes in Polish manufacturing, we add the share of private firms in total number of manufacturing firms $(PRIV)$. We assume that private enterprises have stronger incentives to rationalize and modernize their production than their public counterparts, so that their activities might have affected the relative high-skilled labor demand. Furthermore, we include the variables R&D expenditures' share in sales $(R\&D)$ and the import and export shares in sales $(M$ and $X)$. R&D is supposed to account for technological improvements, and M and X capture the potential influence of international integration and exposure to international competition. Finally, as the total labor cost function condition on total output, it is common practice to include output in this type of the regression. However, due to a high correlation between output (measured by sales) and domestic fixed assets, which enters the regression in levels, we excluded the former variable from regression. Nevertheless, accounting for industry and time fixed effects helps to resolve potential problems arising from omitting output in the regression. Thus our modified estimating equation is

$$WBS_{it}^{HS} = \alpha_1 + \alpha_2 \ln\left(1 + \frac{K_{it}^{FDI}}{K_{it}^{D}}\right) + \alpha_3 \ln K_{it}^{D} + \alpha_4 \ln PRIV_{it}$$

$$+ \alpha_5 \ln R\&D_{it} + \alpha_6 \ln M_{it} + \alpha_7 \ln X_{it} + \varepsilon_{it}. \qquad (10.3)$$

10.5.2 Empirical Results

Table 10.7 reports the two-way fixed effects estimation results for the wage share of high-skilled labor. Column 1 presents the basic specification with the two independent variables: foreign capital share in domestic capital $(1 + K^{FDI}/K^{D})$ and domestic capital (K^{D}). Columns 2 to 4 present the results when adding several control variables to the basic specification. The coefficient on the foreign capital variable is positive and statistically significant in all regressions. Its magnitude ranges from 0.029 to 0.044. What is interesting is its economic significance. We multiplied the most conservative estimate of the coefficient of the foreign fixed assets (0.029) with the log change in one plus the share of foreign fixed assets between 1994 and 2002 (0.534). The obtained number (0.015) is the contribution of foreign capital to changes in relative demand for skills. It implies that FDI can account for at least 16 percent of the observed increase in nonproduction workers' wage share (0.099) in the Polish manufacturing sector between 1994 and 2002.

The coefficient of domestic capital is also positive in all specifications but not statistically significant. The sign of domestic capital coefficient corroborates the theoretical result that any accumulation of capital, domestic or foreign owned, leads to an increase in the relative demand for skilled labor. Its statistical insignificance, however, underscores the special role of foreign capital for the changes in relative high-skilled labor demand.

The inclusion of control variables does not change the results obtained for the basic regressors. *PRIV* has a positive and significant impact on the high-skilled wage share. The result on the *R&D* variable suggests that the increase in the relative high-skilled labor demand was due partly to technological upgrading. The negative coefficient on the import share can be seen from the Heckscher-Ohlin perspective. Given that Poland is low-skilled labor abundant compared to its trading partners, international trade would exert a downward pressure on

Table 10.7
Foreign investors and demand for high-skilled labor in Poland

Dependent variable	Wage bill share of high-skilled workers							
	(1)	(2)	(3)	(4)	(5)	(6)	(7)	(8)
$\ln\left(1 + \frac{K^{FDI}}{K^D}\right)$	0.044*** (0.015)	0.048** (0.014)	0.046** (0.014)	0.029** (0.012)				
$\ln\left(1 + \frac{E^{FDI}}{E^D}\right)$					0.114* (0.062)	0.141*** (0.049)	0.124** (0.048)	0.107*** (0.039)
$\ln K^D$	0.011 (0.016)	0.016 (0.013)	0.016 (0.013)	0.004 (0.013)	0.001 (0.016)	0.007 (0.014)	0.007 (0.014)	0.002 (0.012)
$\ln$ PRIV		0.041** (0.016)	0.036** (0.018)	0.043** (0.018)		0.045** (0.019)	0.042* (0.022)	0.050** (0.019)
$\ln$ R&D		0.008** (0.003)	0.008** (0.003)	0.007** (0.003)		0.006*** (0.003)	0.006*** (0.003)	0.006** (0.003)
$\ln M$				−0.046*** (0.011)				−0.053*** (0.012)
$\ln X$				0.001 (0.017)				−0.003 (0.016)
Year dummies	Yes***	Yes***	Yes***	Yes***	Yes***	Yes***	Yes***	Yes***
Adjusted R^2	0.917	0.920	0.920	0.926	0.910	0.931	0.918	0.949
N	194	192	185	171	194	192	185	171

Note: Parameters are estimated by OLS regressions; *** (**) [*] indicates significance at the 1 (5) [10] percent level; robust standard errors are reported in parentheses; constant and industry dummies are included but for expositional ease are not shown.

Variables are defined as follows: wage bill share = wage bill of nonproduction workers/manufacturing wage bill; $\ln(1 + K^{FDI}/K^D) = \log[1 +$ (foreign fixed assets/domestic fixed assets)]; $\ln(1 + E^{FDI}/E^D) = \log[1 +$ (number of foreign firms/number of domestic)]; $\ln K^D = \log($domestic fixed assets); $\ln$ PRIV $= \log($number of private firms/total number of firms); $\ln$ R&D $= \log($R&D expenditures/sales); $\ln M = \log($import/sales); $\ln X = \log($export/sales).

earnings of high-skilled workers relative to the earnings of low-skilled workers. Nevertheless, the result on the export share is inconclusive.[27] Finally, the inclusion of time dummies is crucial when analyzing the role of outsourcing for the skilled workers' relative demand in Poland. We should not forget that Poland is a transition economy with institutions and the economic system as a whole being still work in progress. The positive coefficient on the year dummies suggests that the transition to a market economy has favored high-skilled workers.

In the remaining specifications of table 10.7 we substitute $(1 + K^{FDI}/K^D)$ with the ratio of the number of foreign to domestic firms $(1 + E^{FDI}/E^D)$. An inspection of columns 5 to 8 shows that the results are robust to this alternative measure of outsourcing.[28]

In table 10.8 we replace the wage share of high-skilled workers as a dependent variable by decomposing it into relative employment and wages of nonproduction workers. As can be seen, the results for the relative employment practically mirror those for the wage share. But the magnitude of the coefficients is twice as high (in the case of R&D, even triple), and the year dummies lose their significance. The regressions with high-skilled workers' relative wages in columns 5 to 8 give a different picture. The coefficients on domestic capital become significant at the 1 percent level, while the influence of privatization becomes negative and not significant. R&D retains its positive sign but it is no longer significant, whereas year dummies are positive and highly significant.

The different results on the time dummies are not surprising. Under the socialist regime, Poland had an extremely compressed wage distribution. Thus, one of the dimensions of the transition process was the liberalization of wage-setting schemes. In the regression with relative wages, significant and positive time dummies may reflect labor market adjustments to a market economy. Meanwhile, relative employment underwent changes that were industry specific and therefore better captured by privatization advances. The main message of this table is the positive and significant impact of foreign capital $(1 + K^{FDI}/K^D)$ on relative wages and the positive though less statistically significant impact on relative employment of nonproduction workers.

10.5.3 Robustness

Some studies also include relative wages of high-skilled workers as an independent variable, arguing that they are of importance by factor

Table 10.8
Foreign investors and decomposed demand for high-skilled labor in Poland

Dependent variables	Relative wages				Relative employment			
	(1)	(2)	(3)	(4)	(5)	(6)	(7)	(8)
$\ln\left(1 + \frac{K^{FDI}}{K^D}\right)$	0.183***	0.180***	0.174***	0.170***	0.083**	0.094**	0.090**	0.045
	(0.042)	(0.045)	(0.045)	(0.051)	(0.041)	(0.039)	(0.035)	(0.033)
$\ln K^D$	0.164***	0.161***	0.162***	0.166***	0.056	0.068	0.069	0.039
	(0.035)	(0.060)	(0.060)	(0.060)	(0.049)	(0.045)	(0.043)	(0.045)
$\ln$ PRIV		−0.023	−0.034	−0.039		0.095**	0.083*	0.102**
		(0.048)	(0.052)	(0.055)		(0.042)	(0.045)	(0.045)
$\ln$ R&D			0.006	0.010			0.027**	0.025**
			(0.011)	(0.012)			(0.010)	(0.010)
$\ln$ M				−0.011				−0.119***
				(0.056)				(0.021)
$\ln$ X				0.005				0.026
				(0.069)				(0.047)
Year dummies	Yes***	Yes***	Yes***	Yes***	Yes	Yes	Yes	Yes
Adjusted R^2	0.773	0.769	0.771	0.775	0.836	0.838	0.837	0.847
N	194	192	185	171	194	192	185	171

Note: Parameters are estimated by OLS regressions; *** (**) [*] indicates significance at the 1 (5) [10] percent level; robust standard errors are reported in parentheses; constant and industry dummies are included but for expositional ease are not shown.

Variables are defined as follows: relative employment = number of nonproduction workers/number of production workers; relative wage = wage of nonproduction workers/wage of production workers; $\ln(1 + K^{FDI}/K^D) = \log|1 + (\text{foreign fixed assets/domestic fixed assets})|$; $\ln K^D = \log(\text{domestic fixed assets})$; $\ln$ PRIV $= \log(\text{number of private firms/total number of firms})$; $\ln$ R&D $= \log(\text{R&D expenditures/sales})$; $\ln$ M $= \log(\text{import/sales})$; $\ln$ X $= \log(\text{export/sales})$.

supply and demand decisions. The relative wages of high-skilled workers are likely to be endogenous in wage share regression, and a failure to control for this may lead to simultaneity bias. So far we have ignored the potential influence of relative wages, but this approach may cause an omitted-variable bias. Therefore, in this section, we include the first lag of relative wages into the regression. The lagging procedure should alleviate the problem of simultaneity.

It is also likely that foreign capital is endogenous. Bruno, Crino, and Falzoni (2004) and Pavcnik (2003) argue that foreign firms invest in some industries because of their high-skill intensity, not the other way around. Tests for exogeneity indeed indicated that foreign capital variable is endogenous. It is therefore necessary to verify the robustness of the OLS estimates with the instrumental-variables method. We add the first, the second, and the third lag of foreign capital variable to the existing set of instruments.[29]

Table 10A.1 in the appendix shows IV-GMM results for the high-skilled workers' wage share. It appears that an increase of relative wages has slightly (statistically insignificantly) retarded the increase of relative demand for nonproduction workers. More important, the coefficients on foreign capital remain positive and statistically significant in all regressions but one. The inclusion of relative wages, however, deprived privatization of their explanatory power. The joint statistical significance of year dummies corroborates the result that the transition process is partly responsible for the increase in nonproduction workers' wage share because it liberalized the wage-setting mechanism.[30]

Turning to Table 10A.2 in the appendix reporting IV-GMM results for relative wage and employment, the inclusion of relative wages to the regression has similar consequences for relative employment as for relative demand. Regarding relative wages, their development was driven mainly by foreign capital and aggregate shocks related to the transition process.

We also carried out the regression with all independent variables lagged one period, as Bruno et al. (2004) did, in order to compare their results with ours. The results for the two approaches differ in the value of coefficients of foreign capital variable. They are higher when using lags. We also reestimated our regressions with panel-corrected standard error estimation (PCSE), which allows correction for contemporaneous correlation across cross-sectional units and for autocorrelation. The results are similar to those presented in this chapter.[31]

10.6 Conclusion

In this chapter we have examined the importance of outsourcing for the labor market outcome in Austria and Poland prior to eastern enlargement. In contrast to other studies on the topic, we find that outsourcing has lowered the skill premium in Austria, the high-income country, while it has increased the wage gap in Poland, the low-income country. We summarize our findings in table 10.9. We also contrast our results with the empirical findings of Feenstra and Hanson (1997) for the United States and Mexico. We report numbers for all four countries prior to eastern enlargement and to NAFTA. Austria and Poland liberalized their trade and investment regime in the 1990s after the fall of communism. Feenstra and Hanson (1997) report their

Table 10.9
Contribution of outsourcing to wage inequality in selected countries

	Poland, 1994–2002	Mexico, 1975–1988	Austria, 1995–2002	United States, 1979–1990
Changes (in percent)				
Outsourcing	70.61[a]	—	50.45[b]	50.98[c]
Wage bill share[d]	34.18	21.35	8.29	19.92
Relative wages[e]	41.39	19.63	−2.00	—
Relative employment[e]	10.23	—	16.89	—
Contribution of outsourcing (in percent)				
Wage bill share[d]	15.7–23.7	52.4–56.2[f]	6.8–13.6	30.9–51.3
Relative wages[e]	15.3–16.4	—	33.0–38.1	—
Relative employment[e]	83.0–173.4	—	18.4–25.2	—

[a] 1 + (foreign fixed assets/domestic fixed assets), manufacturing.
[b] Narrow definition of outsourcing: (imported inputs from the same sector/value added of sector) ∗ 100, mining and manufacturing.
[c] (Imported inputs from the same sector/total nonenergy material purchases) ∗ 100, manufacturing.
[d] (Nonproduction workers' wage ∗ number of nonproduction workers)/((nonproduction workers' wage ∗ number of nonproduction workers) + (production workers' wage ∗ number of production workers)) in manufacturing for Poland, United States, and Mexico, in mining and manufacturing for Austria.
[e] Nonproduction to production workers in manufacturing for Poland, Germany, United States, and Mexico, in mining and manufacturing for Austria.
[f] Outsourcing measured by 1 + (U.S. establishments/Mexican establishments); for U.S. border region only.
Source: Poland: own calculations; Mexico: Feenstra and Hanson (1997); United States: calculations taken from Feenstra and Hanson (1996); Austria: own calculations.

numbers for Mexico for 1975–1988 and for the United States for 1979–1990. Several points are noteworthy from table 10.9.[32]

First, Poland experienced the largest increase in outsourcing compared to Austria and the United States. In the period 1994 to 2002 outsourcing in Poland (as measured by the ratio of foreign to domestic assets) increased by 71 percent; in Austria outsourcing (as measured by the share of imported inputs in percent of value added) increased by 50 percent in the period 1995 to 2002. In the United States outsourcing (as measured by the share of imported inputs in total inputs excluding energy) rose by 51 percent in the period 1979 to 1990. Both low-income countries, Poland and Mexico, experienced an increase in their skill premium, but Poland's rise in the skill premium was more than twice as large (41 percent between 1994 to 2002) compared to Mexico's (19.6 percent between 1975 to 1988). Second, in Austria, the high-income country, relative wages for skills declined by 2 percent in the period 1995 to 2002, but increased by 41 percent in Poland, the low-income country. We suggest that this has happened in Austria because Austria is poor in human capital relative to its trading partners.[33] We also show that in the absence of an active R&D policy pursued by the Austrian government, the decline in the skill premium would have been much more pronounced. Third, in spite of the larger increase of outsourcing in Poland compared to Austria, outsourcing is more important in Austria compared to Poland in explaining the evolution of the skill premium. In Poland outsourcing contributes only 16 percent to the change in the relative wage for skilled workers, while in Austria it contributes 35 percent. In other words, in the absence of outsourcing, relative wages for human capital would have declined by 35 percent less in Austria and would have increased by 16 percent less in Poland.

Appendix 10A: Notes on Calculation of Variables

Wages
Since Austria's wages are recorded according to at most to the social security contribution ceiling, an accurate measure of mean wages is not possible. The capping of high earnings that are highly correlated with nonproduction workers introduces a downward bias in relative wage rates. However, the statistics of the Association of Austrian Social Insurance report different percentile wages for production and nonproduction workers.

Table 10A.1
Definition and source of variables

Variable	Description	Source
Austria		
Wage bill share	Share of nonproduction workers' wage bill in total wage bill	Association of Austrian Social Insurance
Relative wages	70 percentile nonproduction wage relative to 30 percentile production wage	Association of Austrian Social Insurance
Relative employment	Nonproduction workers relative to production workers	Association of Austrian Social Insurance
OUTS	Share of imported inputs from the same NACE two-letter sector in value added	Statistics Austria (input-output table), OECD STAN database
Y	Output (production), deflated by sector-specific producer price indices	OECD STAN database
VA	Value added, deflated by sector-specific producer price indices	OECD STAN database
K/Y	Ratio of gross fixed capital stock to output	OECD STAN database
K/VA	Ratio of gross fixed capital stock to value added	OECD STAN database
R&D L	Share of R&D employment in total employment	Eurostat, OECD STAN database
R&D SUB	Ratio of R&D subsidies to value added	Austrian Research Promotion Organization, OECD STAN database
FDI L	Share of employment in foreign affiliates to total sector's employment in Austria	OeNB, OECD STAN database
Poland		
Wage bill share	Share of nonproduction workers' wage bill in total wage bill	Polish Central Statistical Office
Relative wages	Nonproduction workers' wages relative to production workers' wages	Polish Central Statistical Office
Relative employment	Number of nonproduction workers relative to production workers	Polish Central Statistical Office

$\left(1 + \frac{K^{FDI}}{K^{D}}\right)$	One plus the share of foreign-owned fixed assets in domestic fixed assets deflated by sector-specific producer price indices	Polish Central Statistical Office
$\left(1 + \frac{E^{FDI}}{E^{D}}\right)$	One plus the ratio of number of foreign firms to domestic firms	Polish Central Statistical Office
K^{D}	Domestic fixed assets	Polish Central Statistical Office
PRIV	Share of private firms in total number of firms	Polish Central Statistical Office
R&D	Share of R&D expenditures in sales	Polish Central Statistical Office
M	Share of imports in sales	OECD STAN database
X	Share of exports in sales	OECD STAN database

Table 10A.2
Foreign investors and demand for high-skilled labor in Poland

| Dependent variable | Wage bill share of high-skilled workers | | | |
	(1)	(2)	(3)	(4)
$\ln\left(1 + \frac{K^{FDI}}{K^D}\right)$	0.083*	0.076	0.075*	0.102*
	(0.046)	(0.050)	(0.042)	(0.048)
$\ln \frac{W^S}{W^{US}_{t-1}}$	−0.211	−0.185	−0.275	−0.401
	(0.307)	(0.288)	(0.268)	(0.287)
$\ln K^D$	0.019	0.016	0.023	0.039
	(0.030)	(0.034)	(0.033)	(0.041)
$\ln$ PRIV		−0.014	−0.018	−0.011
		(0.011)	(0.012)	(0.011)
$\ln$ R&D			0.007**	0.010**
			(0.003)	(0.004)
$\ln$ M				−0.007
				(0.016)
$\ln$ X				−0.035*
				(0.021)
Year dummies	Yes*	Yes*	Yes*	Yes*
Centered R^2	0.941	0.942	0.936	0.922
Hansen J statistic	0.472	0.676	0.393	0.211
P value	[0.492]	[0.411]	[0.530]	[0.645]
N	126	124	120	110

Note: Parameters are estimated by instrumental variable regressions (GMM); instruments: first, second, and third lag of log foreign fixed assets share in domestic fixed assets; *** (**) [*] indicates significance at the 1 (5) [10] percent level; robust standard errors are reported in parentheses; constant and industry dummies are included but for expositional ease are not shown.

Variables are defined as follows: wage bill share = wage bill of nonproduction workers/manufacturing wage bill; $\ln(1 + K^{FDI}/K^D) = \log[1 + (\text{foreign fixed assets}/\text{domestic fixed assets})]$; $\ln K^D = \log(\text{domestic fixed assets})$; $\ln$ PRIV $= \log(\text{number of private firms/total number of firms})$; $\ln$ R&D $= \log(\text{R\&D expenditures/sales})$; $\ln$ M $= \log(\text{import/sales})$; $\ln$ X $= \log(\text{export/sales})$.

For calculating the wage bill share and relative wages, we experimented with various approaches: ratios of mean, median, and different percentile wages. Furthermore, we used those alternative calculations as dependent variables for the regression analysis in order to check for robustness. Finally, we decided to use the mean wages for calculating the wage bill of production and nonproduction workers. Therefore, all reported wage bill share regressions show results on the wage bill share of mean wages. For regressions with relative wages as the de-

Table 10A.3
Foreign investors and decomposed demand for high-skilled labor in Poland

Dependent variables	Relative wages				Relative employment			
	(1)	(2)	(3)	(4)	(5)	(6)	(7)	(8)
$\ln\left(1 + \frac{K^{FDI}}{K^D}\right)$	0.325**	0.333**	0.296**	0.385*	0.295**	0.279*	0.256**	0.342**
	(0.159)	(0.169)	(0.148)	(0.217)	(0.144)	(0.156)	(0.124)	(0.153)
$\ln \frac{W^S}{W^{US}_{l-1}}$					-1.304	-1.169	-1.270	-1.622
					(0.930)	(0.883)	(0.807)	(0.897)
$\ln K^D$	0.177	0.186	0.175	0.250	0.115	0.111	0.113	0.164
	(0.123)	(0.134)	(0.122)	(0.175)	(0.095)	(0.105)	(0.098)	(0.126)
$\ln$ PRIV		0.001	-0.011	-0.040		-0.017	-0.030	-0.016
		(0.032)	(0.030)	(0.042)		(0.034)	(0.034)	(0.034)
$\ln$ R&D			-0.002	0.009			0.021**	0.029**
			(0.006)	(0.008)			(0.010)	(0.012)
$\ln$ M				0.124				0.000
				(0.0101)				(0.050)
$\ln$ X				-0.085				-0.085
				(0.069)				(0.066)
Year dummies	Yes***	Yes***	Yes***	Yes***	Yes	Yes	Yes	Yes
Centered R^2	0.816	0.808	0.829	0.827	0.798	0.804	0.782	0.723
Hansen J statistic	0.061	0.020	0.014	0.142	0.480	0.949	0.561	0.316
P value	[0.805]	[0.886]	[0.904]	[0.707]	[0.489]	[0.330]	[0.454]	[0.574]
N	126	124	120	110	126	124	120	110

Note: Parameters are estimated by instrumental variable regressions (GMM); instruments: first, second, and third lag of log foreign fixed assets share in domestic fixed assets; *** (**) [*] indicates significance at the 1 (5) [10] percent level; robust standard errors are reported in parentheses; constant and industry dummies are included but for expositional ease are not shown.

Variables are defined as follows: relative employment = number of nonproduction workers/number of production workers; relative wage = wage of nonproduction workers/wage of production workers; $\ln(1 + K^{FDI}/K^D) = \log[1 + (\text{foreign fixed assets}/\text{domestic fixed assets})]$; $\ln K^D = \log(\text{domestic fixed assets})$; $\ln$ PRIV = log(number of private firms/total number of firms); $\ln$ R&D = log(R&D expenditures/sales); $\ln$ M = log(import/sales); $\ln$ X = log(export/sales).

pendent variable, we calculated the ratio of the 70 percentile wage of nonproduction workers to the 30 percentile wage of production workers.

Imported Intermediate Goods
As in most other countries, input-output tables for Austria are not published annually. The most recent such tables available are from 1995 and 2000. We estimate the input-output tables for the missing years by interpolating the input-output coefficients and multiplying them by imported inputs. These imported inputs result from the interpolated share of intermediate goods in total imports. We receive the total imports by transforming harmonized system (HS) classification import data at the six-digit level to NACE categories at four-digit level. The import data in HS classification are taken from the Eurostat Comext database. Since the data on labor market determine the level of sectoral aggregation, we aggregate the imported inputs to the chosen NACE two-letter level of analysis. Therefore, Austria's imports at the sectoral level formulate the estimated input-output tables for the missing years.

Capital Stock
Gross fixed capital stocks are calculated according to the perpetual inventory method using data on gross fixed capital formation (GFCF), which are deflated by a general price index for investment goods.[34] The initial capital stock for the year 1994, K_{1994}, is estimated by using the values of capital formation in the preceding years, 1990 to 1993:

$$K_{1994} = (GFCF_{1990} + GFCF_{1991} + GFCF_{1992} + GFCF_{1993} + GFCF_{1994}) * 2.$$

The gross fixed capital stocks for the sample period are calculated according to the following simple formula, assuming a constant depreciation rate of 10 percent:

$$K_t = 0.9 * K_{t-1} + GFCF_t.$$

To check the validity of this estimation, we compare the aggregate estimate for NACE D with the net capital stocks provided by Statistics Austria. The sizes of these stocks differ somewhat, but the development is very similar, as the comparison of the tables below with the results in the main text illustrate.

Notes

1. The Brookings Trade Forum in 2005 was devoted to the theme of outsourcing of white-collar workers.

2. For the New International Division of Labor in Europe, see Marin (2006).

3. For an explanation of the evolution of the skill premium in Germany, see Marin and Raubold (2006).

4. In 2003 CEE accounted for 88 percent of total outgoing FDI in Austria but only 4 percent in Germany (see Marin, Lorentowicz, and Raubold 2003). Preliminary results for Germany suggest similar results as in Austria (see Marin and Raubold 2006).

5. For the determinants of outsourcing, see Marin (2006).

6. Marin (2004, table 12) shows that Austria is poor in skills relative to Eastern Europe.

7. Readers should keep in mind that the economic link between Austria and Poland is not as strong as between the United States and Mexico. See table 10.1.

8. See Feenstra and Hanson (1996a).

9. In the literature it is common to weigh the data with the size of the industrial sector. We have experimented with two types of weighting: employment and sales. These regressions yield similar results to those presented here. This is true for the Austrian and the Polish data sample as well.

10. See Geishecker (2002).

11. The considered sectors belong to NACE C and D.

12. See, for example, Feenstra and Hanson (1996b) and Geishecker (2002).

13. Data for capital stocks are available at the aggregated level of ISIC one-letter sectors for the years 1988 to 2000.

14. We also ran all the regressions with investments (gross fixed capital formation) instead of capital stocks; the results are very similar.

15. The regressions are also carried out with data on R&D expenditures relative to value added. The results for the estimated coefficients (not reported here) are very similar to those for R&D employment.

16. For the R&D policy–induced effect on relative wages for skilled workers in Austria, see Marin (1995). She shows that the same policy has contributed to the slowing of the speed by which the pattern of trade moved up the technological ladder in Austria.

17. In the EU-15 countries 7.7 percent of the R&D activity is undertaken by foreign multinationals. See Statistische Nachrichten 6/2004, Statistics Austria.

18. The numbers show averages for 1995 to 2002.

19. For a comparison of Austria's skill endowment with other OECD and Eastern European countries, see Marin (2004).

20. See the appendix for a note on calculating relative wages. Due to missing values on the 70 percentile wages of the mining (NACE C), coke and petroleum (NACE DF), and vehicles (NACE DM) sectors, the sample reduces to thirteen sectors. It results in the reduced sample of ninety-six observations.

21. When using real output as we did in table 10.3 instead of real value added, the coefficients on the variable of interest, the outsourcing variable, and the output and capital-to-output ratio are not affected. Only in the case of relative wages as the dependent variable do the coefficients on both control variables, output and the capital-to-output ratio, become insignificant.

22. In the table we do not show the results on the FDI variable for expositional ease. As in the case of the regressions of the wage bill share as a dependent variable (table 10.3) the estimated coefficients on the FDI variable are negative but significant at the 1 percent level only in the case of relative employment as the dependent variable.

23. $ln(K^D + K^{FDI}) = ln(K^D) + ln(1 + K^{FDI}/K^D)$.

24. Some numbers are not made public for confidentiality reasons.

25. Bruno, Crino, and Falzoni (2004) examine a similar question for the Poland, the Czech Republic, and Hungary. However, they have data on six ISIC industries for only the period 1994 to 2001.

26. Both variables have been aggregated by the Polish Statistical Office from detailed reports provided by domestic and foreign firms in Poland. Feenstra and Hanson (1997), for lack of data, could not directly measure the capital stock in foreign ownership and thus used the number of foreign firms as a proxy. Bruno et al. (2004) measure foreign capital with foreign direct investment stock.

27. For consistency reasons, we included the import and export shares analogously in our regression on Austria. However, the estimated coefficients on both of these variables are statistically insignificant in virtually all specifications and do not change the results of the remaining variables.

28. Replacing K^D with the number of domestic establishments E^D does not change the result substantially.

29. This lag structure maximizes the F-statistic.

30. However, also in the case of Austria, positive F-tests on the joint significance of the included time dummies indicate that a strong time trend underlies the development of the wage bill share.

31. The results of PCSE and regressions with lagged independent variables are available form the authors upon request.

32. When comparing the figures in table 10.9 it is important to keep in mind that in contrast to the United States and Mexico, Poland and Austria have little economic link (see table 10.1).

33. See Marin (2004, table 12) for Austria's relative endowment with human capital.

34. For this calculation, see Egger (2000). We also experimented with alternative calculations of the capital stocks and received fairly similar results.

References

Anderton, B., and P. Brenton. (1998). Outsourcing and Low-Skilled Workers in the UK. Working paper no. 12/98, Centre for the Study of Globalisation and Regionalisation, University of Warwick.

Berman, E., J. Bound, and Z. Griliches. (1994). Changes in the Demand for Skilled Labor within U.S. Manufacturing: Evidence from the Annual Survey of Manufacturers. *Quarterly Journal of Economics* 109, 367–397.

Berman, E., J. Bound, and S. Machin. (1998). Implications of Skill-Biased Technological Change: International Evidence. *Quarterly Journal of Economics* 113, 1245–1279.

Bruno, G. S. F., R. Crinr, and A. M. Falzoni. (2004). Foreign Direct Investment, Wage Inequality, and Skilled Labor in EU Accession Countries. Working paper no. 154, Centre for Research on Innovation and Internationalisation. Universita Bocconi.

Diehl, M. (1999). The Impact of International Outsourcing on the Skill Structure of Employment: Empirical Evidence from German Manufacturing Industries. Kiel working paper 946, Institut für Weltwirtschaft.

Egger, P. (2000). A Note on the Proper Econometric Specification of the Gravity Equation. *Economic Letters* 66, 25–31.

Feenstra, R. C., and G. H. Hanson. (1996a). Foreign Investment, Outsourcing and Relative Wages. In R. C. Feenstra, G. G. Grossman, and D. A. Irwin (eds.), *Political Economy of Trade Policy: Essays in Honor of Jagdish Bhagwati*. Cambridge: MIT Press, pp. 89–127.

Feenstra, R. C., and G. H. Hanson. (1996b). Globalization, Outsourcing and Wage Inequality. *American Economic Review, Papers and Proceedings* 86 (2), 240–245.

Feenstra, R. C., and G. H. Hanson. (1997). Foreign Direct Investment and Relative Wages: Evidence from Mexico's Maquiladoras. *Journal of International Economics* 42, 371–393.

Foreign Investment in Poland. (1999, 2000). *Foreign Trade Research Institute*. Warsaw.

Geishecker, I. (2002). Outsourcing and the Demand for Low-Skilled Labour in German Manufacturing: New Evidence. Deutches Institute für Wirtschatts for schung. Discussion papers 313, DIW, Berlin.

Marin, D. (1995). Learning and Dynamic Comparative Advantage: Lessons from Austria's Postwar Pattern of Growth for Eastern Europe. Discussion paper no. 1116, Centre for Economic Policy Research, London.

Marin, D. (2004). A Nation of Poets and Thinkers: Less So with Eastern Enlargement? Austria and Germany. Discussion paper no. 4358, Centre for Economic Policy Research, London.

Marin, D. (2006). A New International Division of Labor in Europe: Outsourcing and Offshoring to Eastern Europe. *Journal of the European Economic Association, Papers and Proceedings* 4, 612–622.

Marin, D., A. Lorentowicz, and A. Raubold. (2003). Ownership, Capital or Outsourcing: What Drives German Investment to Eastern Europe? In H. Hermann and R. Lipsey (eds.), *Foreign Direct Investment in the Real and Financial Sector in Industrial Countries*. Berlin: Springer-Verlag.

Marin, D., and A. Raubold. (2006). The Declining Prospects for Human Capital in Germany: A Result of the New International Division of Labor? Mimeo., University of Munich.

Polish Information and Foreign Investment Agency. http://www.paiiz.gov.pl/index/.

Pavcnik, N. (2003). What Explains Skill Upgrading in Less Developed Countries. *Journal of Development Economics* 71, 311–328.

Rocznik Statystyczny Przemyslu. *Polska Statystyka Publiczna*. Warsaw.

Rocznik Statystyczny Rzeczpospolitej Polskiej. *Polska Statystyka Publiczna*. Warsaw.

Protsenko, A. (2003). Vertical and Horizontal Foreign Direct Investments in Transition Countries. Ph.D thesis, University of Munich.

Statistik Austria. (2004). Finanzierung der Ausgaben für Forschung und experimentelle Entwicklung in Vsterreich—Globalschdtzung 2004. *Statistische Nachrichten 6/2004, Statistics Austria*, Vienna.

11

Is It Strategic to Attract the Service Activities of Multinational Firms? Some Empirical Evidence

Fabrice Defever

11.1 Introduction

It is well known that many governments provide incentives to attract foreign firms. Barba Navaretti and Venables (2004) offer several examples of such proactive behavior; the U.S. state of Alabama and the Portuguese government, respectively, granted subsidies equivalent to $160,000 and $250,000 per employee to a foreign car producer. These incentives take many forms, including tax cuts, employment, and capital grants.[1]

However, both academics and policymakers seem to have neglected the possibility of attracting service functions associated with production activity. Indeed, the fragmentation of the production process of multinational firms cannot be restricted to the production side. Krugman (1995) considers that the international value chain decomposition is one of the four major aspects of the modern international trade. He calls this phenomenon "slicing the value chain" and includes in his definition a large number of service activities. As noted by the World Investment Report (2001, pp. 72–82): "Historically critical corporate functions like design, R&D, strategic and financial management or the procurement of core inputs have been kept at headquarters. It is possible in theory, however, for TNCs to place each function in a different location to take advantage of different characteristics and thus optimize efficiency for the company as a whole. There is growing evidence that this is taking place."

For policymakers, the attraction of service activities, like headquarters or research and development centers, could be not only an indirect way to strengthen human capital formation and technological capacities, but could also lead to the subsequent location of other parts of the multinational firms' value chain.

Policy instruments are obviously not the only factor that can influence the location choice of multinational firms. Previous investments have also been considered by location theory as essential. For instance, when vertical relationships are strong enough, multinational firms co-locate their activities within the same country. Head, Ries, and Swenson (1995) investigated possible supply relationships or technological spillovers between members of the same industrial *keiretsu*, and Smith and Florida (1994) considered relationships between two distinct parts of the production process. These authors study the investments of Japanese auto-related-parts suppliers and show that they tend to locate near Japanese assembly plants. More recently, Chung and Song (2004) showed that prior investments of Japanese electronics firms in the United States strongly influenced the location choice of their subsequent investments.

Co-location could be an important factor when considering service functions. As noted by Markusen (2005), service activities are likely to be internalized by the firm rather than bought and sold on arm's-length markets, and there may be crucial complementarities among different elements of the production chain. Fragmentation of the production process may generate significant coordination costs, which could be lessened by the co-location of their complementary activities within the same country.

Here I study pre- and postproduction service activities, which have been widely neglected by location theory. Following Defever (2006), I use a unique data set collected by the consulting group Ernst & Young. Data of almost 11,000 location choices were collected at the individual firm level over the period 1997–2002. This data set identifies the location of production plants, as well as the location of several types of service functions, including headquarters and research and development (R&D) centers, logistics, and sales and marketing activities. I consider both fifteen old European Union countries (EU-15) and eight Central and Eastern European countries (CEE-8) as possible location choices.

As a result of the information provided by this data set, I roughly estimate the number of jobs created by multinational firms in both western and eastern Europe during this period in order to underline the importance, in terms of jobs created by multinational firms, of the service activities, especially in western European countries.

Then I empirically analyze the within-firm co-locations between different stages of the value chain. I show that vertical linkages between functions push firms to concentrate affiliate activities within the same country. It is found that service activities are likely to be located in countries where the firm has previously set up a production plant. In addition, R&D seems to exert a very strong, attractive effect on production plant location. Therefore, the proactive attraction of the R&D centers may trigger the location of production plants.

The remainder of the chapter is organized as follows: Section 11.2 presents the database and proposes some empirical evidence on the number of jobs created by the multinational firms. Section 10.3 discusses the econometric model. Section 10.4 explains the dependent and independent variables used. Section 10.5 presents the econometrics results. Section 10.6 discusses the implications for policymakers.

11.2   Data

11.2.1   Description of the Database

Empirical evidence on the number of jobs created by multinational firms and on the co-location of multinational firms' activities will be evaluated using a database of multinational firms' location in Europe over the period 1997–2002, computing more than 11,182 projects.[2]

This EIM (European Investment Monitor) database, developed by the consulting group Ernst & Young, identifies the project-based foreign inward investment announcements that are new, expanding, or co-located in an international context.[3] The main sources of information are newspapers, financial information providers (such as Reuters), and national investment agencies (such as Invest in France Agency). When the consulting group discovers a new project, it tracks it in order to determine the exact location, at the city level. Projects included in the database have to comply with several criteria to be considered an international investment with mobility. The database excludes acquisitions, license agreements, and joint ventures (except in the case where these operations lead to an extension or a new establishment creation). It also excludes retail, hotel and leisure facilities, fixed infrastructures, extraction facilities, and portfolio investments. There is no minimum investment size criterion, but the number of investments with fewer than ten job creation projects is very low.

The investment projects data are at an individual level and provide investments in Europe by European and non-European firms, except for investments in the home country. The database includes the name of the firm, the parent company name, the name and the origin country of the parent company, the country of location, and the sector. There are forty-nine manufacturing and nonmanufacturing sectors in the NACE classification,[4] with subsectors in the automotive, electric and electronic, and chemical sectors. It also includes the function of each investment: unit of production and different service activities, such as headquarters, research and development centers, logistics, or sales and marketing offices.

11.2.2 The Five Functions Considered

I consider the five following functions: production plant, headquarters, R&D centers, logistics, and sales and marketing offices. Other functions are available,[5] but I could not use them due to the limited number of investments.

The headquarters function corresponds to administration, management, and accounting activities localized internationally. It includes decision centers, but the data do not allow us to know exactly their importance in the global decision process, and none correspond to the principal decision center. In fact, investments realized in the home country are not considered in the data set. Therefore, most of these centers correspond to European or regional headquarters (e.g., north of Europe) or are intended for the network organization only at a national level.

Research and development centers can be related to fundamental scientific research and to applied development directly linked to the production process. Data do not allow us to distinguish between centers dedicated to the development of new products and those to the adaptation to the local market of existing products.

Production plants correspond to the whole entity related to the physical production of goods.

The logistics function refers to all entities linked to goods transport, including warehousing (e.g., regional goods distribution). They can be internal to the firm or external logistics, for distributing to customers or suppliers. Logistics can also be viewed as acting as an intermediary between component production and assembly.

The sales and marketing offices include both wholesale trade and business representative offices. Despite the fact that they are not limited by size, the database appears to cover only the biggest investments.

Table 11.1
Total jobs created by function

Function	Number of projects	Average jobs created by project	Job creation observed	Jobs estimated	Total job creation
Headquarters	859	101	54,356	34,542	88,898
R&D centers	1,002	130	98,003	39,247	137,250
Production					
In EU-15 countries	3,912	*159*	438,944	220,151	659,095
In CEE-8 countries	1,304	*316*	280,525	156,736	437,261
Logistics	958	110	62,648	45,067	107,715
Sales and marketing	3,148	39	72,133	52,213	124,346
Total	11,182		1,006,607	547,957	1,554,565

Note: New creations and extensions in twenty-three countries (EU-15 and CEE-8) and on the five functions during the period 1997–2002. European and non-European firms.

11.2.3   Job Creation by Multinational Firms

Before turning to the econometric estimation on the co-location between activities, I present some descriptive statistics on the importance of the jobs created in service and production activities by multinational firms. The database information also includes the number of jobs created in each project. Unfortunately, this information is available for only around 65 percent of the projects (see the "Job Creation Observed" in table 11.1). To complete the information for the 35 percent of the projects with the missing value, I consider the specific project size of activities and then calculate an average number of job creation for each function, as presented in the third column of table 11.1. In the case of the production function, I also distinguish between the project size depending on if it is realized in western or eastern Europe. In fact, average job creation for production plants realized in central Europe appears to be at least twice as large as in the West (on average, 159 jobs created by production plants in the EU-15 and 316 jobs created in the CEE-8). This allows us to complete missing data for projects that do not have information on the number of jobs created (see the "Jobs Estimated" column in table 11.1). This permits us to estimate the total number of jobs created by multinational firms during the period 1997–2002 (the final column of table 11.1). Considering the individual data, the correlation between the reported number of jobs

Jobs created per capita in headquarters

Jobs created per capita in R&D centers

Jobs created per capita in production units

Jobs created per capita in logistics plants

Jobs created per capita in sales & marketing

■ Number of jobs created
30 percent above the
European average

■ Number of jobs created
between 30 percent and
-30 percent around the
European average

□ Number of jobs created
30 percent below the
European average

Table 11.2
Structure of estimated job creation in EU-15 and CEE-8 countries

Function	EU-15	CEE-8	Total
Service activities	421,812	36,397	458,209
Production	659,095	437,261	1,096,356
Total	1,080,907	473,658	1,554,565

Note: New creations and extensions in twenty-three countries (EU-15 and CEE-8) and on the five functions during the period 1997–2002. Manufacturing and nonmanufacturing sectors. European and non-European firms.

created and the number of jobs that would be estimated using this estimation is around 22 percent. This indicates the huge heterogeneity of the data not captured by this simple methodology.[6] This approach is arguably imperfect, but it does allow me to provide some descriptive statistics at an aggregate level not available from other sources. At the microlevel, this estimation is far from being precise enough to be used as a dependent variable.

At an aggregate level, multinational firms located in the twenty-three countries 11,182 investments during the period 1997–2002. My estimation leads to an approximation of more than 1.5 million jobs created during this period.[7] Figure 11.1 shows maps of the geographical distribution of the five functions (headquarters, R&D, production, logistics, and sales and marketing offices) during the period 1997 to 2002. To correct for size, I consider the number of jobs created (using my estimates) for each function divided by the countries' population. In some countries, such as the United Kingdom and Ireland, the number of jobs created is 30 percent above the European average for all the functions relative to their population size. At the opposite end, in Italy and Greece, again relative to their population size, the number of jobs created is 30 percent below the European average for a given population for five activities.

Table 11.2 shows that around 1 million of these jobs have been created in production activities, with one-third being realized in service activities. Notice that production represents 90 percent of the job created by the MNF in Central and Eastern Europe (CEE-8) countries and

Figure 11.1
Number of jobs created by function related to the countries' population
Note: New creations and extensions of European and non-European firms in the manufacturing sector in twenty-three countries (EU-15 and CEE-8) during the period 1997–2002.

only 60 percent in the EU-15 countries. These statistics seem to demonstrate that governments should pay more attention to service activities, especially in western European countries.

11.3 Econometric Model

In order to consider the impact of vertical linkages on location choice, we use individual firm location choices over a set of twenty-three European countries. The most commonly used econometric modeling technique for this type of problem is the conditional logit model (CLM) proposed by McFadden. Each location decision is a discrete choice made among several alternatives.

Although the real underlying profit yielded by alternative locations cannot be observed, one does observe the actual choice of each firm l and the characteristics of the alternative locations. Suppose $R = \{1, \ldots, r, \ldots, o\}$ is the set of possible location countries.

There are two types of determinants of location: country characteristics and previous location of plants defined at the individual firm level. In order to capture the attractiveness of location r to the representative investor (common to all investors independent), we introduce a fixed effect to capture country characteristics for each location, noted θ_r.[8] So each location offers a profit of π_{lr} to the firm l such that

$$\pi_{lr} = \theta_r + \beta X_{lr} + \varepsilon_{lr}, \tag{11.1}$$

where X_{lr} indicates previous investments realized by the firm l in each location choice r, β a vector of coefficients to be estimated by maximum likelihood procedures, and ε_{lr} the unobservable advantage of the location r. The firm l will choose r if the profit at this location is higher than those obtained in any other alternative location. Hence, the probability of choosing r is

$$P_{lr} \equiv Prob(\pi_{lr} > \pi_{lk}) = Prob(\varepsilon_{lk} < \varepsilon_{lr} + \theta_r - \theta_k + \beta(X_{lr} - X_{lk})), \quad \forall k \neq r. \tag{11.2}$$

The crucial assumption of the CLM is that the error terms are independently and identically distributed according to a type I extreme value distribution. It leads to the simple probability of choosing location r:

$$P_{lr} = \frac{e^{\theta_r + \beta X_{lr}}}{\sum_{i=1}^{o} e^{\theta_i + \beta X_{li}}}. \tag{11.3}$$

One of the main assumptions of CLM is to do with the independence of irrelevant alternatives (IIA), which implies that the relative probability of choosing one country is independent of the destination choice set: working on a subsample or on the whole sample should produce the same results (except, of course, the loss of information in the omitted decision). But unobserved characteristics of the choosers and unobserved correlations across element choices can generate a form of IIA assumption violation (Train 2003). The introduction of country fixed effects removes some forms of the IIA violation. Due to a limited period of time of our dependent variable, this methodology does not permit us to introduce country characteristics variables. Therefore, we will consider variables defined not only at the country level but also at the firm level. Also, we should be careful that unobserved characteristics of the choosers do not make some choices closer substitutes than others. To test the robustness of our results, we would have to consider different subsamples.

11.4   Dependent and Independent Variables

11.4.1   Construction of the Dependent Variable

We consider as a possible location choice twenty-three countries of the enlarged Europe. In order to study the possible co-location of all functions, including production, we consider only the manufacturing sector and exclude other sectors (essentially service sectors).[9] In addition, we are able to distinguish projects between actual creations (also known as greenfield) and extensions (e.g., brownfield). This latter category is not directly linked to the location choice determinants. Consequently, we use only actual creations for the construction of the dependent variable.

Considering only manufacturing sectors in the twenty-three European countries, the creation of greenfields represent 5,138 investments. One would expect that the fragmentation of the production process drives the different parts of the value chain to be located in accordance with countries' characteristics. From table 11.3, we can observe that production investments in the CEE-8 countries represent 81 percent compared to 48 percent in the EU-15.

During the period 1997–2002, of the 2,858 parent companies acting in manufacturing sectors that created new establishments in the twenty-three countries, 2,496 created new establishments for only one function. Of the rest of the sample, 240 firms realized investments

Table 11.3
Structure of new investments in manufacturing sectors in EU-15 and CEE-8 countries

Function	EU-15	CEE-8	Total
Headquarters	327	9	336
R&D	572	47	619
Production	1,841	1,032	2,873
Logistics	408	83	491
Sales and marketing	712	107	819
Total number of investments	3,860	1,278	5,138

Note: New creations in the manufacturing sectors in twenty-three countries (EU-15 and CEE-8) and on the five functions during the period 1997–2002. European and non-European firms.

in two types of activities, 75 in three, 24 in four, and 23 in all five functions studied. Some firms realized an impressive number of investments. For example Ford Motor Co. had thirty-seven new establishment announcements during the period 1997–2002.[10]

11.4.2   The Independent Variables

Co-location Variables
We introduce co-location variables between functions in order to consider national vertical linkages between stages of the value chain. In fact, these within-firm linkages are likely to encourage multinational firms to co-locate functions to save coordination costs. In this study, we consider only national co-location. To do this, we build five co-location variables—one for each function f. We build the historic establishment for each parent company and for each function in each country r. To do that, we take into account all the projects of the sample—greenfield and brownfield. More precisely, we include all the establishment extensions for each firm (which represent about one-third of the database projects) realized during the period 1997–2002 and that were not created by the firm during this period.[11] This allows us to consider these investments as anterior investments, to which we will add the new establishment creations realized by the firm during the years before the specific investment studied. In order to study precisely the history of location in a specific site, we would have to consider for each function only one possible investment for each parent company and for each city.[12] Finally, we consider that the variable takes the value 1 if the function f has been previously implanted in

Table 11.4
Dependent and independent variable descriptions

Variables	Definition	Year
Y	Location choices among 23 European countries of European and non-European firms from manufacturing sectors (greenfield only)	1997–2002
Co-location variables		
Headquarters co-location	1 if a headquarters has been located in the past in country r and 0 otherwise (greenfield and brownfield)	1997–2002
R&D co-location	1 if a R&D function f has been located in the past in country r and 0 otherwise (greenfield and brownfield)	1997–2002
Production co-location	1 if a production plant has been located in the past in country r and 0 otherwise (greenfield and brownfield)	1997–2002
Logistics co-location	1 if a logistics activity has been located in the past in country r and 0 otherwise (greenfield and brownfield)	1997–2002
Sales and marketing co-location	1 if a sales activity has been located in the past in country r and 0 otherwise (greenfield and brownfield)	1997–2002

the country by one of the affiliates of the parent company and 0 otherwise.[13] This will allow us to consider the within-firm co-location between functions. Table 11.4 summarizes the variables that will be used.

11.5   Econometric Test

Considering the location choice of new investments in the manufacturing sector, this section introduces co-location variables between functions within the same parent company in a specific country. We do not include the diagonal of the subdivided network variables (for which setting up a function f would have been explained by the presence of the same function by other affiliates). In fact, we are more interested in vertical linkages than within-function co-location. Conditional logit estimation with country fixed effect (table 11.5) leads to two main results: (1) within-firm vertical linkages tend to locate services activities in the same country as production plants and (2) R&D centers and production plants seem to be strongly attracted by each other.[14]

The four service functions surrounding production are all attracted by the production location. R&D and logistics have high and significant

Table 11.5
Co-location between functions in the east and west of Europe

Variables	Dependent variable: Location choice				
	Head-quarters	R&D	Production	Logistics	Sales and marketing
Headquarters co-location		0.16 (0.22)	−0.09 (0.16)	−0.06 (0.36)	−0.27 (0.27)
R&D co-location	0.05 (0.28)		0.93[a] (0.11)	0.11 (0.29)	−0.04 (0.22)
Production co-location	0.47[b] (0.22)	0.74[a] (0.13)		0.78[a] (0.16)	0.07 (0.16)
Logistics co-location	−0.54 (0.40)	0.19 (0.24)	0.27[c] (0.14)		−0.08 (0.28)
Sales and marketing co-location	0.08 (0.35)	0.01 (0.20)	−0.25 (0.17)	0.44 (0.30)	
Country fixed effect	Yes	Yes	Yes	Yes	Yes
Number of choosers	336	619	2,873	491	819
Number of choices	23	23	23	23	23
Log likelihood	−684	−1,430	−7,425	−1,180	−2,032

Note: Standard errors in parentheses: [a], [b], and [c] represent respectively 1 percent, 5 percent, and 10 percent significance levels. Dependent variable: Location choice in 23 countries (EU-15 and CCE-8) and of the five functions during the period 1997–2002. New creations of European and non-European firms in the manufacturing sector.

coefficients associated with production co-location variables, while headquarters is only weakly significant and sales and marketing is not significant. For example, of the 392 firms that had already established at least one production plant and decided to locate a new R&D facility, 211 chose the country of a previous production plant location.

The second important result of the introduction of vertical linkage variables is the co-location between R&D and production plants. In fact, those functions are highly attracted to each other, and the strong vertical linkages between activities are likely to lead to strong co-location between these two activities. R&D is the only service activity that has a significant attractive effect on production. More specifically, with a 1 percent significant coefficient of 0.93, a firm is more likely to locate its production plant in a country in which it already has an R&D center located. So we can clearly identify a co-location aspect between R&D and production, which could be driven by R&D (R&D co-location variable has the highest coefficient). In terms of number of projects, of the 2,873 production location choices, 153 of these facilities were established in a country where the parent company had previously located a R&D center. This low number is due to the fact only a small number of firms decide to locate R&D facilities abroad. More precisely, of the firms that decide to realize an investment in production activity, only 503 firms previously had an R&D center located in one of the 23 countries considered and 344 when considering only the EU-15 countries. Considering the 23 countries, around 30 percent (153 firms of 503) chose the R&D host country to locate their production plant. When considering only the EU-15 countries, these firms represent around 38 percent (132 firms of 344). These statistics permit us to understand the high coefficient of the R&D co-location (see table 11.5).

The inclusion of country dummy variables allows the use of a conditional logit specification in the presence of some forms of IIA violation. In order to consider the robustness of these results using a country fixed-effect setup, I reestimated the model using a variety of subsamples, where each subsample is chosen to remove a potential violation of the independence assumption. Notably I run the econometric model considering (1) only EU-15 and (2) all countries but excluding both France and the United Kingdom, which together account for 35 percent of new investments in manufacturing sectors. In both cases, the coefficients on the parameters of primary interest remain remarkably stable.[15]

11.6 Implications for Policymakers

Some policy implications can be taken from this analysis. First, it provides some statistics demonstrating the importance of multinational firms' investments and job creation in service activities. Services account for one-third of all jobs created by multinational firms in the enlarged Europe. Taking into account the EU-15 countries only, this ratio increases to 39 percent. Financial incentives are largely devoted to production plant attraction, but when my estimations are considered, it seems reasonable to pay more attention to service activities also, specifically in modern service economies.

I empirically analyzed the co-location of the different stages of the value chain between affiliates of multinational firms. Using a country fixed-effects conditional logit, I showed that firms are likely to locate several service activities in countries where they have already located a production plant. The location of a production plant leads to subsequent investment in service activities.

This work also highlights some strategic aspects of location for policy makers. Notably, some functions could have strategic aspects for both multinational firms and host countries. Attracting an R&D center largely increases the probability of the firm's choosing the same country for locating its production plant. In addition, the results seem to demonstrate that unlike R&D centers, headquarters do not have any attractive effect on the affiliates' production plant location choice, which could revise policy orientation through privilege subsidies to R&D.[16]

Of course, this policy advice mainly applies to the attraction of the largest firms with multiple locations. In addition, only a small number of firms decide to locate R&D facilities abroad. This limits the policy action to a limited, but well-defined, number of projects. Finally, because the time dimension of the data set is limited, prediction of the co-location of activities is probably more applicable to firms expanding their location rapidly in Europe during a short period of time.[17] Firms that decide to locate a few pieces of their value chain simultaneously are possibly more likely to choose a location for an activity based on their knowledge of the future location of other activities.

Notes

The study of the quality of the database was carried out at the Invest in France Agency under the supervision of Fabrice Hatem and Edouard Mathieu. I thank them for their help. I am very grateful to the consulting group Ernst & Young and, more specifically, to Barry Bright and Mark Hughes. Many thanks to Rodolphe Desbodes, Fabian Gouret, and the participants at the CESifo Summer Institute Workshop, "Recent Developments in International Trade: Globalization and the Multinational Enterprise," Venice International University, San Servolo, July 18–19, 2005. Three referees provided helpful comments, for which I am particularly grateful. The observations and viewpoints expressed are solely my responsibility.

1. There are many arguments against government incentives. Notably it can be argued that they distort competition or are an inefficient way to attract multinational firms, especially when they give rise to costly international bidding. I will not discuss these aspects. Instead, I will consider the need for governments to attract FDI as given. Subsequent literature has tended to find that corporate taxes and other incentives have a significant effect on the location of multinational firms, but the evidence is far from conclusive and still largely disputed. See notably Head, Ries, and Swenson (1999) and Devereux and Griffith (1998).

2. The complete database includes 13,109 projects when one considers all countries and all functions available. I will limit the descriptive statistics to five functions and twenty-three countries: the fifteen "old" European Union countries (EU-15) and the eight central and eastern European countries (CEE-8) that joined the European Union in 2004, but excluding Malta and Cyprus. Other countries were available, including Russia and Tur-

key, but they represent a small number of investments. The five functions considered are described in the next section.

3. See www.eyeim.com.

4. Classification of Economic Activities in the European Community.

5. Contact center, education and training, Internet data center, testing and servicing, and service center. These functions represent 770 projects.

6. Also considering country-specific project size could have strongly increased the correlation (at least by construction), but some countries account for a very low number of investments in service activities. Using the same data set, Hatem and Defever (2003) approximated the number of job created by multinational firms for the period 1998–2002 using a much more complex methodology. They calculated the average number of jobs created depending on the function of the project, the sector of the firms (for the production activity only), and the type of the project (creation or expansion of establishment). They also calculated capital intensity by sector (or by function in the case of service activities) and used the investment amount of the project, when either was available, to approximate the size of the project in order to complete the job creation information. They considered three groups of countries (east, northwest, and southwest) that could differ in terms of project size. At an aggregate level, their results are comparable to ours.

7. Because there is no other comparable data set, it is difficult to see how exhaustive the data set is. The Invest in France Agency (AFII) is providing a similar data set, Bilan France, but only for France. This organization is part of the French Ministry of the Economy, and the quality and the exhaustiveness of the data set seem higher. It includes the number of jobs created for each operation with a minimum size criterion of ten jobs. For the period 1997–2002, the Bilan France includes 2,813 projects leading to a total of more than 169,000 new jobs created. The EIM data set has no minimum of investment size criterion, but the number of investments with fewer than ten jobs created is very low. For the period 1997–2002, the EIM data set includes 1,958 investments for France, with a total of 96,690 jobs created and reported. The difference in terms of number of projects between the two databases seems mainly explained by the better reporting of small projects in the Bilan France. After completing the missing value using my methodology, I obtain a total of 179,191 jobs created. Difference in terms of methodology prevents an individual projects comparison. Also it is difficult to compare time periods directly, as E&Y generally integrates investments in its data set more rapidly.

8. In practice, I will run five independent regressions—one for each function—in order to estimate country fixed effect for each type of investment. In fact, each activity could be affected differently by country characteristics; therefore, different country fixed effects must be estimated.

9. We consider the service function of a manufacturing sector, for example, the headquarters of an automotive company, but not any project of the service sectors, for example, the headquarters of a financial sector firm.

10. Two headquarters, five R&D centers, twenty-two production plants, one logistics center, and seven sales and marketing offices.

11. A site extended in 2000 with no creation reported during the period 1997–2002 would be considered as anterior to 1997. It is important not to consider the same project several times. For example, a production plant created in 1999 and extended in 2001 is considered as existing since 1999.

12. I count as just one all the projects in a specific function and in a particular city (the most detailed geographical level) for each parent company. For example, if a firm decides to locate two production plants in the same city, I consider this investment once. This allows establishing an investment history at city level and avoids counting the same project several times.

13. In the case of a joint venture, I consider an investment for each parent company engaged in this investment (recall that I consider only joint ventures that lead to an extension or a new establishment creation).

14. As noted in the econometric model section, unobserved characteristics of the choosers might affect the IIA assumption. One way to relax this assumption is to introduce individual random effects and estimate a mixed logit model (Brownstone and Train 1999). Using the same data set, Defever (2006) provides estimation implementing a mixed logit. Introducing country variables instead of country fixed effects produces the same result.

15. As I implement five independent regressions with country fixed effects, I took into account the fact that different types of activities can react differently to country characteristics. It is also possible that some country characteristics can encourage not only the location of two functions simultaneously but also the co-location itself. For example, a country with a good communication sector can encourage co-location independent of the interaction between functions and country characteristics. To explore the robustness of these results, I ran a unique regression with all investments independent of the type of activity. Because each type of activity can react differently to country characteristics, I have introduced five times twenty-three country fixed effects, so I still have specific country fixed effects for each function. These results stay mainly stable. In order to study the hypothesis that some country characteristics could be at the origin of the co-location of activities, I introduced another set of country fixed effects shared by all investments, independent of their type of function. This fixed effects should integrate country characteristics, which could influence the co-location of activities, but my results stay mainly stable with the change of specification.

16. Although it is not the main purpose of this chapter, policy variables such as taxes could be interesting to study. Using the same setup as Defever (2006), I included a tax variable. I have been able to collect corporation tax data for all twenty-three countries of the enlarged Europe. Even so, it is important to notice that to my knowledge, no data set computes comparable data for all these countries, and so it is not clear if they are fully comparable. When implemented, this variable had a significant (at 10 percent) and positive coefficient (inverse sign of our expectation) in the case of headquarters location choice, negative (at 10 percent) in the case of sales and marketing, and not significant for the other functions. My co-location variables were mainly stable with the introduction of this variable.

17. In fact, my co-location variables could indicate that there is no previous investment by a firm, when in reality there is previous establishment realized before 1997 and not extended during the period 1997–2002. In this case, my estimate coefficients could be biased and mainly contain information about firms that are busy expanding.

References

Barba Navaretti, G., and A. J. Venables. (2004). *Multinational Firms in the World Economy.* Princeton, N.J.: Princeton University Press.

Brownstone, D., and K. Train. (1999). Forecasting New Product Penetration with Flexible Substitution Patterns. *Journal of Econometrics* 89(1), 109–129.

Chung, W., and J. Song. (2004). Sequential Investment, Firm Motives and Agglomeration of Japanese Electronics Firms in the US. *Journal of Economics and Management* 13(3), 539–560.

Defever, F. (2006). Functional Fragmentation and the Location of Multinational Firms in the Enlarged Europe. *Regional Science and Urban Economics* 36(5), 658–677.

Devereux, M. P., and R. Griffith. (1998). Taxes and the Location of Production: Evidence from a Panel of US Multinationals. *Journal of Public Economics* 68, 335–367.

Hatem, F., and F. Defever. (2003). La france face aux nouvelles tendances de l'investissement international en europe. *Accomex* 54, 36–44.

Head, K., J. Ries, and D. Swenson. (1995). Agglomeration Benefits and Location Choice: Evidence from Japanese Manufacturing Investment in the United States. *Journal of International Economics* 38, 223–257.

Head, K., J. Ries, and D. Swenson. (1999). Attracting Foreign Manufacturing: Investment Promotion and Agglomeration. *Regional Science and Urban Economics* 29, 197–218.

Krugman, P. (1995). Growing World Trade: Causes and Consequences. *Brookings Papers on Economic Activity* 1, 327–342.

Markusen, J. R. (2005). Modeling the Offshoring of White-Collar Services: From Comparative Advantage to the New Theories of Trade and FDI. Working paper no. 11827, National Bureau of Economic Research, Cambridge, Mass.

McFadden, D. (1984). *Handbook of Econometrics*, vol. 2. Amsterdam: Elsevier/North-Holland.

Smith, D., and R. Florida. (1994). Agglomeration and Industry Location: An Econometric Analysis of Japanese-Affiliated Manufacturing Establishments in Automotive-Related Industries. *Journal of Urban Economics* 36, 23–41.

Train, K. (2003). *Discrete Choice Methods with Simulation*. Cambridge: Cambridge University Press.

World Investment Report. (2001). *Annual Report: Promoting Linkages*. New York: UNCTAD.

Index

Acemoglu, D., 69–78
Acquisitions, 1, 5, 32
  efficiency and, 26
  greenfield case and, 25–26
  merger gains and, 33–34
  OECD data and, 30–31
  oligopoly model and, 25–31
  price-cost margin and, 28–29
  synergy and, 26
  trade liberalization and, 29–30
  UNCTAD and, 25–26
Agglomeration
  benchmarking methods for, 90, 95
  break analysis and, 103–106, 112–114
  core-periphery outcome and, 89–90
  equilibrium and, 93–94
  Forslid-Ottaviano model and, 95–110
  government spending and, 89–110
  Nash equilibrium and, 91
  positive externalities and, 93–94
  production factors and, 89–90
  race-to-the-bottom hypothesis and, 92–95
  symmetric equilibrium and, 100–103
Aghion, P., 69–78
Alabama, 259
Amerighi, Oscar, 117–153
Amiti, M., 201
Andersson, F., 90–91, 96
Anselin, Luc, 180, 188
Antras, P., 68
Arm's length principle, 260
  Italians and, 199, 220
  oligopoly model and, 117–126, 131–132, 137–142, 145, 147
Asset specificity problem, 5
Association of Austrian Social Insurance, 236, 249

Austria, 7
  capital stock and, 254
  Feenstra-Hanson model and, 235–241
  integration of, 227
  outsourcing and, 225–232, 236–241, 248–249
  relative employment regressions and, 240–241
  research and development (R&D) and, 237–241
  skilled labor and, 227–232, 236–241, 248–249
Autarky, 29–30, 98, 156–157
Autoregressive patterns
  constant returns to scale (CRS) and, 175, 177–178
  empirical specification and, 178–181
  inbound FDI and, 173–194
  inverse distance function and, 180–181
  OECD data and, 174, 181–186
  omega effect and, 180, 186
  partial equilibrium model and, 174–194
  spatial lag and, 180–192
  spillover and, 181
Average treatment effect on treated (ATT), 207–208, 217, 218–220
Aw, B., 203

Backward induction, 124–125
Balassa index, 31
Baldwin, Richard E.
  agglomeration and, 89–91, 93, 96–97, 100, 110
  liberalization and, 39
  new economic geography and, 89–90
Baltagi, Badi H., 173, 181

Banking, 158–159
Barba Navaretti, Giorgio, 7, 199–223, 259
Barry, Frank, 24–25, 39
Bartelsman, E. J., 117, 122
Beetsma, R. M. W. J., 117, 122
Belderbos, René, 17–18
Bellak, C., 204
Bellman, L., 204
Benchmarking, 90, 95
Bergstrand, J. H., 173
Berman, E., 235
Bernard, A., 203
Blomström, M., 178, 200
Blonigen, Bruce A., 7, 200
  autoregressive patterns and, 173–197
  liberalization and, 57
  trade costs and, 24
Blundell, R., 206
Boeing, 67
Bound, J., 235
Braconier, H., 21, 57, 200–201
Brainard, L., 17, 21, 179, 200
Brakman, Steven
  agglomeration and, 89–116
  liberalization and, 39
  multinational enterprises (MNEs) and, 1–9
  trade costs and, 30
Break analysis
  agglomeration and, 103–106, 112–114
  Forslid-Ottaviano model and, 103–106
Breusch-Pagan test, 235–236
Brülhart, M., 90
Bruno, G., 200, 247
Bureau Van Dijck, 208

Canada, 21
Carr, D. L., 4, 17, 179
Castellani, Davide, 7, 199–223
Caves, R. E., 173
Celtic tiger, 24
Central and Eastern European Countries (CEE), 227
Centro Studi Luca d'Agliano, 208
China, 225
  fragmentation and, 167–168
  knowledge-capital model and, 41, 58–60
Chung, S., 203, 260
Clausing, K. A., 117
Clerides, S. K., 203
Coase, R., 4

Cobb-Douglas production function, 44–45, 71
Communication technology, 159
Communism, 227
Complex integration strategies, 31–32
Computers, 67
Concentration, 14–19
Conditional logit model (CLM), 266–267
Constant elasticity of substitution (CES), 42, 71
Constant returns to scale (CRS), 175, 177–178
Contracts
  incomplete, 71–74
  outsourcing and, 67–84
  product innovation model and, 71–74
  product variety and, 74–84
Costa Dias, M., 206
Coughlin, C., 181
Cournot competition, 124
Cournot model, 45–47
Crino, F. R., 247
Criscuolo, C., 204
Cross-border mergers and acquisitions (M&As), 32
  efficiency and, 26
  greenfield case and, 25–26
  merger gains and, 33–34
  OECD data and, 30–31
  oligopoly model and, 25–31
  price-cost margin and, 28–29
  synergy and, 26
  trade liberalization and, 29–30
  UNCTAD and, 25–26
Czech Republic, 225

Daimler-Chrysler, 95
Davies, Ronald B., 7, 57, 173–197
Deardorff, Alan V., 6–7, 155–169
Defever, Fabrice, 7–8, 21–22, 259–275
Delgado, M., 203
Dell, 67
Demand, 71–72
Devereux, M., 93
Difference-in-difference (DID) estimators
  Italian study and, 200, 205–208, 217–220
  propensity score matching and, 205–208
  switching firms and, 206–208
  total factor productivity and, 205
Digital television, 67
Dixit, A. K., 3, 5, 156
Dixit-Stiglitz model, 3–4

Doms, M., 204
Dunning, J., 2, 14, 205
Dutch Ministry of Economic Affairs, 95

Eaton, J., 179
Eckholm, K., 201
Economic and Monetary Union (EMU), 89
Economic geography, 6
  benchmarking and, 90, 95
  conditional logit model and, 266–267
  dependent variable and, 267–268
  endogenous formation and, 40
  equilibrium and, 40, 100–103
  Forslid-Ottaviano model and, 95–110
  fragmentation and, 155–168
  Herfindahl index and, 49–54
  independent variable and, 268–269
  knowledge-capital model and, 39–62
  liberalization effects and, 47–57
  limitations of, 39
  new, 89–90, 93, 95–110
  outsourcing and, 155–168 (see also
    Outsourcing)
  parent market proximity effect and, 174
  race-to-the-bottom hypothesis and, 93
  research and development (R&D) and,
    39–40
  service functions and, 259–272
  studies on, 39–40
  world Edgeworth box and, 40–41
Economic Report of the President, 183
Economies of scale, 13, 26, 217
Efficiency
  agglomeration and, 96–97, 101, 109
  cross-border mergers and acquisitions
    (M&As) and, 26
  economies of scale and, 217
  Forslid-Ottaviano model and, 95–110
  Italian study and, 202, 210, 217
  outsourcing and, 67, 76
  product variety and, 74–83
  service functions and, 259
Egger, P., 39, 173, 200, 206
Eichengreen, B., 1
Einhorn, B., 68
Ekholm, K., 21, 39, 41, 50, 60, 62, 173, 200
Elasticity
  constant elasticity of substitution (CES)
    and, 42, 71
  demand and, 71–72
  labor and, 72–74
  product innovation model and, 71–74

product variety and, 74–83
  supply and, 72–74
Electronics sector, 67
Elitzur, M., 118
Enforcement policy
  Amerighi model and, 121–143
  competition and, 130–132, 137–140, 147
  corporate profit effects and, 128–129
  country comparison of, 118
  economic integration and, 132–137
  equilibrium and, 137–140, 147–149
  exports and, 124, 126–129, 127–128
  noncooperation and, 119
  personnel costs and, 123
  symmetric tax rates and, 130–132
  transfer pricing and, 117–149 (see also
    Transfer pricing)
Engardio, P., 68
Equations
  acquisition gain, 27
  Amerighi model, 121–123, 125–128, 131–
    139
  break analysis, 103–104, 112–113
  Cobb-Douglas production function, 44–45
  comparative statics, 80
  conditional logit model, 266
  difference-in-difference (DID) estimators,
    206–208
  direct liberalization effect, 145–147
  enforcement policy competition, 147–149
  equilibrium, 78–80, 101–103, 125–128,
    143–145
  Euler, 72, 77–78
  Feenstra-Hanson model, 235, 237, 243
  Forslid-Ottaviano model, 96–99, 110–112
  innovation networks, 76–77
  knowledge-capital model, 42, 44–47
  merger gains, 33–34
  offshoring gains, 20
  operating profits, 32, 74–75
  partial equilibrium model, 176–179, 186,
    188
  probit regression, 210
  product innovation model, 72
  Ramsey, 72
  relative profitability, 20
  service function model, 266
  steady state stability, 84
  symmetric equilibrium tax rate, 143–145
  tariff-jumping, 20–21
  trade cost, 15, 20–22, 27, 32
  transfer pricing, 121–139

Equilibrium, 2, 5
  agglomeration and, 93–94
  break analysis and, 103–106
  constant elasticity of substitution (CES)
    and, 71
  economic geography and, 40
  enforcement policy and, 137–140, 147–
    149
  equations for, 78–80, 101–103, 125–128,
    143–145
  exports and, 126–129
  factor price equalization (FPE) and, 54,
    56, 61–62
  Forslid-Ottaviano model and, 97–109
  Herfindahl index and, 49–50
  home sales and, 126–129
  innovation networks and, 70, 74–83
  inverted-U shape and, 70–71
  knowledge-capital model and, 42, 44–45
  liberalization effects and, 47–57
  migration and, 62
  Nash, 91, 144
  outsourcing and, 74–83
  partial equilibrium model and, 174–194
  product variety and, 74–83
  proximity-concentration trade-off and,
    14–19
  public goods and, 100–103
  supply and, 78–80
  symmetric, 100–103
  tax competition and, 130–135, 143–145
  transfer pricing and, 117–137
Ernst & Young, 260–261
Euler equation, 72, 77–78
Europe, 5, 7
  autoregressive patterns and, 189–192
  barrier reduction and, 13
  benchmarking and, 90, 95
  export-platform gain and, 24–25
  fall of communism and, 227
  Forslid-Ottaviano model and, 105
  Italian study and, 199–220
  Japanese electronics firms and, 17–18
  outsourcing and, 225–254
  partial equilibrium model and, 189–192
  proximity-concentration trade-off and,
    17–19
  race-to-the-bottom hypothesis and, 92–
    95
  service functions and, 260–266
  stylized tax facts and, 92–95
  tax harmonization and, 89–110

  transfer pricing and, 141
  transport costs and, 17–18
European Investment Monitor (EIM), 261
Export-platform foreign direct investment
    (FDI), 22–25, 31–32, 173
Exports
  banking technology and, 158–159
  enforcement policy and, 127–128
  equilibrium and, 126–129
  FDI complements and, 18–19
  inbound FDI and, 173–194
  incentives and, 127–128
  of jobs, 155 (see also Outsourcing)
  proximity-concentration trade-off and,
    14–19
  tariff-jumping and, 20–21
  transfer pricing and, 124, 126–129 (see also
    Transfer pricing)
  transport costs and, 17–18, 21
  vertical vs. horizontal FDI and, 19–22
Expropriation, 2

Factor mobility, 1–2, 6, 232
  Elitzur-Mintz model and, 118
  Haufler-Schjelderup model and, 118–119
  liberalization and, 40, 54, 62
Factor price equalization (FPE), 1
  knowledge-capital model and, 54, 56, 61–
    62
  liberalization effects and, 54, 56
  tariffs and, 2
Falzoni, A. M., 200, 247
Farinas, J., 203
Feenstra, R. C., 56, 67–68, 232, 248–249
Feenstra-Hanson model
  Austria and, 235–241
  Breusch-Pagan tests and, 235–236
  framework of, 232–235
  heteroscedasticity and, 235–236
  ordinary least squares (OLS) analysis
    and, 235
  outsourcing and, 235–243, 248–249
  Poland and, 242–243
  White test and, 235–236
Firm location. See Economic geography
Florida, R., 260
Foreign direct investment (FDI)
  acquisitions and, 1, 25–31
  Austrian study and, 227–232, 236–242,
    248–249
  cross-border mergers and acquisitions
    (M&As) and, 25–34

Dixit-Stiglitz model and, 3–4
economies of scale and, 13, 26, 217
European Investment Monitor (EIM) and, 261
export-platform, 22–25, 31–32, 173
factor mobility and, 1–2, 6, 40, 54, 62, 118–119, 232
greenfield case and, 25–26
growth of, 1, 13
horizontal, 4–5, 19–22, 31
importance of, 1
inbound, 173–194
intraunion barriers and, 22–25
Italian study and, 199–220
knowledge-capital model and, 4, 6, 39–62, 96
offshoring gain and, 20–21 (see also Outsourcing)
OLI approach and, 2–6, 14–19, 24, 67–84, 117–149
outward concentration and, 41
Poland study and, 227–232, 242–249
proximity-concentration trade-off and, 14–19
returns to scale and, 39, 42, 60, 73, 96–97, 160, 175, 177–178, 206
service functions and, 259–272
spatial lag and, 180–192
tariff-jumping and, 20–21
theory and, 5–7
trade costs and, 13–34
transport costs and, 21
vertical, 5, 19–22, 31
Fors, G., 200
Forslid, R., 173
  agglomeration and, 90–91, 96
  liberalization and, 39, 41, 50, 60, 62
Forslid-Ottaviano model, 111
  agglomeration and, 95–110
  break analysis and, 103–106, 112–114
  capital and, 96–99
  consumption factors and, 96–97
  description of, 95–99
  economic geography and, 97
  equilibrium and, 97–109
  freeness-of-trade parameter and, 98
  government spending and, 95–110
  manufacturing sector and, 95–110
  monopolistic competition and, 98
  public vs. private sector and, 95–106, 110
  research and development (R&D) and, 97

simulation results of, 106–109
symmetric equilibrium and, 100–103
Fragmentation, 6–7
  banking technology and, 158–159
  country effects from, 158–161
  global effects of, 161–168
  Heckscher-Ohlin (HO) model and, 160
  market distortion and, 159–160
  Ricardian model and, 158
  service functions and, 260
  specialization and, 160
  Stolper-Samuelson theorem and, 160
  tariffs and, 159–160, 162
  United States and, 167–168
France
  outsourcing and, 232
  race-to-the-bottom hypothesis and, 94–95
  service functions and, 261, 271, 273n7
  stylized tax facts and, 92
Fujita, M., 39

Gao, T., 39, 60, 62
Garretsen, Harry
  agglomeration and, 89–116
  liberalization and, 39
  multinational enterprises (MNEs) and, 1–9
  trade costs and, 30
Germany
  outsourcing and, 225–226
  race-to-the-bottom hypothesis and, 94–95
  stylized tax facts and, 92
Gimme Shelter, 132
Girma, S., 203–204, 206
GlaxoSmith-Kline, 67
Globalization, 5
  fragmentation effects and, 161–168
  outsourcing and, 155–168, 225–254 (see also Outsourcing)
  tax harmonization and, 89–110
  transfer pricing and, 117–149
GOLE (General OLigopolistic Equilibrium) model, 5
Gorg, H., 201, 206
Government spending
  agglomeration and, 89–110
  break analysis and, 103–106, 112–114
  capital mobility and, 92–93
  enforcement policy and, 117–140
  Forslid-Ottaviano model and, 95–110
  model for, 95–110
  race-to-the-bottom hypothesis and, 92–95

Government spending (cont.)
  simulation results and, 106–109
  stylized facts about, 92–95
  subsidies and, 95, 238–239, 259, 272
  symmetric equilibrium and, 100–103
Gravity models
  data set and, 181–184
  empirical specification and, 179–181
  European results and, 189–190
  OECD results and, 184–186
  robustness and, 186–189
  standard, 179–180
Greece, 93, 265
Greenaway, D., 206
Greenfield case, 25–26
Griffith, R., 93
Griliches, Z., 235
Gross domestic product (GDP)
    measurement
  export-platform gain and, 25
  liberalization effects and, 47
  partial equilibrium model and, 179–180,
    183, 190
  post-World War II era, 13
  race-to-the-bottom hypothesis and, 94–95
  tax rates and, 93
  world trade/foreign direct investment
    (FDI) comparison and, 1
Grossman, G., 68–71, 83

Hanley, A., 201
Hanson, G. H., 56, 232, 242, 248–249
Harmonized system (HS) classification,
    254
Haufler, A., 118–119
HCL Technologies, 67
Head, K., 200, 260
  autoregression and, 174, 179, 181–183
  liberalization and, 57
  trade costs and, 24
Headquarters, 262, 265
Heckman, J., 206
Heckscher-Ohlin-Samuelson (HOS)
    models
  factor price equalization (FPE) and, 54
  fragmentation and, 160
  international factor mobility and, 1–2
  liberalization effects and, 54
  Polish outsourcing and, 243, 245
  proximity-concentration trade-off and,
    18–19
  vertical vs. horizontal FDI and, 19–22

Helpman E., 4–5, 203
  autoregression and, 174–175
  outsourcing and, 68–71, 83
  trade costs and, 19
Herfindahl index, 49–54, 61
Heteroscedasticity, 235–236
Hewlett-Packard, 67
Hoffmann, Anders N., 6, 39–65
Hold-up problem, 5, 73
Home employment, 200
Home sales, 126–129
Homoscedasticity, 235–236
Hong Kong, 60
Host countries, 5, 7, 59, 234
  autoregressive patterns and, 173–194
  constant returns to scale (CRS) and, 175,
    177–178
  fragmentation and, 155
  OECD data and, 174, 181–186
  omega effect and, 186
  partial equilibrium model and, 174–194
  production and, 176–178
  service functions and, 271–272
  spatial lag and, 180–192
  spillover and, 181
  trade costs and, 14, 18–25
  transfer pricing and, 119, 142
Hotelling's lemma, 32
Human capital. See Labor
Hungary, 225

Ichimura, H., 206
Imperfect competition, 3–4, 39–40, 60, 160
Independence of irrelevant alternatives
    (IIA), 267
India, 67, 225
Information
  knowledge-capital model and, 4, 6, 39–
    62, 96
  leakage of, 68–69
  outsourcing and, 67–84
  Reuters and, 261
  specialization benefits and, 68–70
Innovation networks, 6
  demand and, 71–72
  entry costs and, 70
  equilibrium and, 70
  governance costs and, 68
  information leakage and, 68–69
  inverted-U shape and, 70–71
  model for, 71–74
  organizational structure and, 68, 74–83

outsourcing and, 67–84
product innovation model and, 71–74
product variety and, 74–84
specialization benefits and, 68–70
steady state stability and, 84
supply and, 72–74
vertical integration and, 70, 74–83, 85n2
Intellectual property, 155–156
Intraunion barriers, 22–25
Inverse distance function, 180–181
Inverted-U shape, 70–71
Invest in France Agency (AFII), 261,
273n7
Ireland, 17, 24, 265
ISIC (International Standard Industry
Classification), 242
Italy, 7, 265
Aida data set and, 208–210
arm's length principle and, 199, 220
average treatment effect on treated (ATT)
and, 207–208, 217, 218–220
Bureau Van Dijck and, 208
Centro Studi Luca d'Agliano and, 208
construction of counterfactual, 210–217
data description and, 208–210
difference-in-difference (DID) estimators
and, 200, 205–208, 217–220
empirical setting and, 203–205
evaluation problem and, 205–208
firm issues and, 199, 201–202
first-time investors and, 200
horizontal investment and, 201–202
Kolmogorov-Smironov statistics and,
217
nearest-neighbor matching and, 213
ordinary least squares (OLS) estimation
and, 207
performance analysis and, 201–205
Politecnico of Milan and, 208
probit regression and, 210
production growth and, 202
propensity score matching and, 205–208
Reprint data set and, 208–210
research and development (R&D) and,
200, 202, 209–210
results of, 217–220
stylized tax facts and, 92
subsidiary observations and, 203–205
switching firms and, 203–210, 215, 217
total factor productivity and, 205, 210–
211, 217–220
vertical investment and, 202

Japan, 17–18, 24–25, 181, 260
Jensen, B., 203–204
Job creation, 263–266, 273n6
Jones, R. W., 18, 155, 161, 166
Jungnickel, R., 204

Keen, M., 90
Keiretsu, 260
Kerry, John, 167
Kierzkowski, H., 161, 166
Kind, H. J., 119–120, 124, 141
Klemm, A., 93
Kneller, R., 203, 206
Knowledge-capital model, 4, 6
capital and, 62n2
China and, 41, 58–60
constant elasticity of substitution (CES)
and, 42
Cournot model and, 45–47
economic geography and, 39–40
equilibrium and, 42, 44–45
factor-intensity assumptions and, 42–47
factor price equalization (FPE) and, 54,
56, 61–62
firm types and, 42
Forslid-Ottaviano model and, 96
Herfindahl index and, 61
liberalization effects and, 47–57, 61–62
relevant data for, 57–60
research and development (R&D) and, 42
structure of, 41–47
world Edgeworth box and, 48, 63n8
zero-profit conditions and, 45–47
Kokko, A., 178
Kolmogorov-Smironov statistics, 217
Konings, J., 200
Kraay, A., 203
Krogstrup, S., 93
Krugman, P., 259
agglomerization and, 89–97, 100, 110
liberalization and, 39

Labor
activity intensity and, 43–47
Austria and, 227–232, 236–241, 248–249
Breusch-Pagan tests and, 235–236
civil vs. non-civil servants, 98–99
elasticity and, 72–74
Feenstra-Hanson model and, 232–243
Forslid-Ottaviano model and, 95–110
fragmentation effects and, 158–168
Herfindahl index and, 49–54, 61

Labor (cont.)
  intraunion barriers and, 22–25
  IV-GMM results and, 247
  job creation and, 263–266, 273n6
  knowledge-capital model and, 39–62
  liberalization effects and, 47–57
  Mexico and, 228, 232, 248–249
  migration and, 62
  mobility and, 92–95
  outsourcing and, 67–84, 155–168 (*see also*
    Outsourcing)
  Poland and, 227–232, 242–249
  product variety and, 74–83
  real wages and, 41, 63n5, 160, 166
  relative employment regressions and,
    225–232, 240–241, 252–253
  service functions and, 259–272
  skilled, 7, 21–22, 40–60, 114n8, 225–249
  supply and, 72–74
  taxation and, 92–95
  United States and, 232
  unskilled, 40–60, 225–232
  vertical vs. horizontal FDI and, 19–22
Lach, S., 203
Lai, E., 68
Lancaster, K., 162
Liberalization
  cross-border mergers and acquisitions
    (M&As) and, 29–30
  direct effects of, 145–147
  economic geography and, 40–41
  economic integration and, 132–137
  effects of, 47–57
  enforcement policy and, 128–143
  factor mobility and, 40, 54, 62
  factor price equalization (FPE) and, 54,
    56
  Herfindahl index and, 49–54, 61
  knowledge-capital model and, 39–62
  profit increase and, 134
  relative endowment locus and, 48–49
  Rutherford's subsystem and, 48
  symmetric equilibrium tax rate and, 134–
    135
  transfer pricing and, 117–149 (*see also*
    Transfer pricing)
  world Edgeworth box and, 47–48, 63n8
  zero-profit conditions and, 45–47
Licenses, 3–4, 261
Lichtenberg, F., 201
Lipsey, R. E., 162, 200
Location. *See* Economic geography

Logistics, 262, 265
Lorentowicz, Andzelika, 7, 225–258

McFadden, D., 266
McLaren, J., 68
Mansori, K. S., 119
Manufacturing sector
  break analysis and, 103–106
  co-location choices and, 267–269
  Forslid-Ottaviano model and, 95–110
  service functions and, 259–272
Maquiladoras (low-skilled workers), 232
Marchand, M., 90
Marin, Dalia, 7, 200, 225–258
Mariotti, S., 200
Markets
  barrier reduction and, 13
  constant returns to scale (CRS) and, 175,
    177–178
  cross-border mergers and acquisitions
    (M&As) and, 25–31
  economies of scale and, 13, 27, 217
  Europe and, 18 (*see also* Europe)
  export-platform gain and, 22–25, 31–32,
    173
  foreign, 2 (*see also* Multinational
    enterprises (MNEs))
  Forslid-Ottaviano model and, 95–110
  inbound FDI and, 173–194
  liberalization effects and, 47–57
  North American Free Trade Agreement
    (NAFTA) and, 228, 248
  offshoring gain and, 20–21 (*see also*
    Outsourcing)
  operating profits and, 14–19, 32
  parent market proximity effect and, 174,
    179–180, 183–193
  proximity-concentration trade-off and,
    14–19
  service functions and, 259–272
  trade costs and, 13–34 (*see also* Trade
    costs)
  transfer pricing and, 117–149
Markusen, James R., 205, 260
  autoregression and, 173–174, 179, 182
  economic geography and, 39–65
  fragmentation and, 161, 166
  knowledge-capital model and, 39–62
  multinational enterprises (MNEs) and, 4,
    6
  trade costs and, 17–18, 21
Martin, R., 204

Maskus, K., 4, 17, 57, 179, 182
Matching problems, 5, 13
  Italian study and, 200, 205–214, 217–220
  outsourcing and, 69, 73–74, 80–83
Maximum-likelihood procedure, 180
Mayer, T., 24, 174, 179, 183
Melitz, M., 175, 203
Mergers. *See* Cross-border mergers and
  acquisitions (M&As)
Mexico, 228, 232, 248–249
Meyer, B., 207
Midelfart Knarvik, K. H., 119, 201
Migration, 41, 61–62
Mintz, J., 118
Monopolies
  Forslid-Ottaviano model and, 98
  operating profits and, 32
  product innovation model and, 73
  proximity-concentration trade-off and,
    14–19
  transfer pricing and, 119–120
Motorola, 67
MP3 players, 67
Multinational enterprises (MNEs), 7–8
  attracting, 259–272
  conditional logit model and, 266–267
  constant returns to scale (CRS) and, 175,
    177–178
  Cournot competition and, 124
  disadvantages of, 2–3
  Dixit-Stiglitz model and, 3–4
  economic geography and, 6, 39 (*see also*
    Economic geography)
  endogenous formation and, 40
  Herfindahl index and, 49–54, 61
  historical perspective on, 13
  integration effects and, 31–32, 132–137
  Italian study and, 199–220
  job creation and, 263–266, 273n6
  knowledge-capital model and, 39–62
  OLI approach and, 2–6, 14–19, 24, 67–
    84
  outsourcing and, 67–84 (*see also*
    Outsourcing)
  parent market proximity effect and, 174
  partial equilibrium model and, 174–194
  personnel costs and, 123
  proximity-concentration trade-off and,
    14–19
  service functions and, 259–272
  subsidies for, 259
  tax harmonization and, 89–110

  trade costs and, 13–34 (*see also* Trade
    costs)
  transfer pricing and, 117–149 (*see also*
    Transfer pricing)
Mundell, R. A., 18
Murphy, A., 200
Mutinelli, M., 200

NACE (Nomenclature general des
  Activités Economiques), 236–237, 254,
  262
Naghavi, Alireza, 6, 67–87
Nash equilibrium, 91, 144
Naughton, Helen T., 7, 173–197
Neary, J. Peter, 5–6, 13–38, 89
Netherlands, 232
New economic geography (NEG), 89–90,
  93. *See also* Economic geography
  Forslid-Ottaviano model and, 95–110
  symmetric equilibrium and, 100–103
New Trade Theory, 166
No-black-hole condition, 113
Norbäck, P.-J., 57
Norman, V., 156
North American Free Trade Agreement
  (NAFTA), 228, 248
Notebook PCs, 67

Obstfeld, M., 1
Offshoring. *See* Outsourcing
Ó Gráda, C., 17
Ohyama, M., 156
Oligopoly model, 6
  acquisitions and, 25–31
  cross-border mergers and acquisitions
    (M&As) and, 25–31
  proximity-concentration trade-off and,
    14
  transfer pricing and, 117–149 (*see also*
    Transfer pricing)
OLI (ownership-location-internalization)
  approach, 2–6
  export-platform gain and, 24
  outsourcing and, 67–84
  proximity-concentration trade-off and,
    14–19
  transfer pricing and, 117–149 (*see also*
    Transfer pricing)
Omega effect, 180, 186
Operating profits, 14–19, 32
Ordinary least squares (OLS) estimation,
  207, 235, 247

Organization for Economic Cooperation
  and Development (OECD), 30–31
  inbound FDI and, 174, 181–186
  outsourcing and, 236–249
  stylized tax facts and, 93
  transfer pricing and, 117–118, 121, 149n4,
    150n8
Ottaviano, Gianmarco, 6, 67–87, 96
Outsourcing
  Austria and, 225–232, 236–241, 248–249
  Breusch-Pagan test and, 235–236
  capital stock calculation and, 254
  constant elasticity of substitution (CES)
    and, 71
  Euler equation and, 72
  Feenstra-Hanson model and, 232–243
  fragmentation gains and, 155–168
  heteroscedasticity and, 235–236
  information leakage and, 68–69
  intellectual property issues and, 155–156
  inverted-U shape and, 70–71
  investment integration and, 225–232
  Italian study and, 199–220
  offshoring gain and, 20–21
  organizational structure and, 68, 74–83
  Poland and, 225–232, 242–249
  product innovation model and, 71–74
  product variety and, 74–84
  Ramsey problem and, 72
  relative employment regressions and,
    225–232, 240–241, 252–253
  relative wages and, 225–232
  research and development (R&D) and,
    67–69, 72–74, 81–84
  specialization benefits and, 68–70
  steady state stability and, 84
  Stolper-Samuelson effect and, 226
  utility maximization problem and, 71–72
  vertical integration and, 71–83, 85n2
  White test and, 235–236

Panel-corrected standard error estimation
  (PCSE), 247
Parent countries
  autoregressive patterns and, 173–194
  constant returns to scale (CRS) and, 175,
    177–178
  inverse openness and, 195n6
  OECD data and, 174, 181–186
  omega effect and, 186
  partial equilibrium model and, 174–194
  production and, 176–178
  service functions and, 259–272
  spatial lag and, 180–192
  spillover and, 181
Parent market proximity effect, 193
  alternate weighting schemes and, 186–
    189
  data set for, 183
  defined, 174
  European results and, 189–192
  empirical methodology and, 179–180
  OECD results and, 184–186
Partial equilibrium model
  alternative weighting schemes and, 186–
    189
  constant returns to scale (CRS) and, 175,
    177–178
  empirical specification and, 178–181
  Europe and, 189–192
  inbound FDI and, 174–194
  OECD data and, 174, 181–186
  omega effect and, 180, 186
  robustness and, 186–189
  spatial lag and, 180–192
  spillover and, 181
Pavcnik, N., 247
Pavelin, S., 25
Peeters, J., 93
Peralta, S., 119–120, 124, 132
Personnel costs, 123
Pfaffermayr, M., 173, 200, 204, 206
Pharmaceutical companies, 67
Philips, 67
Piscitello, L., 200
Pisu, M., 203
Poland, 7, 225
  Feenstra-Hanson model and, 242–243
  Heckscher-Ohlin (HO) model and, 243,
    245
  outsourcing and, 242–249
  research and development (R&D) and,
    242–245
  size of, 227
  skilled labor and, 227–232, 242–249
Policy, 7
  agglomeration and, 89–110
  antidumping, 18
  attracting multinational enterprises
    (MNEs), 259–272
  benchmarking and, 90, 95
  enforcement, 117–149 (see also
    Enforcement policy)
  government spending and, 89–110

Italian study and, 199–220
liberalization, 39–62
North American Free Trade Agreement
    (NAFTA) and, 228, 248
Politecnico of Milan, 208
Portugal, 93, 259
Price-cost margin, 28–29
Principal-agent problem, 5
Probit regression, 210
Procter & Gamble, 67–68
Production, 7
  attracting multinational enterprises
      (MNEs) and and, 259–272
  Austria and, 227–232, 236–241, 248–
      249
  banking technology and, 158–159
  benchmarking and, 90, 95
  break analysis and, 103–106
  Cobb-Douglas function and, 44–45, 71
  constant elasticity of substitution (CES)
      and, 71
  constant returns to scale (CRS) and, 175,
      177–178
  demand and, 71–72
  Dixit-Stiglitz model and, 3–4
  economic geography and, 39 (see also
      Economic geography)
  economies of scale and, 13, 26, 217
  export-platform gain and, 22–25, 31–32,
      173
  Feenstra-Hanson model and, 232–243
  final assembly and, 39
  Forslid-Ottaviano model and, 95–110
  fragmentation effects and, 155–168
  government spending and, 89–110
  host countries and, 176–178 (see also Host
      countries)
  imperfect competition and, 3–4, 39–40,
      60, 160
  inbound FDI and, 173–194
  induced capital flows and, 18–19
  Italian study and, 199–220
  knowledge-capital model and, 39–62
  OLI approach and, 2–6, 14–19, 24, 67–84,
      117–149
  organizational structure and, 74–83
  outsourcing and, 67–84, 155–168, 225 (see
      also Outsourcing)
  parent countries and, 176–178
  Poland and, 227–232, 242–249
  product innovation model and, 71–74
  product variety and, 74–84

proximity-concentration trade-off and,
    13–19
quality issues and, 69
service functions and, 259–272
supply and, 72–74
tax harmonization and, 89–110
total factor productivity and, 205, 210–
    211, 217–220
vertical integration and, 69
weaker product differentiation and, 70
Profits
  banking technology and, 158–159
  Cobb-Douglas production function and,
      44–45
  constant elasticity of substitution (CES)
      and, 71
  cross-border mergers and acquisitions
      (M&As) and, 25–34
  export-platform gain and, 22–25, 31–32
  factor price equalization (FPE) and, 54,
      56, 61–62
  fragmentation effects and, 158–168
  inbound FDI and, 173–194
  knowledge-capital model and, 39–62
  liberalization and, 134 (see also
      Liberalization)
  markup revenues, 46–47
  maximization of, 74–76
  operating, 14–19, 32
  price-cost margin and, 28–29
  product variety and, 74–83
  tax competition and, 129–137
  trade costs and, 13–34
  transfer pricing and, 117–149 (see also
      Transfer pricing)
  weaker product differentiation and, 70
  zero-profit conditions and, 45–47
Propensity score matching, 205–208
Proximity-concentration trade-off, 14–19.
    See also Parent market proximity effect
Public goods
  break analysis and, 103–106
  Forslid-Ottaviano model and, 95–106
  simulation results and, 106–109
  symmetric equilibrium and, 100–103
  tax harmonization and, 89–110

Quantity decisions, 124–129

Race-to-the-bottom hypothesis, 92–95
Raimondos-M ller, P., 119
Ramsey problem, 72

Raubold, Alexander, 7, 225–258
Rauch, J., 5
Raybaudi-Massilia, Marzia, 39, 50, 60, 62
Real wages, 41, 63n5, 160, 166
Relative endowments, 48–49
Research and development (R&D)
  attracting multinational enterprises
    (MNEs) and, 261, 269–271
  Austria and, 237–241
  economic geography and, 39–41
  Forslid-Ottaviano model and, 97
  Italian study and, 200, 202, 206, 209–
    210
  knowledge-capital model and, 42
  outsourcing and, 67–69, 72–74, 81–84
  Poland and, 242–245
  product variety and, 74–83
  proximity-concentration trade-off and,
    14
  service functions and, 261–262, 265, 269–
    272
  specialization benefits and, 68–69
  supply and, 72–74
  vertical integration and, 74–83
Return on investment (ROI), 209–210
Returns to scale, 206
  agglomerization and, 96–97
  autoregression and, 175, 177–178
  constant returns to scale (CRS), 175, 177–
    178
  fragmentation and, 160
  liberalization and, 39, 42, 60
  outsourcing and, 73
Reuters, 261
Reynolds, R., 27
Ricardian model, 158
Ries, J., 181, 200, 260
Riezman, R., 68
Riker, D., 200
Roberts, M., 203
Rowthorn, R. E., 15
Ruano, S., 203
Ruffin, R., 155
Rutherford's subsystem, 48

Salant, S., 27, 29
Sales and marketing, 262, 265
Samsung, 95
Samuelson, P. A., 155, 159
Scharf, K., 119
Schjederup, G., 118–119
Segev, E., 181

Service functions
  conditional logit model and, 266–267
  database analysis of, 260–266
  dependent variable and, 267–268
  econometric model for, 266–267
  fragmentation and, 260
  headquarters, 262, 265
  interdependent variables and, 268–269
  job creation and, 263–266, 273n6
  location decisions and, 259–261, 269–
    271
  logistics, 262, 265
  policy implications and, 271–272, 274n16
  research and development (R&D) and,
    261–262, 265, 269–272
  sales and marketing, 262, 265
  value chain and, 259–261, 267–268, 271–
    272
Sianesi, B., 215
Sinn, H.-W., 89
Sleuwaegen, L., 18
Smith, D., 260
Song, J., 260
Spain, 93
Spatial lag
  autoregressive patterns and, 180–192
  OECD sample and, 184–186
  U.S. inbound FDI and, 181–184
Specialization, 166
  agglomeration and, 90
  fragmentation and, 160
  outsourcing and, 67–70, 73, 76, 81, 83
  Stolper-Samuelson theorem and, 160
  trade costs and, 27, 30
Spillover, 174, 178, 181, 194, 260
Standard gravity model, 179–180
STAN database, 237
Statistics Austria, 254
Steady state stability, 84
Stiglitz, J., 3, 5
Stolper-Samuelson theorem, 160, 226
Strobl, E., 201
Subsidies, 95, 238–239, 259, 272
Supply
  equilibrium and, 78–80
  innovation and, 76–77
  product innovation model and, 72–74
  product variety and, 74–83
  vertical integration and, 74–83
Sweden, 21–22
Swenson, D., 181, 260
Switzer, S., 27

Symmetric tax rates, 130–132, 134–135,
    143–145
Synergy, 26

Tamura, A., 179
Tariff-jumping, 20–21
Tariffs, 2, 18
    factor price equalization (FPE) and, 2
    fragmentation and, 159–160, 162
    offshoring gain and, 20–21
Tax competition
    economic integration effects and, 132–137
    enforcement policy and, 130–132
    Nash equilibrium and, 144
    symmetric rates and, 130–132, 134–135,
        143–145
    transfer pricing and, 129–137
Taxes, 6
    attracting multinational enterprises
        (MNEs) and, 259
    break analysis and, 103–106, 112–114
    capital mobility and, 92–95
    competition and, 129–137
    corporate profit effects and, 128–129
    economic integration and, 132–137
    EU harmonization of, 89–110
    Forslid-Ottaviano model and, 95–110
    government spending and, 89–110
    labor mobility and, 92–95
    positive externalities and, 93–94
    race-to-the-bottom hypothesis and, 92–95
    stylized facts about, 92–95
    symmetric equilibrium rates and, 130–
        132, 134–135, 143–145
    transfer pricing and, 117 (see also Transfer
        pricing)
Taylor, A. M., 1
Technology
    banking, 158–159
    communication, 159
    fragmentation effects and, 158–168
    outsourcing and, 67–84
Todd, P., 206
Total factor productivity, 205, 210–211,
    217–220
Trade
    autarky and, 29–30, 98, 156–157
    factor mobility and, 1–2, 6, 40, 54, 62,
        118–119, 232
    Forslid-Ottaviano model and, 95–110
    fragmentation gains and, 155–168
    globalization and, 161–168

Italian study and, 199–220
    lessons from gains in, 156–157
    medieval, 13
    New Trade Theory and, 166
    North American Free Trade Agreement
        (NAFTA) and, 228, 248
    outsourcing and, 155–168 (see also
        Outsourcing)
    service functions and, 259–272
    standard theories of, 1–2
    Stolper-Samuelson theorem and, 160
Trade costs
    acquisitions and, 25–31
    cost equations for, 32
    cross-border mergers and acquisitions
        (M&As) and, 25–34
    economic geography and, 6, 39
    export-platform gain and, 22–25, 31–32
    imperfect competition and, 39
    intraunion barriers and, 22–25
    knowledge-capital model and, 39–62
    liberalization and, 29–30, 39–62
    offshoring gains and, 20–21
    operating profits and, 14–19, 32
    product variety and, 74–83
    proximity-concentration trade-off and,
        14–19
    returns to scale and, 39
    tariff-jumping and, 20–21
    transfer pricing and, 117–140
    transport costs and, 17–18, 21
Train, K., 267
Transfer pricing
    Amerighi model and, 121–143
    arm's length principle and, 117–126, 131–
        132, 137–142, 145, 147
    backward induction for, 124–125
    corporate profit effects and, 128–129
    Cournot competition and, 124
    economic integration and, 132–137
    equilibrium and, 117–137
    European Union (EU) and, 141
    exports and, 124, 126–129
    home sales and, 126–129
    Kind model and, 119–120
    noncooperation and, 119
    OECD and, 117–118, 121, 149n4, 150n8
    personnel costs and, 123
    quantity decisions and, 124–129
    taxes and, 117–118, 129–137
    United States and, 117
Transport costs, 17–18, 21

Trionfetti, M., 90
Tybout, J. R., 203

United Kingdom, 17, 94–95, 265, 271
United Nations Conference on Trade and
   Development (UNCTAD)
 benchmarking and, 95
 knowledge-capital model and, 58
 liberalization effects and, 58
 trade costs and, 25–26, 31, 35n10
 World Investment Report, 58–59, 259
United States
 attracting multinational enterprises
   (MNEs) and, 259
 export-platform gain and, 24–25
 fragmentation and, 167–168
 inbound FDI and, 174–194
 North American Free Trade Agreement
   (NAFTA) and, 228, 248
 proximity-concentration issues and, 17
 service functions and, 260
 skilled labor and, 232, 248–249
 transfer pricing and, 117
 transport costs and, 21
Utility maximization problem, 71–72

Value chain
 outsourcing and, 232
 service functions and, 259–261, 267–268,
   271–272
van Marrewijk, Charles, 6, 30, 39, 89–116
Van Pottelsberghe de la Potterie, B., 201
van Ypersele, T., 119
Venables, A. J., 39, 259
Viner, J., 157

Waddell, Glen R., 7, 173–197
Wagner, J., 206
Wang, P., 68
Wauthy, X., 119
Wei, S., 201
Weichenrieder, A. J., 119
Welfare
 agglomeration and, 99, 103, 109
 factor mobility and, 1–2, 6, 40, 54, 62,
   118–119, 232
 fragmentation and, 156–167
 liberalization and, 41, 56–57
 transfer pricing and, 117–149 (*see also*
   Transfer pricing)
White test, 235–236
Williamson, O. E., 4–5

World Bank, 60
World Edgeworth box, 63n8
 economic geography and, 40–41
 knowledge-capital model and, 48
 liberalization and, 47–48
 World Investment Report (UNCTAD), 58–
   59, 259
World War II era, 13

Yeaple, S., 17, 21, 173, 175, 203

Zanfei, A., 204
Zero-profit conditions, 45–47
Zilibotti, F., 69–78